MW01284476

MEMOIR
OF A
MANGLED
MIND

MEMOIR
OF A
MANGLED
MIND

How Concealing My
Dissociative Identity Disorder
Unleashed Multiple Personalities

Steven Simmons Shelton, MA, JD

STEVEN
SHELTON

Published in Palm Bay, Florida, by Steven Shelton

Author Website: https://TheMangledMind.com

Library of Congress Control Number: 2024922557

Available formats:
ISBN 978-1-965446-12-6 (hardcover with dust jacket)
ISBN 978-1-965446-17-1 (hardcover without dust jacket)
ISBN 978-1-965446-13-3 (trade paperback)
ISBN 978-1-965446-14-0 (ebook)
ISBN 978-1-965446-15-7 (hardcover, large print edition)
ISBN 978-1-965446-16-4 (trade paperback, large print edition)

First Edition
10 9 8 7 6 5 4 3 2 1

For my husband, Grant.

Your unconditional love
made this book possible.

For Estelle and Cliff.

I'm the son you never had, and
you're the parents I desperately
wanted. You might be gone, but the
love you gave me will never go away.

Trademarks Mentioned

Honigman®, the surviving legal entity of HONIGMAN MILLER Schwartz and Cohn, is a registered trademark of HONIGMAN LLP, a Michigan (USA) limited liability partnership.

IBM® is a trademark of INTERNATIONAL BUSINESS MACHINES CORPORATION, a New York (USA) corporation.

JCPenney® is a trademark of PENNEY IP LLC, a Delaware (USA) limited liability company.

Jenner & Block® is a registered trademark of JENNER & BLOCK LLP, an Illinois (USA) limited liability partnership.

Judge Judy® is a registered trademark of BIG TICKET TELEVISION INC., a Delaware (USA) corporation.

Little Orphan Annie® is a trademark of TRIBUNE ENTERTAINMENT COMPANY, LLC, a Delaware (USA) limited liability company.

Mail Boxes Etc.® is a registered trademark of UNITED PARCEL SERVICE OF AMERICA, Inc., a Delaware (USA) corporation.

M*A*S*H® is a registered trademark of TWENTIETH CENTURY FOX FILM CORPORATION, a Delaware (USA) corporation.

McDonald's® and Egg McMuffin® are registered trademarks of MCDONALD'S CORPORATION, a Delaware (USA) corporation.

Montgomery Ward® is a registered trademark of MONTGOMERY WARD, INC., a Wisconsin (USA) corporation.

Motel 6® is a registered trademark of G6 HOSPITALITY IP LLC, a Delaware (USA) limited liability company.

Pepto Bismol® is a registered trademark of THE PROCTOR AND GAMBLE COMPANY, an Ohio (USA) corporation.

Post-It® is a registered trademark of 3M COMPANY, a Delaware (USA) corporation.

Snickers® is a registered trademark of MARS, INCORPORATED, a Delaware (USA) corporation.

Taubman® is a registered trademark of THE TAUBMAN COMPANY LLC, a Delaware (USA) limited liability company.

The Beverly Hillbillies® is a registered trademark of CBS BROADCASTING INC., a New York (USA) Corporation.

Contents

Author's Note

S ome readers will find this memoir too traumatic to read. I include scenes of being raped—as a child and adult—and attempting suicide. I present the details as sensitively as possible given the circumstances.

Sexual assault, especially of children, is rarely depicted in nonfiction work to the extent I do here. The incidents are an integral part of my story, not gratuitous scenes meant to be titillating or to serve prurient interests.

At its heart, this memoir is a true, first-hand account of dissociative identity disorder (formerly called multiple personality disorder) resulting from childhood trauma. The story unfolds through my eyes at the ages the events occurred.

For more than twenty years, I resisted writing this memoir because doing so would require me to relive the trauma and all my failures in managing the resulting mental disorder. I hurt many people during the events covered here—and disappointed even more. In the end, I decided telling my story might encourage others in similar situations to make better decisions and to seek mental health treatment in a timely manner.

I present the events of this book—which took place over a thirty-year time period—to the best of my recollection. The dialogue is conveyed in the spirit of what happened rather than verbatim.

For privacy reasons, I changed the identities and identifying characteristics of most people involved. I use the real names of those who are deceased, gave me permission, or are members of my immediate family.

As for those who sexually assaulted me—as a child and adult—you know who you are. This book isn't about justice for me. For that, you'll have to answer to your own conscience and to a higher power. I would say, "May God have mercy on your soul," but, of the many things I wish for you, mercy is nowhere to be found.

Steven Simmons Shelton

Memoir of a Mangled Mind

Chapter 1

I'm the Monster

June 6, 1984
Detroit, Michigan
Age 24

When I was eleven years old, Aunt Estelle told me—after I screamed in my sleep—that monsters weren't real. She lied. The shadowy figures who pursued me in my nightmares, often leaving me lying on a sheet soaked in urine, didn't stay in my dreams. They also took the form of people at home, at school, and everywhere else I went—except when I was with her. I didn't say anything about the real monsters because all the darkness surrounding me might scare her away.

That memory flooded me as I found myself standing in an unknown bedroom, naked but for my eyeglasses, holding what appeared to be a chef's knife in my right hand. The silver blade shimmered in the small amount of streetlight coming through a gap in the curtains.

The four-poster bed in front of me held someone—undoubtedly some random guy from a bar—but all I could make out was the back of his head on the pillow. A light snoring sound told me he was alive.

Where the fuck am I? What the hell is going on?

If he woke up and caught me with a weapon, I'd be in deep shit. I had to ditch it, get dressed, and vamoose.

A cursory search of the darkened room came up empty, so my clothes had to be elsewhere. The first door I opened led to a walk-in closet. No more closets for me. The second one revealed a hallway. Careful not to make a sound, I pulled the door closed behind me before turning right and heading toward a dim glow in a far-off room. I bumped into the wall a few times until I found the living room, convinced the mystery sleeper would come to see what made the noise.

More light from the street shined through the windows, revealing an end table with a lamp, which I turned on. The kitchen stood at the far end of the room, with a bar jutting from the wall. On the counter sat a wooden block holding a set of kitchen knives.

Relief washed over me when I found where the weapon belonged. If the stranger sleeping down the hall learned the danger I presented, would he go to the police? Would he come after me? I wiped my fingerprints off the utensil before sliding it into the empty slot.

When I left the guy's house, I took off in the direction of the brightest glow on the horizon. Twenty minutes later, I stumbled upon downtown Royal Oak. Then I had to walk almost three miles south on Woodward to where Detroit bus service began. I didn't reach my apartment until after 3 a.m.

After I awoke mid-morning, I tried without success to work on the incompletes I'd received in my graduate school classes the previous semester. Hepatitis B had quarantined me for weeks. Not until yesterday morning did the doctors clear me to enter society once again. I had no blackouts for the ten weeks of isolation. So much for that.

The question of the knife hounded me, keeping me from concentrating on my overdue organizational communication paper. Lord, someone needed to put out a user manual for multiple personalities.

My two alters—Wayne and Mark—had controlled my life for years. I understood why Wayne picked up random tricks at bars. He was, after all, a sex-starved man-slut who had abandoned me during many sexual encounters. But Mark had always been the violent one, so the knife had to be his idea, didn't it? Yet, he had only ever gotten aggressive when someone posed a threat to us. Was the sleeping guy dangerous? If so, how?

By evening, I couldn't sit still. Kris, my roommate, had gone home to Utah for the summer, leaving me alone in the drab apartment. I had to get out—mingle, dance, and maybe have sex with someone while I was aware of it.

Gay men liked to party hard, and we wanted variety. The Detroit area had a hot bar for every night of the week. On Mondays, we went to Gigi's for its go-go boys and drag queens. Tuesdays, the E-RAMP. Wednesdays, BACKSTREET. Thursdays, TIFFANY'S. Fridays, MENJO'S. Saturdays, back to BACKSTREET. Sundays, TIFFANY'S once again, this time for brunch—sliders from WHITE CASTLE—and afternoon dancing. Sunday night, we returned to MENJO'S. We called this "the circuit."

Thanks to Wayne's voracious sexual appetite, I'd found myself "waking up" at all of those bars at one point or another, sometimes in various stages of undress. Wayne's constant bar hopping left me broke, tired, and—as I discovered several weeks earlier—temporarily infected.

With Kris gone and my loins antsy, I decided to catch a bus to TIFFANY'S, located at Six Mile Road and Woodward. I'd been going there since moving to Detroit the previous August—sometimes when Wayne dumped me there, and at other times of my own volition. Compared to the other circuit bars, TIFFANY'S was tiny with a main area of only twenty-by-forty feet. Somehow, a hundred men or more packed its small space every Thursday night.

The place didn't fill up until 10 p.m., but I tried to arrive before the cover charge began. I strolled in and settled on a bar stool.

"Look who the cat dragged in." Bob, the manager, placed a coaster in front of me." Where did you disappear to?"

"School kicked my ass last semester." He and I had developed a casual friendship, but not close enough to warrant disclosure of my bout with hepatitis.

"Welcome back. What can I get you?"

"Just a draft. I'm broke as usual."

Bob filled a mug and set it on the coaster. "Are you working this summer?"

"Not until August."

"Would you be interested in doing some work here?"

A job that didn't interfere with summer classes sure would help. "It depends. I do have school."

"Well, I'm looking for someone to clean the bar after closing every Saturday night. I pay fifty a week to scrub the floors, table surfaces, bar, and the restroom."

"What about the fuck room?" The bar had an infamous hidden room behind the jukebox where guys went for sexual adventures. A two-way mirror overlooked the small dance floor. I'd been in there a few times with different guys but found it nasty, even by my nonexistent standards.

"No need. Another guy comes in on Mondays to sanitize it. In addition to cleaning the place, I also need someone to bus tables and run drinks on Thursdays and Sundays. It would just be for tips, but you'll make a lot if you wear those tight, white shorts." He leaned over the bar, looked down toward my crotch, and smiled.

This might be the answer to my financial woes. Would Mark and Wayne behave while I worked? I'd be running around a bunch of horny men while wearing shorts so tight you could tell I was circumcised. Wayne might enjoy himself a little too much, but he did that already.

"Sure, I'll do it."

"Great." Bob handed me a wet rag and a towel. "You can start tonight."

So much for relaxing. As the bar filled, so did my pockets. By 1:00 a.m., the green paper money and silver coins showed through my sweat-soaked shorts. A bar stool opened up, so I sat for a short break.

"Hey, Wayne," a sexy, deep voice from behind me said over the loud music. As I turned, dizziness hit me, and the room spun. *Shit, here we go.*

Waking up from a blackout always disoriented me. When the mental fog lifted, I took in my surroundings. Oh, hell no.

Once again, I stood naked in the same bedroom, next to the same four-poster bed, holding the same knife, with the same snoring coming from the mystery sleeper.

Fuck. *What the hell is going on? Did he do something? For God's sake, why abandon me here like this with a knife in my hand? None of this makes sense.*

Don't be an idiot, Steve. This is your chance to save the guy's life—again. Mark wants to kill him.

I had to put the knife back in the kitchen and escape as soon as possible.

"Come back to bed," a deep voice mumbled—the same one from the bar.

Shit. Afraid he would look up and see me with the knife, I stuffed it between the mattress and box springs. "Sorry, I need to go."

"Okay. I had fun," he said, still not turning in my direction.

Why the hell did I leave the knife under the mattress? That was beyond stupid. The guy would find it and figure out I put it there. What would he think?

I stumbled around the darkened room until I found my clothes on a chair in the corner, my shoes on the floor. After getting dressed and making sure I had my wallet and keys, I left the house.

An hour later, I sat on a Detroit bus heading to my apartment. I couldn't keep doing this. My other personalities were either going to kill someone or cause someone to kill us.

Monsters *were* real, and I had become one.

Chapter 2

Fitting In

I'd be starting high school in the fall. This could be the last summer mowing lawns if I got a real job once I turned sixteen in December. One sweltering day in early June, I rode my ten-speed bike by an old tennis court on the Wilkinson property just up the hill from our house. Their home once served as Greenwood Schools many years earlier.

Four students a year ahead of me in school—two cheerleaders and their boyfriends—were playing doubles. I got off my bike and sat to watch. The two guys had teased me relentlessly over the years, so I didn't know what possessed me to stop.

The tennis court was nothing but a concrete slab rising four inches above the grass. When trying to hit a ball bouncing wide or long off the court, the players sometimes fell when they stepped down from the slab. I found it difficult not to laugh.

After a while, I got up to leave.

"Steve, don't go," Carolyn, one of the cheerleaders, said. "Here, you try." She stepped off the court and held out her racket. I shook my head and kept walking.

I don't want to give them another reason to humiliate me at school.

"Sissy Simmons doesn't know how to play," her boyfriend, Fred, said. "She might hurt herself."

Hearing the awful nickname nauseated me. All four laughed—and continued to do so for several seconds, including making references to limp wrists.

"Sure, I'll give it a try." I'd never held a tennis racket, and I was pretty sure they knew that.

For the next half hour, no matter where I stood on the court, one of the other players found a way to hit me with the ball. Even Fred—whom I got stuck with as a partner—slammed one into me when he got the chance. After three games, I'd had enough.

"Stick to knittin', Miss Simmons," Fred said, "because you'll never be a tennis player."

As I rode away, his words ate at me. I decided to prove him wrong, to show him that I belonged. With my mowing money, I bought a cheap racket and practiced hitting balls off the carport wall at home.

For months, I hit forehand and backhand strokes off the brick wall. When I found the Wilkinson court unoccupied, I practiced serving the ball. I wasn't very good at any of it—yet.

―――――――――

December rolled around, and I finally turned the magical age of sixteen. I'd been learning to drive since before my parents' divorce the previous year. Mom took off work the Friday morning after my birthday so I could get my driver's license. She handed me the car keys when we got inside the DMV in downtown Greenwood.

"Don't wreck it," she said, as if the words would stop me from having an accident. That was why they called them "accidents."

The examiner—a man with a huge potbelly he used as a desk—instructed me to drive around the town square, make a few turns through side streets, and parallel park next to the courthouse. I got him back to the DMV alive, so he passed me.

Inside, the clerk took my learner's permit and gave me a temporary license—nothing more than a piece of paper. She said the real one would be mailed to me in a week or two. Mom snatched the keys from me as soon as we got outside.

"No, you're not drivin' us home," she said, "so don't bother askin'."

It sucked having a driver's license and no car. My older brother, Mike, bought a Mustang when he turned sixteen, but he'd saved every nickel from our lawn-mowing business. I spent all my money on junk food, gifts for Mom, a bicycle, and tennis equipment. Borrowing Mike's car was out of the question.

Two weeks later, Dad asked me to go with him to Fort Smith, ten miles northwest of Greenwood. He rarely came around anymore, so his request made me more curious than anything else. We climbed into his 1950 green Chevy pick-up truck—which he had painted with a roller and can of exterior paint—and drove toward the city.

Thirty minutes later, he pulled the truck into a used car dealership. The building once served as a drive-in restaurant like Arnold's on *Happy Days*. The dozen covered parking spaces contained the "finest used cars in Fort Smith," if the sign on the roof was to be believed.

With me a few steps behind, Dad approached a black 1965 Ford Mustang and inspected the outside. What was it with my family and that car? Mom smashed her 1966 model into a ditch in May—drunk driving, of course—and Mike's was a 1967 version.

"What do you think of it?" Dad asked.

"It's nice." The body didn't have any dents, although the paint had a few scratches. The tires looked new. However, the inside told a different story. The black seats had cracked, and the dash looked as if someone had set it on fire.

Maybe if Dad bought this car, he'd give me his truck. It wasn't my style, but I was a driver in need of wheels. Desperation trumped pickiness.

A salesman approached us. He and Dad laughed and made small talk. The guy handed a set of keys to Dad, who got in the car and started the engine. Some described their cars as purring like kittens. This car sounded like a cat with pneumonia.

"It just needs a tune-up," the salesman said. "The automatic transmission runs smoothly, and the brakes are new."

I found the guy's toothy smile to be off-putting. He had all the genuineness of Mister Haney on *Green Acres*.

"The dash and seats are messed up," I said.

"Arkansas summers will do that to a black car," the salesman said through his fake grin.

"That's just surface stuff." Dad got out of the car and handed the keys back to the salesman. "How much will you take for it?"

"Bobby, for you, five hundred dollars, which includes tags and—"

"Deal."

I followed them into the office where they completed paperwork. Dad pulled a wad of twenties from his pocket, counted out a bunch, and gave them to the salesman. He didn't want to pay child support, but he had money to throw around. Pathetic. When the salesman stacked the tags, paperwork, and keys on the desk, Dad picked them up and held them out toward me.

"Happy birthday."

What? I had to be dreaming. Dad had never personally given me a present, never acted like I existed. I'd known for years that Mom bought the gifts and scribbled his name on them. With the keys, tags, and paperwork in my hands, I jumped up and down.

"*Woo hoo.*"

The sound bounced off windows covering three walls of the room that once served as the restaurant's lobby.

"You'll have to pay for the gas and upkeep, so you gotta get a job," Dad said.

"I don't mind," I said. "Thank you." He'd hugged me only once before—after the tornado in 1968—so we shook hands.

The next day, I drove back to Fort Smith to look for a job. A cafeteria manager hired me, and I reported to work later that day. I had to place dishes on a conveyor belt that ran through the dishwasher and then stack the clean ones on racks. After hours of slipping on a wet floor and falling several times, I said "fuck that." I finished my shift and quit.

I applied for a job at WINTON's IGA the next day. After Mom and I had a bad experience with one of the store's sackers the year before, I didn't want to work there, but I needed a job.

The manager, Frank, hired me on the spot. I would bag groceries on weekends and some evenings after school. During breaks, I could work full time. With my job, school, and extracurricular activities, I wouldn't be home much—something I welcomed with utter joy.

My car meant freedom. Despite how the interior looked, I loved my Mustang. I no longer depended on others to drive me around, nor did I have to walk or ride my bicycle as much. I discovered places to have fun in Fort Smith—including the public tennis courts at Creekmore Park.

My best friend—Sean—and I still hung out together, but my secrets wedged a distance between us. He knew how bad I had it at home because his parents also drank too much. But he knew nothing about my sexual activities—not that I had a choice in them. Embarrassment, shame, and fear served as my censors.

In January, despite the cold weather, I began taking tennis lessons at Creekmore from a local pro named Farrell Graves. He taught me on Tuesday evenings as long as the courts weren't covered in ice or snow.

With the weekly lessons, my play improved dramatically, which led to Creekmore players inviting me into their inner circle. At any given time, these newfound friends—most of them my age—would be at the courts. They knew me as "Steve, the tennis player," not as "Sissy Simmons."

In the spring of 1976, I made the Greenwood High School tennis team. A player increased his team ranking by challenging and beating the one immediately above him. I ascended in rank until I could challenge Fred. He laughed at me in front of the coach, who smiled and shook his head. Coach Davidson knew how I played, but Fred hadn't been paying attention.

The other team members stood on the sidelines as I trounced my nemesis. I beat him again the following week when he tried to regain his spot. At least the asshole stopped calling me "Sissy Simmons." By the end of the season, I became the team's top player.

When school let out in May for the summer, life looked good. I had an old car, a job, and the number one spot on the tennis team.

I finally fit in.

Chapter 3

Losing Time

June 1976
Greenwood, Arkansas
Age 16

A day off from bagging groceries meant tennis. When I didn't work, my Fort Smith buddies and I usually stayed on the Creekmore Park courts from mid-morning until late in the evening. Just as I readied to leave the house at 9 a.m., the telephone rang. With Sharon watching TV, I had to answer it.

"Simmons residence."

"Steven, it's your mother." I chuckled. She always introduced herself on the phone like that, as if I didn't know who it was. "Mike's workin' late, so stay with Sharon until I get home. Ball practice is at six, and I don't wanna have to track her down."

"I can't today. I'm playin' tennis."

"I wasn't askin'."

"Mom, she can take care of herself." My sister was almost twelve. She stayed by herself all the time. "It's my only day off this week."

"Don't argue with me. Stay there and watch your sister."

I got warm all over, and my head buzzed. "*I'm going to play tennis.*"

"Steven Wayne Simmons, don't you *ever* raise your voice to me. I'm still your mother, and I'm tellin' you to stay home with your sister."

"Fine." I slammed the receiver and stomped down the hallway to my bedroom. Why did she always treat me like this? She had never seen me play tennis, but she even formed a softball team so Sharon could play.

The room suddenly spun like it did after I'd been playing on hot courts all day. I lay on the bed and fell asleep. When I awoke, I found my sister in the living room, sitting in the tattered recliner, still watching television.

"I'm tellin' Mama," she said as soon as I walked in. "You're in so much trouble."

"What are you talkin' about?" I dropped on the couch. She'd already ruined my day off. If she wanted to argue with me, I was ready and willing.

"You were supposed to be watchin' me," she said.

"I was in my room. That's good enough."

"No, you weren't. You took your tennis bag and left."

The little liar. I had to park in the front yard after work yesterday. My car would still be there, so I jumped up to the picture window to prove it. *What the hell?* Someone had moved my car to the street.

"You little shit. You drove my car."

"Now you're lyin'. I don't even have a key."

I checked my right pocket where I usually carried my car key—and there it was. Then I realized my clothes had changed. Instead of the white shorts and T-shirt from earlier in the morning, I had on red shorts and a gray shirt. I dashed down the hallway to my room and checked my tennis bag. The new can of balls I bought the day before had been used.

I didn't really go play tennis without remembering any of it, did I? How was that possible?

Come on, Steve. You know how.

I had to ask my friends if I'd been there—and do it without looking crazy.

That's what you're worried about, isn't it? You don't want people to know. They'll put you in a straitjacket.

This can't be happening again. It's been two years.

Don't think about it, Steve. Let it go.

I'm going to Creekmore when Mom gets home. I have to know.

"Please don't say anything," I asked my sister. "You didn't want me here, anyway."

"Okay, but you owe me one."

When Mom walked through the door at 5:30 p.m., I slipped out of the house with my tennis gear and drove to Fort Smith. My hands shook as I pulled onto the gravel lot rising four feet above the courts at Creekmore Park. *Please let this be the first time they've seen me today.* Three of my tennis buddies were playing Canadian doubles. I got out of the car and slammed the door shut. Rob looked up and waved.

"Hey, look who's back," he called out.

A sharp pain hit me in the stomach. *Oh, shit. Sharon isn't lying. I'm losing time again.*

Chapter 4

Let Me Eat Cake

NOVEMBER 1967
GREENWOOD, ARKANSAS
AGE 7

I **loved going to school**. My second-grade teacher, Mrs. Smith, had gray hair and wore dresses with lots of flowers on them. She was old enough to be someone's granny, but Mrs. Smith didn't dip snuff or smell funny. At least she wasn't crazy like Granny on *The Beverly Hillbillies*, although we did have a few Jethros in my class.

Every day we had two recesses on the playground—a big yard in front of the school building. I didn't hang around the other boys in my class. All they did was throw footballs and pretend to be police cars or fire trucks. I had more fun jumping rope with my friends Kathie, Jeannie, and Sheila.

As we played one day, someone yelled, "Sissy Simmons!"

I stopped, letting the rope hit my leg as I stood on the sidewalk. Whoever said it had to be talking about me because nobody else in the second grade had my last name. Who did it?

"Sissy Simmons!"

Marla.

She was next to the flagpole, pointing at me and laughing. Why did she call me that? Was it because I played games with girls instead of the stupid things the boys did? I hadn't done anything to her. The teasing spread across the yard as more kids said it over and over.

"Sissy Simmons!"

"Sissy Simmons!"

I hid behind a bush, but the shrub didn't block the sound. Why were they being mean to me? When recess ended, I dashed into the building. Maybe they would forget about it. Maybe they wouldn't do it again.

That night, I didn't tell Mama or Daddy about being made fun of. The name embarrassed me.

The next day at our first recess, I waited until the others had gone to the playground before I left the classroom. Then I dilly-dallied through the building to the exit. As I walked down the steps to the yard, somebody hollered the name again—and others joined in.

Try to ignore them.

Over on the sidewalk, Kathie and Jeannie swung a rope while Sheila jumped. I headed toward them.

"Sis-sy Sim-mons," Sheila began singing in rhythm with her feet hitting the ground. "Sis-sy Sim-mons."

I froze. Why would she say it, too? I backed up and sat on the steps. When Kathie and Jeannie added their voices to the chant, I wanted to die. *God, please make them stop. Please.* The four of us had played together at every recess since we started first grade. Why were they calling me that bad name, too? I pulled my knees to my chest, hid my face, and bawled.

"Stevie, come inside with me *right now*." Mrs. Smith grabbed my arm and pulled me up.

"But I didn't do anything."

"Back to the room *now*."

It took forever to walk past the other classrooms. What was I in trouble for? I hoped she wouldn't paddle me.

"Sit right there." She pointed at the chair next to her desk and gave me a tissue. "Here, wipe your eyes and stop cryin'."

I dried my face and blew my nose.

"Stevie, remember this. Sticks and stones can break your bones, but words will never hurt you."

"You're wrong." Every time someone said "Sissy Simmons," my stomach twisted and hurt.

"If you ignore them, they'll stop."

"*No, they won't.* I ignore them *now*, but they ain't stoppin'."

"'Ain't' isn't a word."

"Yes, it is. It's spelled a-i-n-t. I found it in the dictionary." How could a teacher not know that?

"Just because a word is in the...never mind. Listen, they'll stop teasin' you if you don't pay any attention to them. Now I don't want to see you cryin' anymore. It upsets the other kids."

The other kids? Is she kidding? I'm not doing anything to them. They're *making fun of* me. "But I don't *mean* to bawl. It just happens."

"If I catch you doin' it again, I'll send you to the office. The principal will call your mother to come get you."

Mama would spank me for sure. "Please, don't tell her about this. I promise I ain't gonna do it again."

The recess bell rang. "Now go to your seat and remember what we talked about."

I didn't look at the others when they came back inside. How could I make them like me again? After lunch, I came up with an idea. The bell rang at the end of the day, and I ran to the car in order to beat Mike there. I climbed into the front seat.

"Can I have a birthday party?" If the kids in my class came to our house for cake and ice cream, they would *have* to be nice to me. They might stop others from calling me names, too.

"Who would you invite?" Mama asked. "You don't have friends."

Randy used to be my friend. Then he asked me to spend the night, and I wet the bed. He wouldn't be my friend anymore after that.

"Kids in my class said they'd come." I touched my nose to see if it had grown like Pinocchio's.

"They did? Who?"

"A lot of them. Please?" I didn't like lying to her, but she'd never let me have a party if I told her the truth.

"Nobody's comin' to a party. Just forget about it."

"Please? I *promise* they'll come."

"Fine, but you have to help."

"*Yes.*"

When we got home, Mama drew an invitation. It even had a map to our house. She gave me a sharp pencil and some blank paper.

"Here. Use the pencil in case you make mistakes. You can invite ten classmates."

Does she expect me to make the invites? I'm not very good at drawing. "But I can't write as good as you."

"You said you'd help."

"Okay. I'll do the best I can."

I worked hard all weekend. My hand hurt, but I finished making twenty-five invitations. I hid the extra ones in my notebook so Mama wouldn't see them. On Monday, I handed them all out, even to the mean kids.

"You're invited to my eighth birthday party." I practiced saying it so I wouldn't mess up. "It's at one o'clock on December second. That's my birthday. It's a Saturday. I even drew a map on the back. Mama's makin' a cake with chocolate icin', and we'll have ice cream and play games. I hope you can come."

I got the invitations passed out before school ended. Some of my classmates threw the papers away, but others put them in their notebooks.

After Thanksgiving, Mama and I started getting ready for the party. She baked the cake in two round pans. When they cooled, she wrapped them in plastic and put them in the freezer.

Daddy brought the Christmas tree inside. I made chains from colored construction paper. We wrapped them around the tree, but I made extra ones to hang in the kitchen for my party. Mama gave me balloons to blow up. Daddy had to tie the ends because I kept letting them go. When they flew across the room, my little sister giggled and chased them.

On the morning of my party, someone shook me awake.

"Steven, we got a lot of stuff to do today," Mama said, "so get up."

I ran to the kitchen because she always made me chocolate gravy on my birthday. She'd also give me my present after I ate.

When I got to the dining room table, Mike and Sharon were eating Cap'n Crunch. Someone already filled another bowl with it and put it on the table.

"Where's my chocolate gravy?"

"You're gettin' a cake today," Mama said. "That's enough chocolate."

"What about my present?"

"You're havin' a party," she said. "Be happy with that."

After breakfast, Daddy and Mike went squirrel hunting while I helped Mama hang the paper chains and balloons. When she made the chocolate icing, I licked the beaters.

I didn't eat anything for lunch so I'd have lots of room for cake and ice cream. She stuck eight candles on the cake and put it on the table. I tried to stick my finger in the icing, but she slapped my hand away.

"You had enough already," she said.

"I'm gonna go watch out for them." I dragged a chair to the front door and stood on it to look through the little window at the top. My legs got tired, so I had to sit. I wondered what presents I would get.

"Mama, is it time yet?" When she didn't answer, I went to the kitchen.

"Is it time yet?" I repeated.

"I told you nobody would come." She took a puff on her cigarette.

"They'll be here. They promised." I checked my nose, but my lies hadn't made it grow.

"The party was supposed to start more than an hour ago. You wasted my time and money. Now help me clean up."

Mama picked up the cake and carried it to the kitchen. I caught up to her as she removed the candles.

"Please leave 'em on. I wanna blow them out." I'd never had my own birthday cake before.

"I'm savin' the candles and ice cream for your sister's birthday," she said. "You fibbed to me."

"But Sharon will only need three. Can't I just have one?" I wanted to make my birthday wish.

"Steven Wayne, just drop it."

"Can I at least have some cake?" I'd been thinking about it all week. Even if she wouldn't let me have the ice cream, I could still celebrate my birthday—although, without candles, it was just a cake.

She handed me a fork and plate. "Eat the whole thing, for all I care. Then get rid of those silly decorations."

I ruined my birthday by fibbing to Mama. All I wanted was to make the other kids like me. Now they'd tease me even more.

With no appetite for the cake, I put the fork and plate away. It took me a while to take down the balloons and paper chains. Afterward, I went to my bedroom and lay down.

"Happy birthday to me."

Chapter 5

A Whore's Best Friend

July 1976
Fort Smith, Arkansas
Age 16

A **month had passed since** my blackout, and I hadn't been sleeping. Every night, I had the same nightmare—the one I used to have as a kid. In it, a dark shadow chased me no matter where I was—at home and at school. It even found me at work. After running from him for what seemed like hours, I awoke, sweating. I even wet the bed two nights, something I hadn't done since I was fourteen.

I'd lost my appetite and, along with it, my energy. Even playing tennis—the one thing I could count on to take my mind off of shit—had become a tedious chore. But I still tried. Today, though, I should have stayed in bed.

"Nice shot," I said after Rob passed me with a return down the line. He and I usually had close matches, but not this one. My ground strokes either went wide, long, or in the net. I double-faulted at least once every service game.

Even though I tried to concentrate on the game, I couldn't. Why did I start losing time again? I used to space out when guys forced me to have sex but never for hours. That last happened with Danny—two years ago.

I checked my watch every chance I got to ensure I knew the time. Each morning, I counted the money in my wallet to make sure none had disappeared. I even wrote down the mileage on my car and paid closer attention to the clothes I wore. If I skipped forward in time, I wanted to know about it.

Despite my gut screaming at me to tell someone, I didn't. What if others found out?

They'll put you in the loony bin, that's what.

"Forty fifteen," Rob called out. "Match point."

Behind the baseline, I bounced on the balls of my feet and crouched. His go-to serve had always been a wide slice to my forehand rather than anything down the middle to my strong backhand. As I leaned slightly to my right, he tossed the ball in the air and went into motion. The flat serve hit the middle line and whizzed past me. I had no chance of reaching it.

After retrieving the ball, I strolled to the wooden bench at the side of the court. Rob put a towel on the hot slats to prevent third-degree burns when we sat. I fished two jars of Lemon Lime Gatorades from the ice chest and handed him one.

"Sorry I wasn't much competition today."

"Man, you were gnarly. Did you forget to put strings in your rackets?"

"Don't get used to it." Maybe I should check my equipment to see if he was right.

We chugged our drinks. The tangy, cold liquid gave me brain-freeze as it soaked my dry throat. I fought off the sting while finishing the bottle's contents. He and I dropped the empties into our bags. I opened Rob's ice chest and pulled out two more.

"You just need to get laid—to leave the V train behind."

"I told you I'm past that." *Way* past that, but he could never know the truth about when, where, and how I lost my virginity.

"Man, until you give details, it never happened." Rob picked up an old tennis ball someone had left behind and slammed it over the fence. It bounced past the tracks used by the little train to take kids around the park. "Who was she?"

"Another time, maybe." I picked up both of our tennis bags. "I gotta go."

With Rob a step behind me carrying his ice chest, we left the now-empty courts. Only crazy people like us played in this heat. It had to be well over a hundred degrees on the concrete. Fifty yards away, screaming kids splashed in the Creekmore pool. They had the right idea, although public pools gave me the heebie-jeebies. Sleeping in pee-soaked sheets for so many years had been bad enough—as I'd been recently reminded. Who wets their bed at age sixteen?

I took the steps two at a time up to the gravel parking lot. We had gotten there early enough to snag spaces in the front row overlooking the courts. Once the pool opened, the lot filled quickly.

"Steve, slow down. You gotta hot date or somethin'?"

"I have to work at three." That gave me forty-five minutes. Then it would be six hours of bagging groceries and cleaning the store's floors.

Rob put the ice chest in his trunk while I tossed the equipment bags in our respective back seats. The heat bore down on me like a heavy, hot quilt. Sweat drenched my clothes and socks. A slight breeze offered no relief from the heat as it blew dust around, forming a muddy film all over me. If we'd stopped playing an hour earlier, I could've driven home for a shower.

"Man, you gonna go to work smellin' like that?"

He had me there. My deodorant had worn off hours ago. "I'll just clean up in the restroom."

"Dude, be careful down there or you might get your cherry popped by some guy named Bubba."

"Funny. See ya later." I climbed into my car and started the engine. The hot vinyl seat burned the back of my legs. One of these days, I'd remember to put a towel down first.

The restroom was a standalone building located between the swimming pool and park administration office. Some of the other players joked about the place being "homo central," although I never asked them how they knew. I parked the car and grabbed my duffel bag from the trunk. The bag contained a change of clothes and supplies I'd need to clean up with.

Why couldn't the restroom door have a lock on the inside? Once I made sure nobody lurked in the place, I pulled a towel and washcloth from the bag. I removed my shirt and washed the grime off my arms and torso, paying special attention to the funky pits. I doused myself with Right Guard and prayed I'd done enough so Frank wouldn't send me home for stinking up the store.

I stepped out of my shorts and underwear to clean from the waist down. When the door swung open and someone whistled, I would say I shit my pants, but I didn't have any on. Instead, I dropped the washcloth and reached for my towel.

"Woo-hoo. Will you take a gander at *that.*"

A man who had to be as old as my dad stood inside the doorway. He was about my height—six feet—and had a buzz cut, like he was in the military or something. The tight blue jeans and T-shirt showed off the body of someone who spent as many hours in the gym as I did on the tennis courts. I held the towel in front of my crotch.

"Sorry. I have to go to work and was tryin' to clean up."

"Son, why in tarnation are you 'pologizin? You got nothin' to be sorry for. What's your name?"

Dizziness hit me, and I leaned against the sink to keep from falling. The man said something else, but I couldn't make out the words. *What's happening to me?*

———————

The clanging of an alarm snapped me awake. The soft mattress hugged me, making me not want to move. *This isn't my bed.* I sat up and found my eyeglasses on the nightstand next to me. Clothes that appeared to be mine—jeans and a white, short-sleeved dress shirt—hung on the back of a chair six feet away. Lifting the covers confirmed I was naked.

Where the hell am I?

Steve, you need to get out.

"Wayne, you wanna cup of joe?" a man called out.

Is he talking to me? *If so, why is he using my middle name?* I waited for someone else to answer, but they didn't.

"No thanks." *I have to go.* As I tried to come up with a plan to escape, a nude man walked into the bedroom—the guy from the Creekmore restroom. He had a rock-solid body and an impressive manhood. He might be as old as Dad, but he was gorgeous.

Stop looking at him.

"If you change your mind, the pot's in the kitchen. I'm gonna shower. Wanna join me?"

Does he know I'm only sixteen, like in the Dr. Hook song?

I had to leave—and fast. According to my watch, it was 7 a.m.

Damn, this blackout lasted all night. If I didn't show up for work yesterday, Frank will kill me.

"No coffee for me. I have to get to work."

"You *are* workin', baby."

The man zipped across the room and slid under the covers, grabbing my ass as I jumped out of bed. I snatched my clothes off the back of the chair and ran. Out the bedroom and down a hallway I went. There had to be an exit somewhere. From the sound of feet slapping on the hardwood floor behind me, the guy was close behind.

"I paid for two days. Your ass is mine 'til this evenin'."

No, it's not.

If I didn't find a way out, he'd catch me—and it didn't take much imagination to guess what he'd do next. I flew around a corner and came face to face with a red front door. I turned the deadbolt, pulled the door open, and dashed out. With my junk flapping in the breeze, I took the front steps two at a time down to his sidewalk.

Screw modesty.

Naked, I ducked behind a bush at the corner of his house. Although I didn't think the man would follow me outside, I still dressed quickly.

Son-of-a-bitch. I didn't grab my shoes and socks. Thank God I kept an extra pair of both in my tennis bag.

I found my car parked across the street. Operating the brake and gas with bare feet, I drove aimlessly through the neighborhood until I found Rogers Avenue, a familiar street. Guessing which way to turn, I steered left in hopes it would lead me to I-540. I soon found the interstate overpass and took the south entrance.

Something the guy said hit me—my ass was his for two days, until this evening.

Please, let today be Friday. I pushed the button on my watch to show the date. Saturday, July 10. *Holy shit.* The car swerved onto the shoulder, almost hitting a light pole. *Stay on the road, Steve.* More than a day and a half—gone. I must have missed my Thursday and Friday shifts. *Frank is going to fire me for sure.*

I exited the highway and turned right toward Winton's. On Fridays and Saturdays, I had the prime shift of eight to four, so at least I would be on time. What would I say to my boss? I had to salvage my job, even if it meant groveling.

If you tell the truth, Steve, nobody's gonna believe you. And if they do, they'll call you a whore and toss you in the nuthouse.

Winton's didn't open until 9 a.m., and only a handful of employees went in at 8 a.m. to get the store ready. After parking, I wiped my feet and slipped on clean socks along with my backup tennis shoes. To delay facing Frank's wrath, I sat in the car until 7:55 a.m. *Do I still have a job?*

I crossed the parking lot to the store entrance and knocked on the glass. Frank looked up from his desk in the office and smiled—which I found to be odd given I'd been AWOL for two days. When he unlocked the automatic door, I stepped back so it could swing out.

"I wasn't expectin' you today," he said. "I guess you're feelin' better."

Not the greeting I imagined. For some reason, he assumed I'd been sick. I could work with that.

"Yeah, I am. Sorry I missed work."

"Luke's coverin' your shift. I didn't expect you back 'til tomorrow."

Missing three days of work would hurt my wallet, but at least I didn't lose my job. I nodded at Frank and turned to leave.

"Wait. Go clock in. I can use extra hands today."

"Thanks. Appreciate it."

I passed the office and headed down the produce section on my way to the time clock. Sam, the produce manager, had the hose out spraying the vegetables. When I stuck the car key into my right pocket, I discovered folded paper.

Two one-hundred-dollar bills.

My stomach churned—so I ran past the meat counter and through the opening to the stock room. I barely made it to the bathroom when everything in my stomach came up. Thank God the toilet didn't have a lid. The heaving continued in waves until my dry throat burned.

Once I finished and rinsed my mouth, I flushed and leaned against the wall. Then I noticed the familiar pain of sexual activity—either that or someone had shoved a bottle up my ass. The adrenaline from escaping the man's house must have covered it up until now. I'd sold myself like a common streetwalker.

I didn't talk much during my entire shift. My body went into automatic mode—bagging groceries like a robot, packing jars and cans in the paper bags without any conscious action while my mind focused on the herd of elephants in the room.

How could I have prostituted myself? If Mom knows I didn't come home, what will I tell her? What if others find out what I did? Why am I losing time again?

Two coworkers asked if something was wrong, probably because I wasn't my usual talkative self.

"I'm still not feeling a hundred percent," I responded, taking advantage of the reason I apparently told Frank.

Despite my distractions, I didn't break anyone's eggs or smash their bread or drop jars of mayonnaise. I finished my shift without incident and clocked out at 4 p.m.

On the way home, the tepid air blowing through the open windows did little to cool me off. By the time I turned down our dead-end street, sweat had soaked my shirt. Seeing Mom's Chevy Impala in the driveway didn't help matters. She was supposed to be coaching my sister's softball team in a tournament at Ben Geren Park this weekend.

Just like my car, our house had no air conditioning. Instead, we had a water cooler fan in the front doorway during the summer. The fan pulled air through filters with water running over them. It didn't cool the house very much, but the blowing air would always give me goosebumps when I stood in front of it.

With the front entrance blocked, we had two ways to get into the house: the sliding glass door at the back of the house, and the door connecting the carport to the kitchen. Anyone sitting at the table could watch both—and I found Mom there, a lit cigarette dangling from her lips.

"Steven Wayne, where the hell have you been?"

She took a drag and tapped the ashes into a coffee can on the table. At least she didn't have a beer or mixed drink in front of her. No telling how long she'd been waiting for me.

"What happened to the tournament?"

"I asked you a question. Sharon said you haven't been home since Thursday."

"You know I work Thursday, Friday, and Saturday." I hoped the answer would be sufficient as I turned to leave the room.

"Steven Wayne Simmons, don't you walk away from me."

When she said my full name, I cringed. All I wanted to do was wash the smell of that...*man*...off me, but I stopped and turned to take my punishment. This wasn't going to go well for me.

Mom got out of the chair and approached. She left a trail of smoke and ashes from the cancer stick in her right hand. God, I despised the smell of cigarette smoke. When she got an arm's length away, she looked up at me.

"Where were you?"

"Staying with someone."

Steve, you technically didn't lie to her, but it's best not to say, "I don't remember."

"You called Sharon on Thursday and said you'd be gone until this afternoon, but you didn't say where you'd be. I even called your work. They said you were sick."

Oh, boy. Now I knew how a mouse felt when the trap closed on it. "I needed a day off."

"You left your sister here by herself for *two nights*. And you lied about working. All you care about is yourself, just like your daddy."

Mom had raised her voice at me before, but never this loudly. Over her shoulder, my dog, Major, stared at us from the other side of the sliding glass door. Did she put him out there just before I got home? His ears stood straight, and he bared his teeth. I'd raised him to be gentle and loving, but he was a loyal Doberman. He'd probably protect me when necessary.

"Steven Wayne, are you listenin' to me?"

My biggest flaw had always been an inability to keep my mouth shut when I should.

"*I'm* selfish? Where were *you*, huh? You party every night and sleep God knows where. You can't expect *me* to be the parent around here. *You're* her mother, *not me*."

I regretted my words when the palm of her hand hit my face, knocking my eyeglasses across the room. Major scratched at the door, trying his damnedest to get in. He growled deeper than I'd ever heard. I stood frozen, unwilling to believe she'd slapped me.

"Havin' you kids ruined my life."

The words ripped a hole through me. Her eyes showed no remorse, just stern truthfulness. Mom often said crazy shit when she'd been drinking, but I smelled no alcohol on her breath. She must have meant every sober word.

How can she blame us for her unhappiness? What did we do? What did I do?

Mom went into the living room, leaving me standing there. Once I found my eyeglasses, I opened the sliding glass door and stepped outside. Major spun round and round with his tongue hanging out. He always looked happy to see me, his stumpy tail wagging like crazy I didn't know what I'd do without him.

I lowered myself onto the top step and held my arms open wide. All ninety-five pounds of him jumped on me like he was nothing more than a toy poodle. With his front legs on my shoulders, Major gave me a much-needed hug. I wrapped my arms around him, buried my face in his neck, and sobbed.

If I had somewhere to go, I'd take him with me and leave without hesitation. Aunt Estelle—Mom's older sister—and Uncle Cliff would take me in, but they didn't like dogs.

You also can't stay with them because of your blackouts. You can't put them at risk.

When Mom and Dad split up, he moved in with her hairdresser, so I couldn't stay there—as if I'd ever live with him anyway.

I had to go do something, so I grabbed my tennis bag from the bedroom. Major shadowed me, not leaving my side. After making sure he had food and water inside, I squatted in front of him at the carport door.

"Thanks for worryin' about me. You're the only one who'd miss me, aren't ya?" He licked the side of my face, which made me smile.

As I closed the door behind me, he whimpered and barked.

I'll never abandon you.

Chapter 6

Babysitting Fee

Whon the alarm woke me, I checked my watch. Thank God. It was the right day of the right year. The left side of my face throbbed, but I had only myself to blame for running my mouth. After getting dressed, I went to brush my teeth—and the reflection in the mirror repulsed me.

Whore.

Even if I didn't remember selling my "services" to the man from the restroom, I did. How could I come back from that? I was, and would forever be known as, a prostitute—at least to me. *Was this the first time?* Maybe I'd pimped out my ass to others and never noticed. The reality of blackouts left me pensive and paranoid.

I didn't know what to do. If I told someone the truth, they wouldn't believe me. It all sounded like a convenient excuse for bad behavior.

After feeding Major, I drove to work. Paying attention while driving proved difficult as my situation haunted me. Why, after two years, was I suddenly losing hours and days at a time?

Suddenly? Stop lying to yourself.

The times before weren't even blackouts. I just spaced out sometimes when guys had sex with me.

What about the fifth grade?

Even that blackout happened when—

Why am I arguing with myself? I don't like to think about all those guys because I...miss them.

Steve, you're pathetic.

I miss the way they held me and treated me special.

You're an idiot. They raped you.

I'm broken. Scared.

Miraculously, I didn't run off the road, hit anyone head-on, or rear-end any cars. I went to work that day...and the next...and the next. For the remainder of the summer, I picked up extra shifts when available. Frank didn't care so long as I didn't go over forty hours a week. What I didn't do was play tennis. I had no desire to be near the Creekmore Park restroom, a mere hundred yards from—and in full view of—the tennis courts.

Not surprisingly, Mom didn't mention anything about hitting me. The words "I'm sorry" and "I apologize" weren't in her vocabulary. Instead, when anyone brought up something she did, Mom's response would be "that's in the past," as if those words eliminated the need for contrition. I'd witnessed her saying that to Dad and Aunt Estelle on several occasions.

Mom's refusal to show regret must be why she didn't want to talk about Tom, our babysitter in Kentucky. We lived there briefly after she and Dad divorced each other the first time in the early '60s. Tom—a neighbor—volunteered to look after me and Mike while Mom worked. I never understood why she didn't question the motives of an adult man who wanted to babysit two boys—ages four and five— for free, especially after he worked all night.

"Why didn't you stop Tom?" A year ago, I blurted out those words while Mom and I shucked corn on the front porch. I'd wanted to bring it up many times—and apparently decided that was the moment.

"I don't know what you're talkin' about." She continued pulling off the corn husks without looking at me.

"He molested me, and you knew about it." I broke out in a cold sweat in the hundred-degree weather.

"Don't be silly." She lit a cigarette, took a drag, and resumed working. "You were too young to remember somethin' like that."

I might have been only four years old, but I recalled a lot of things from the six months we lived in the other state—such as her taking me and Mike to the submarine races at the river, and me sleeping on the floorboard of her Corvair when we moved there. I even knew Tom's name and the fact he didn't charge her for babysitting. Nobody had ever told me those things, so how could she say I'd been too young to remember the man having sex with me?

"Mom, you walked *in* on us."

"Stop makin' stuff up." She threw a cob of corn into the bucket and took another drag off her cigarette. "You probably just dreamed it."

Making stuff up? The incident burned itself into my four-year-old brain. I wasn't too young to have memories of significant events, but I *was* too young to understand the enormity—the depravity—of what Mom did. While Tom had me doing...things...to him on the bed, she opened the bedroom door and walked in. Maybe she came home early from work, or he lost track of time. As she stood there, I kept my hands on his private parts and looked at her.

Did she stop Tom? Throw him out? Call the police? Ask if I was okay? Tell me it was wrong?

Nope.

Without saying a word, she turned and left the room, closing the door behind her. How could she do that to her son? How could she do that to *me*? *I know what I saw. I remember what she did.*

At age four, I didn't see anything wrong with what Tom and I did. She didn't say anything to the contrary—not then or any day since. That incident turned out to be the last thing I remembered about Kentucky—and I'd never forget it.

Mom's denial on that hot August day last year left me empty inside as I sat on the front porch with her, hoping she'd say something to comfort me, anything to make sense of what I remembered. But she lit a cigarette and picked up another ear of corn to clean, moving on with her work as if our conversation never took place. So typical of her.

I got up and went into the house before saying something I shouldn't. Arguing with her never accomplished anything. Besides, what if she was right? What if I imagined it all?

Steve, stop second-guessing yourself. You remember it as if it happened yesterday.

If I told her about my blackouts, she'd accuse me of making them up, too. Or, worse, she'd put me in a mental hospital to get me out of the way. If Mom discovered I had sex with all those guys in Greenwood, she'd kick me out of the house—especially if she learned I'd prostituted myself.

I had no option other than to keep my blackouts a secret. None. Telling anyone would put me at too much risk.

Please, God, make them stop. Let me be normal.

Chapter 7

When Sybil Met Eve

October 1976
Greenwood, Arkansas
Age 16

O nce school started in September, I barely had any time for myself. Mike went away to college in August, which left my sister and I to fend for ourselves when Mom wasn't home. In addition to my classes, I had to work weekends, do homework, attend yearbook staff meetings, and serve as football team manager. My only salvation was I got good grades without having to study beyond reading and doing the class assignments.

Working with the football team—which I'd done since the seventh grade—proved problematic. I couldn't avoid being near naked guys strutting around the locker room and showers. What if I blacked out and made a pass at one of them? Or, worse, what if I prostituted myself again? If word got out at school, I would...kill myself.

I no longer recognized the person in the mirror—the one who hadn't picked up a tennis racket since July, the one who snapped at classmates and got into arguments over pointless issues. The guy staring back at me was moody, angry, and scared.

At lunch one day in early October, I sat across from Charlie, one of my casual friends at school. My best friend, Sean, joined us. The mystery casserole tasted better than it looked, and we had a delicious-looking doughnut for dessert.

"When's Mrs. Johnson announcing who's doing the skit?" I asked. The French Club planned to take part in the Foreign Language Festival in Little Rock in two weeks. We'd be performing "Le Petite Chaperon Rouge," or "Little Red Riding Hood." I'd auditioned for the role of the wolf—the male lead—and considered myself a shoo-in because I nailed the pronunciation and emphasis.

"She already posted the list," Charlie said. "I thought you knew. I'm the wolf and—"

"What?"

My French was a hell of a lot better than his. The teacher had a particular disdain for me. I rarely paid attention in class, yet I received excellent scores on exams. When she would hand back our tests, she'd give me "the look"—a piercing glare with a steeled frown. The woman probably assumed I cheated.

"She picked you for the poetry competition."

"Poetry?"

The dizziness I feared hit me. I leaned forward—elbows on the table—to balance myself.

Oh, God, not again.

———————

No matter how many times I "awoke" in an unexpected place, I found it unnerving. I found myself sitting on a bench at football practice. What happened during the past two hours?

What on God's green Earth was wrong with me?

The players ran drills as the coaches yelled at them.

"Hit the showers," Coach Sadler called out, signaling the end of practice and the beginning of my job.

As I did after every practice and game, I put the equipment away and went to gather wet towels in the locker room. From ten feet away,

Charlie looked at me and shook his head. *Uh, oh. What did I do?* His frown and clenched jaw told a story I didn't want to hear.

When I got to my locker in the classroom building, Sean approached—laughing. "I can't believe you did that."

"Did what?" Maybe playing stupid would get the answers I needed.

"Oh, come on. That innocent look doesn't work on me."

"What did you see?" Answering a question with a question could work.

"You leaned across the table and smashed a doughnut in Charlie's face."

Ouch. Not good at all. "Mrs. Johnson gave him *my* role in the French Club skit. She gave *me* a stupid poem to read."

"It's not *his* fault."

I leaned against the wall and closed my eyes for a second. "You're right. I'll apologize to him."

Damn. I have to fix this—and soon. When you didn't have many friends—even if they weren't close ones—you couldn't risk alienating them. After class, I caught Charlie in the hallway.

"Can we talk?"

He backed up a step, his eyes wide. "It depends. Do you have more doughnuts?"

Ah, a joke. Maybe I could repair this after all. "Look, I'm sorry."

"I've never seen you act like that. Are you on drugs or something?"

"I'm just stressed out." *Talk about understatements.*

He pulled a book from his locker and slammed the door shut. "You need professional help."

Tell me something I don't know. I went to French class and sat far away from Charlie. When the bell rang at the end of the period, I stayed behind and went up to the desk.

"Mrs. Johnson, could I get a copy of the poem for the competition?"

She handed me several pages stapled together. "You should be able to do this easily."

Then why didn't she give me the lead in the skit?

Let it go, Steve. Just let it go.

Over the next two weeks, I recited the poem hundreds of times. Mrs. Johnson recorded it with her voice and put it in the French lab so I could listen to her saying it correctly. My delivery had to be perfect for the poem to sound authentically French.

When the week of the Foreign Language Festival arrived, my alarm clock went off on Monday morning as usual. I opened the dresser drawer to get socks when I noticed a copper mug next to my wallet and keys on top. Engraving on one side read "1st Place, French Poetry, 1976, AFLTA."

Oh, great. Now I'm even dreaming about the competition. But everything was too real. On a whim, I checked my watch. It was Monday the—

What the hell?

Monday the twenty-fifth—not the eighteenth. This can't be. The competition took place last week. I lay on the bed and closed my eyes, tears running down the side of my face and into my ears. How could I lose an entire week?

Cut the crap, Steve. You keep forgetting about the fifth grade.

Stop reminding me!

I was losing my mind—and had absolutely no idea what to do. If I told someone, they'd want to know when and how it started. Then they'd find out *everything*. I'd be the laughingstock of the town.

The only thing I could do was pretend the blackout never happened. *I guess I'll be answering lots of questions with questions.*

After a few minutes, I wiped my eyes and finished putting on my clothes. I waited for Sharon to finish breakfast —I had no appetite—and then drove us to school. Acting normal came naturally, although I was far from it. As I learned information about what happened the previous week, I absorbed it. Blackout Steve—as I decided to call the "me" who did things during the lost time—had turned in all the homework and taken tests. Luckily, none of my Monday classes had exams or pop quizzes.

In French class, Mrs. Johnson gave me "the look" when she handed out the results of Friday's exam. My other self received a perfect score.

Wow. It's a good thing he took the test instead of me because the questions were hard.

Dumb ass, it was you. You just don't remember.

The week passed quickly as I caught up on my schoolwork. Although Blackout Steve had done well the week before, I hadn't completed any of the reading or done the homework myself. That meant twice as much work.

I remained active in the French Club despite my disdain for Mrs. Johnson over the skit fiasco. With my busy schedule, I didn't get to spend much time with Sean except at lunch and club meetings. Ironically, I needed his friendship more than ever, yet I couldn't tell him why it was so important to me.

At a French Club meeting the last week of October, Mrs. Johnson passed out some paperwork.

"Some members suggested we take a trip to France next summer," she announced, eliciting "oohs" and "aahs" from other students.

"I put together a package that includes airfare and lodging. It does *not* include meals or incidentals. You'll have to pay for everything yourself."

Of course we do. There's always a catch.

"We need at least ten people. How many are interested?"

Twelve students raised their hands. I doubted anyone expected me to. After Mom filed for divorce two years earlier, I got free meals at school along with the kids from other poor families. The lunchroom had two lines where students paid the cashier before going into the kitchen to get our trays. Those of us who got free ones had to walk between the lines so the woman could mark us off a list.

On more than one occasion, I caught other students snickering, whispering, and pointing at me. Once I got a job at Winton's, I paid for my lunch to avoid the free line.

So, when Mrs. Johnson asked who was interested in going to France, I didn't want to be the poor person people felt sorry for or teased. When Sean put up his hand, so did I.

"Steve must think it's free," someone behind me said, followed by giggles.

Although I couldn't afford it by myself—despite my savings—I needed only a few hundred dollars. Maybe Mom could help me.

Are you a comedian now? She'll never give you money for the trip, and you know it. She'd have to cut back on cigarettes and booze.

I have to try.

Somehow, I had to find the courage to ask her. In the meantime, I wanted some semblance of normalcy in my life. The blackouts continued to rattle me, keeping me from concentrating on school and work.

On Saturday, October 30, I decided it was time to go back to Creekmore Park. My shift at work ended, so I went to the WINTON'S bathroom to change into my tennis clothes. Standing in the tiny space reminded me of being on my knees with my head over the toilet bowl. I got out of there fast and headed to my car.

The ten-minute drive to the courts seemed like hours. At every turn and stoplight, I wanted to change direction and go anywhere but there. *Why am I doing this to myself?*

When I arrived, the sight of Rob, David, and other tennis friends made me smile. It took every bit of willpower I could muster not to look at the restroom building. I stood on the retaining wall overlooking the concrete-surfaced courts. Rob ran over to me.

"Son of a gun. Where the hell have you been?"

"I took a break." My destructive life hadn't tainted my Fort Smith friends yet. I had to keep it that way.

"Grab your racket and join in. Use the one with strings this time."

With the men's restroom in sight, I pushed through the distraction and had fun. We played late into the evening, even as the November temperatures dropped. Being on the court with my friends invigorated me.

The next day—Halloween—I slept late because I had the rare Sunday off work. When I opened the door to the hallway, the pungent smell of cigarette smoke announced Mom's presence. Her car hadn't been in the driveway when I got home late the night before, so she must have come that morning. I hadn't had a chance to ask her about the trip to France. Maybe she'd be in a good enough mood for me to bring it up.

I discovered her and Sharon sitting at the dining room table. My sister had her head buried in a big bowl of Cap'n Crunch.

"Hey, Mom. Surprised to see you." *Yeah, surprised you aren't nursing a hangover at Harry's.* Major scratched on the glass door, so I slid it open to let him in. A rub behind his ear sent his short tail into wag overdrive.

Since August, Mom had been dating Harry, a guy she met in a bar, of course. Like her, he drank heavily and smoked constantly. She soon spent every night at his apartment on the far side of Fort Smith near Van Buren. It had been months since she showed up at the house and cooked us a meal or washed the clothes or did anything a normal mother would have done for her children. I had become the *de facto* head of the household, and it sucked.

While part of me *wanted* to be happy for her, I couldn't stand the guy. The way he stared at me without smiling made hairs stand up on the back of my neck. I shouldn't joke about them getting hitched. Any marriage between those two would make *The Poseidon Adventure* look like *Gilligan's Island.*

I got a bowl from the cabinet and filled it with cereal. Major nudged me with his head, a sign he wanted to play—as always.

"Steven, I came down to tell you and Sharon somethin'," Mom said.

"Let me guess. I'm gonna have a brand-new daddy."

"As a matter of fact, we're gettin' married."

I flinched at the news, causing me to miss my bowl with the milk. *You had to go and say it, didn't you?* The white liquid poured on the counter and ran down the front of the cabinets.

"Damn it." While Major lapped up what hit the floor, I grabbed a kitchen towel to mop up the milk. "I don't understand what you see in him."

Steve, when will you learn to keep your mouth shut?

"It's none of your business," Mom said.

"Isn't it? He's an alcoholic, and he hates us." I rinsed the towel and got on my knees to wipe the cabinets and floor. The heat inside me expanded as my anger increased. How could she bring a man like that into our family?

"You don't know him. He's even gonna buy me a Corvette after we're married."

What utter bullshit. *Lord, protect me from what I'm about to say.*

"Sure. The man who drives a beat-up Oldsmobile and lives in a cheap apartment is gonna buy you a Corvette. He's full of crap."

The sound of her chair scraping on the floor made me stand, but I didn't turn to give her an easy target to hit again. A moment later, a door slammed shut down the hallway.

It's her life. She's gonna do whatever she wants no matter what you say.

"Way to go," Sharon said.

"Yeah, I'm quite stupid sometimes."

Mom left after lunch. I wanted to feel bad for upsetting her, but I couldn't. Marrying Harry would be a huge mistake. Was it any of my business? Maybe I should keep my nose out of her love life and worry about my own problems.

Are you sure? Whatever she does will affect you for at least two more years.

It couldn't be worse than the blackouts.

But you're not trading one for the other. You'll have both to contend with.

Wintry weather kept me off the tennis courts the first two weeks in November. On Sunday, November 14, I worked on supper while Sharon occupied herself with the TV.

After we ate our macaroni and cheese, Sharon and I watched *Sonny & Cher*. She conked out about halfway through the show, so I shuffled her off to bed. With Mike at college, I no longer had to argue with him about what we watched.

While thumbing through the *TV Guide*, I came across a two-part movie on NBC called *Sybil*. It was about a woman who had sixteen separate personalities. She'd have blackouts during which her other personalities would do things. It was based on a book by Flora Rheta Schreiber.

Reading the description gave me chills.

For the next two hours, I couldn't take my eyes off the show. Sybil bounced in and out of blackouts, waking up without any memory of what happened. The character could have been me. When at the hospital with Dr. Wilbur, Sybil wanted to know if she had hurt anyone. I understood her fear and anguish.

After school the next day, I headed to the Greenwood Public Library. Standing at the counter, Miss Maestri, the librarian, flashed me a big smile when I walked through the door. Her mother lived next door to us and had let use her garden—larger than a basketball court—since we moved into the new house.

"Good afternoon, Steve, what can I do you for?"

"I'm looking for a book called *Sybil.*"

"You and half the town." She pulled a hardcover book off a cart behind her. "I promised this to someone, but they don't need it until Saturday. Can you return it by then?"

"Absolutely."

She stamped the due date on the inside back cover of the book. "Hope you enjoy it."

Could I actually have multiple personalities? It would sure explain everything.

"Thanks. Uh, do you have any other books like this?"

"Have you seen the movie *The Three Faces of Eve?*"

"Never heard of it."

"It's an old movie also based on a book. We don't have it, but I can get it through interlibrary loan."

She pulled a form from under the counter and slid it to me, along with a pen. After completing it, I rushed home, isolated myself in the bedroom, and started reading *Sybil.* The more of the book I consumed, the more it terrified me.

The second part of the movie aired that evening. Afterward, I crawled into bed and continued with the book. Sybil had been abused, including being sexually assaulted with kitchen utensils by her mother. Her brain created something called "alternating selves" to shield her from the trauma she experienced. Her "alters" began living their own lives. That left Sybil with missing time—and absolutely no memory of what the other personalities had done. The doctors called it multiple personality disorder (MPD).

I've never experienced abuse like that. Maybe I don't have MPD. Nobody beat me. The sex wasn't exactly torture, although some of it did hurt. Was that enough to cause the disorder?

Steve, you're in so much denial. Those guys raped you.

But I usually enjoyed the sex—at least the parts I remembered. How could it have psychologically damaged me?

Don't be stupid. If you blacked out, you have no idea what anyone did to you then.

If I have multiple personalities, what kind of life can I have? People will be afraid of me.

They might as well put you in a mental hospital and throw away the key.

I'll be teased and ridiculed.

Face it, Steve. You'll never have a normal life if people find out. You're a freak.

Once I finished the book, I lay frozen in bed. *Am I like Sybil?* Most of my memories were like objects in my peripheral vision that went unnoticed unless I focused on them. Part of me wished I had a brain tumor, something I could understand, but that surely would have killed me by now.

I wanted to share with Sean all I learned about multiple personalities—to tell him everything that had been happening to me—but it would scare him off. Our five-year friendship had been the longest I'd ever had, and it didn't involve sex.

Maybe I can discuss it with a teacher.

They'll call your mom, and you don't want her to know. She'll have you institutionalized because you'll be too much trouble.

I'll just pretend there's nothing wrong with me.

Was keeping it a secret the only solution? I didn't know what else to do.

The Saturday before Thanksgiving, I got home and found Mom at the dining room table, a cigarette dangling from her mouth. She had papers spread in front of her and was writing something on a yellow pad. An overflowing ashtray and a half-full bottle of beer flanked the papers. I sat in one of the uncomfortable wooden chairs around the table and pretended to be interested.

"Whatcha workin' on?"

"Plannin' the weddin'." She took a long drag on the cigarette and blew smoke on the papers. The cloud rolled over the table and hit me. I couldn't believe she still planned to marry that alcoholic creep.

"How's it goin'?" It turned my stomach to make small talk with her.

"It's goin'."

"When is it?"

"Don't know yet. March, maybe. We hope to use Harry's clubhouse."

Wonderful. Afterward, we can have a potluck dinner and go swimming in the cement pond. She could at least take her eyes off the legal pad and look at me.

"Our French Club is going to France next summer, and I wanna go." Since I got my job, I didn't ask her for money—and she never offered.

Mom put down the pen and chuckled. "You need to stop hangin' around those rich friends of yours."

"You don't even know who my friends are." *Steve, be nice.* "It won't cost that much."

My right hand shook as I removed the folded paper from my back pocket and handed it to her. It listed all the relevant information, including the price and dates.

"Do you think I'm made of money?"

Exactly the response I expected. "I can pay for two-thirds of it from savings. And I'll save more to pay for my meals. I just need someone to cover the rest. It won't be due until next May."

When she signed the form and handed it back to me, I couldn't believe it.

"Uh, thank you."

"I ain't payin' more than that."

"That's all I'll need." The trip could take my mind off the blackouts and my screwed-up family.

You're making a big mistake. What if you get to Europe and Blackout Steve decides to go off on his own?

Then maybe I'll disappear and never be found.

Chapter 8

Choose Me

With a new year ahead, I tried to think positively. My plans included taking the ACT for college, qualifying for the state tennis tournament, and traveling to France. I might have an entire year of happiness—although I'd be satisfied with one semester.

In December, I emptied my savings to pay the trip deposit and insurance. I also sent in the application for my passport. Since then, I'd been setting aside money for the "incidentals," as Mrs. Johnson put it. Everything would be set once Mom made the final payment. The prospect of getting away from Arkansas for three weeks made me giddy. It didn't hurt that I'd be in Europe—with my best friend, at that.

Next year, I'd be off to college. Mom and Dad never spoke to me about my college plans. They couldn't afford to pay for it anyway, which meant I'd have to rely on scholarships and financial aid like Mike did. I decided to attend the University of Arkansas because it charged low tuition to state residents. They also didn't require the SAT, which saved me time and money.

The ACT went smoothly. I took the standardized exam early so there'd be plenty of time to retake it if I bombed. School had always been easy for me, which is the only reason I ranked near the top in my class.

On Saturday, April 2, I drove to Fort Smith for an event I'd dreaded for months: Mom's wedding. I didn't mind the concept of her getting married, but she had no business being with that drunkard. My gut told me it wouldn't end well for any of us.

I parked at Harry's apartment complex and meandered until I found the clubhouse. About twenty people stood around with drinks in hand. Only one person wore a suit. He had to be the pastor. Everyone else wore casual clothes—including me with shorts and a T-shirt. Mom told me to "come as you are," so I did.

Generic wedding music began playing from a portable stereo next to the wine fountain. Carrying a bouquet of mixed flowers and wearing a tiara of braided daisies, Mom strolled in and stood next to Harry. A proverbial train wreck played out in real time as two drunk conductors steamed toward each other. Once the bride and groom exchanged vows, the room erupted in applause. I had the urge to slap myself and scream, "*Wake up.*"

To reach the happy couple, I pushed my way through the crowd.

"Congratulations." I tried to sound upbeat, sincere, and loving, but it probably came across as bitchy sarcasm.

"Now you have someone who'll set some rules," Harry said.

He rarely joked, so I chuckled—until I noticed his rigid jaw and lack of smile. I got chills on my arms, and a knot formed in my stomach. Harry, a little shorter than my six feet, outweighed me by at least seventy-five pounds. I could outrun the morbidly obese alcoholic who smoked four packs a day, but he'd catch me if I stumbled.

I wolfed down two slices of pepperoni pizza with a Coke. From the long line at the self-serve bar, I figured most guests preferred a liquid meal. I'd never tasted alcohol. Nobody from school had ever invited me to a party, so I didn't have any opportunities to imbibe. Besides, my parents' drunken brawls had always turned me off to it. Given the "happy" occasion, I decided to give it a try.

I moseyed up to the white-wine fountain and filled a plastic cup. The liquid smelled sour, like vinegar but not as sharp or pungent. If alcoholism was genetic, the odds didn't look good for me. I didn't want to end up like my parents—miserable, bitter, and lonely, always searching for something or someone to fill the void. Mom just filled hers with someone as miserable and bitter as she was.

Oh, what the hell. Why not? I brought the wine to my lips and sipped. The cold liquid tasted tangy, but it warmed my throat as I swallowed. A second sip followed—and then a third. I neither liked nor disliked the drink, but it caused my body to tingle and relax. In one final gulp, I emptied the cup and tossed it in the trash.

Soon I understood why people drank. It took only one cup to dull my worries. I wanted another—and another and another. The more numb I could get, the happier I'd be. But I didn't need a ticket for driving while intoxicated (DWI), so I stopped at one cup and got out of there before I gave in to temptation. Despite all the shit in my life, alcohol made me mostly not care. Could wine be the answer to my blackouts?

The week after the wedding, my ACT results arrived. I scored far above the minimum required to attend my chosen college. In seventeen months, I'd finally be free from this inbred cesspool of a town.

My tennis obsession kept me in the team's top spot the entire season. That gave me confidence that I'd make it to the district finals, thus qualifying for the state competition. On the first day of the district tournament the week after Mom's wedding, I arrived in great shape and ready to win. Midway through my quarter-final match, I flew ahead 4-0. I'd played my opponent twice during the regular season meets and had easily beaten him both times.

A severe cramp struck my left calf as I changed courts in between games. When I was twelve, a surgeon removed varicose veins around my ankle on the same leg. Larger ones appeared below my knee in the years since.

Although I didn't want to retire from the match, my calf muscles seized every time I stretched to reach a ball. My promising run in the tournament came to an abrupt halt. The season ended with a whimper instead of the bang I'd hoped for.

Dropping out of the competition upset me, but wine went a long way to ease the disappointment. Weeks earlier, I used a pencil and eraser to turn my driver's license into the perfect fake ID. The DMV replaced it after I claimed to have lost my wallet. So, on the way home from the tournament, I bought a bottle of wine at a Fort Smith liquor store. I drowned my sorrows that night in the confines of my bedroom—a pity party with me as the guest of honor.

In late April, I had two weeks to make the final payment for my trip to France. At 10 a.m. on Saturday, I stopped by Mom and Harry's apartment to get a check from her. Because he worked every other Saturday and had been off the previous one, he wouldn't be there—which is what I preferred. Mom opened the door, a drink and cigarette in her right hand.

"What are you doin' here?"

"Hello to you, too, Mom."

I walked past her to find Harry watching TV from his recliner. So much for avoiding him.

"Hey, Harry. Got the day off, huh?" Making small talk with the bastard turned my stomach, but I did the minimum to keep the peace.

"Mind your own fucking business," he said.

Thank goodness the asshole couldn't see me roll my eyes. "Mom, can we talk?"

She led me around the corner to their galley kitchen where she added Bacardi to her glass.

"I stopped by to get the check for my French trip."

"What check?"

"For the French Club trip. It's due soon." Her bloodshot eyes told me the story of her morning.

"Oh, that." She gulped half of her drink. "I don't have it."

My chest felt heavy, constricted. *Calm down, Steve. Arguing with her when she's drunk will get you nowhere.*

"Mom, I asked you about this *months* ago." My voice cracked. Coming here had been a terrible idea. "You promised me."

The highball glass slammed on the counter, splashing on me and sending a piece of ice flying across the linoleum countertop to the floor.

"Harry got a DWI, so we needed it."

"Are you telling me the man who's gonna buy you a Corvette needed the few hundred dollars you promised to *me?*" *You should never have married that piece of shit.*

"What the fuck is going on in here?"

Harry had sneaked up behind me. Great. I sure didn't want my stepfather to poke his nose where it didn't belong.

"Nothing. I'm leaving." I pushed past him to escape the dingy, smoke-filled apartment. If I stayed there any longer, I'd say something to make things worse.

Thanks to Harry, I'd lose everything paid toward the trip. I'd been looking forward to getting away from this godforsaken family for just a little while. Freedom in a foreign land. Now Harry's inability to stay sober had tubed my plans.

When I got home, I played with Major for a half hour to calm my nerves. Then I remembered the trip insurance. I found the policy brochure and sat on the bed to read the section on hospitalizations. The insurance covered all deposits for the trip if hospitalization and/or surgery prevented me from going.

"Major, I can get my money back."

He spun around in the center of my bedroom, his tongue hanging out. Then he jumped up next to me. I held him in a tight hug. "You're always here for me."

I put my plan into motion by calling Mom the next day—hoping she would be sober.

"I need you to call Dr. Bailey tomorrow to set up an appointment for me."

"What for?"

"My varicose veins. If I have surgery, I can get the deposit back for my trip to France." Silence on the other end of the call worried me.

After reneging on her promise to pay for part of my trip, the least she could do was help with this. It wouldn't cost her anything because Dad's health insurance still covered me.

"I can't take off work."

"You won't need to. Doctor Bailey has seen me before without you there."

Thankfully, Mom called on Monday and made the appointment for Tuesday. As I expected, Dr. Bailey referred me to a surgeon who could see me that Friday morning. Mom grumbled about having to miss work, but the surgeon took less than five minutes to examine my. His nurse gave me a letter saying I'd have surgery in June and be on restricted activities for four weeks after that. I telephoned the travel insurance company and filed my claim.

I'd rather be going to France, but that wasn't what bothered me most. Mom broke her promise—and she did so because of her alcoholic husband. I always wanted to believe she'd do the right thing and be supportive.

For once, I wanted her to choose *me*.

Chapter 9

Price of Friendship

Not long after my birthday party, we moved into our new house a few blocks from the town square. Mama and Daddy built it on land Granny had used for her garden. Mike and I still had to share a room, but I got my own bed—the top bunk. Sharon landed her own bedroom.

When we unpacked, I found Mama's old typewriter. It weighed almost as much as me. I carried it to the kitchen table while she cooked dinner.

"Can you learn me how to use this?" I asked.

"You're still learnin' to write. Maybe in a few years."

"It's not fair. I know I can do it."

"Fine, but you'll have to teach yourself. There should be manuals in the same box as the typewriter."

I found the books and began doing the lessons. My fingers couldn't reach all the keys—and I had to press them real hard to make words on the paper. Every day, I came home and watched Dark Shadows. Afterward, I practiced typing until it was time to set the table for dinner.

One day, I typed my math homework. When I handed it to Mrs. Smith, she stared at me real funny.

"Stevie—"

"It's Steve. Stevie is for little kids." My brother said the same thing when I called him Mikey. She laughed, but I wasn't trying to be funny.

"Fair enough. Steve it is. Your mother shouldn't be doin' your homework."

Why does she think Mama did my homework?

"It's math, Mrs. Smith. I'm better at it than she is."

From her laughter, she thought that was funny, but I was just telling the truth.

"Okay, she shouldn't be typin' your homework."

"She don't do that either."

"Didn't do that."

"That's what I said. She don't do my typin'. I learned myself how to do it."

"You taught yourself."

"Why do you keep repeatin' what I say?" Mrs. Smith was sure acting squirrelly. Maybe I should go to the principal's office and get help.

"No, Stevie—"

"Steve."

"Right, right. Steve. You said, 'I learned myself how to type.'"

"I did learn myself. Are you feelin' okay, Mrs. Smith?"

"I'm fine. When you used the word...you know what? Never mind. Just don't type your penmanship lessons."

"How could I do that?" *She's not making sense. I can't type my handwriting*

After that day, I typed a lot of my assignments—except for penmanship.

In March, we started having tornado drills every week. When we heard the alarm, we had to get under our desks. It seemed silly. If a tornado could lift a house and carry it all the way to Kansas, how would hiding under a desk help? We did the same drill for a nuclear war. One day, we watched a film about atomic bombs. They made humongous explosions and wiped out everything. I raised my hand before the film finished.

"Steve, do you have a question?" Mrs. Smith asked.

"Yes, ma'am. How is sittin' on the floor gonna protect us from that?" I pointed at the screen where a test bomb had destroyed everything around it. The other kids laughed, but she didn't answer my question.

One Friday afternoon in April, Mama picked us up early from school.

"I have a bad feelin' about the weather," she said when we got in the car.

On the way home, I craned my neck out the window to watch the dark clouds. We had bad storms all the time, but I'd never seen Mama act worried. She drove kind of crazy, just like she did on the highway. When we got home, Mike and I stayed outside between the carport and Granny's house so we could watch the skies.

"Don't go anywhere," Mama said. "And I mean it."

Black clouds passed overhead slowly. Everything got quiet. Even the birds shut up. Then it thundered—at least it sounded like thunder, but the rumble didn't stop. I never heard anything like it. The wind almost knocked us over. Mama opened the carport door.

"Get in the house."

Mike and I ran past her into the kitchen.

"What's that thunder?" I asked.

"It's a tornado," she said. "Help me open all the windows."

We went through the house as fast as we could to push up the windows. I didn't know why she wanted us to open them, but she was old—almost thirty—so she had probably seen a lot of tornadoes.

In the living room, I stopped in front of the picture window. Outside, large limbs flew down the street. The tops of the trees in our front yard nearly touched the ground as they bent in the stiff wind. My brother yanked my arm, making me jump.

"We gotta go," he said.

I nodded and followed him. We ran to the hallway where Mama waited for us. She pushed us into our bedroom. "Get on the floor next to your sister."

The lights went out. Mike and I sat on the floor under a window with Sharon between us. Mama got on her knees, pushed us down flat, and lay on top of us. Her body trapped me. I couldn't breathe.

It was just like when I got a chunk of hot dog stuck in my throat right after we moved into the new house a few months earlier. When I began choking on it, Mama threw me on the floor, sat on my stomach, and dug the wiener out with her fingers. She had saved my life.

Lying on top of us, she was trying to protect us from the tornado, but I didn't care. I had to get out from under her, so I pushed on the wall and wiggled backwards to escape. She grabbed my belt and pulled me back.

"Stop it, Steven."

I shut my eyes and peed my pants. God, please get me out of here. I can't breathe.

The tornado lasted forever. Then it got quiet. When Mama finally got off of us, I opened my eyes. We followed her to the kitchen where she picked up the phone—and shook her head.

"It's dead. We better check on Granny."

We found her coming through the gate between our houses. I'd never seen an old woman move that fast.

"That twister was big," Granny said. "A lotta people are gonna be hurt. Where's Bobby?"

I ran up and gave her a hug. God, please let Daddy be okay. Last month, he fell off a telephone pole and broke his leg. Ever since then, he worked at the office downtown.

"He's at work," Mama said. "That's all I know."

Although the tornado didn't blow away any houses around us, it knocked down trees and telephone poles throughout the neighborhood. We stood in the front yard waiting for Daddy. He suddenly appeared at the end of our street—climbing over the fallen trees and wires. The cast covered his entire left leg, but he practically ran down the street to us.

When he reached our yard, Daddy put his arms around us and squeezed—the first time he ever did that.

The next day, the paper said the tornado had killed at least eleven people and destroyed most of the town. Even though we had no electricity, Mama and Daddy let two families who lost their homes come live with us for a while. One family had two girls in the fifth and sixth grades, and the other one had a boy named Allen who would be in the tenth grade next year.

With twelve people living in our house, it got crowded. We had to put my top bunk on the floor because it was too hot without the attic fan. Allen slept between Mike's bed and mine.

The tornado got school canceled for the rest of the year. Because electricity would be out for weeks, we had to keep our food in ice chests. Every day, the Red Cross handed out free water and ice at the town square. The moms cooked on camp stoves they set up on the carport. We ate a lot of fried baloney sandwiches, but I didn't mind.

The girls were snooty, but Allen said I could hang around with him. Two days after he moved in, I showed him the old rock quarry on the other side of Granny's house. It was nothing more than a big crater with tons of loose rocks in it.

We climbed down to the bottom. Once there, we decided to build a fort by stacking rocks for walls and placing big flat ones on the top as a roof. Thank goodness Allen was strong because some of them were heavy. We finished building our hideaway, with the inside big enough that we could sit without hitting our heads on the ceiling.

Allen told me about playing on the basketball team and his plans to get a car when he turned sixteen. I didn't have anything exciting to share with him because my life was pretty dull.

"Why do they call you Sissy Simmons?" he asked.

His out-of-the-blue question caused my stomach to twist in knots. Why did he have to ruin our fun? "Who told you?"

"I heard it around."

"A girl started it last year. I don't know why she did it."

He put his arm around me and pulled me close. "Don't worry, I won't call you that. We're friends, right?"

I nodded. It was nice having a friend. We crawled over the rocks to get out of the fort. When he stood, Allen groaned and put a hand on his back.

"What's wrong?"

"Sleepin' on the floor, I guess."

"I'll swap. You can use my bed."

"That's okay. I don't wanna be a bother."

We stopped at the pool of water in the bottom of the quarry. I called it Crawdad Lake because it had so many of them in it. When I sat on a rock, Allen got on his knees and poked the water with a stick.

"When we first moved here, kids teased me because of my long hair," he said. "Some called me a girl, so I understand what it's like."

"Daddy called me a girl once." Did others get teased like I did? Maybe I wasn't alone. "I don't mind switchin' beds with you."

"We could always share. We're both skinny."

"I can't do that." I still wet the bed sometimes, but I couldn't tell him that.

"Why not? I promise not to bite."

Don't tell him.

"I might wet the bed." You went and done it. "It's why I have plastic under my sheet."

Allen looked at me and laughed. I kicked a rock into the water and ran to where we had climbed down into the quarry. As I jumped over rocks and pulled myself up the dusty side, I bawled like a little kid. How could he laugh at me?

"Why in tarnation are you leavin'?" he called out, but I ignored him.

By the time I made it to the top, he caught up with me. I tried to walk away, but Allen grabbed me by the shoulder and turned me around.

"I just thought what you said was funny because—"

"It wasn't funny."

"—because I wet the bed until the third grade."

"You still shouldn't have laughed at me."

"Sorry about that. Won't happen again."

Do I believe him? I have to. He's the only friend I have. "Okay, we can share my bed."

That night, I didn't drink anything after supper. Daddy put lanterns in the living room and kitchen so we could read or play games, but I had gotten tired of canasta and gin rummy.

When it came time for bed, Allen crawled in first and moved over against the wall. I put on my pajama bottoms and slid under the covers next to him. It seemed weird having someone lie against me.

The following night, I went to bed before him. It took me a while to fall asleep because of the noise from our parents' drinking beer and playing cards. Allen woke me later that night. I started to say something, but he put his hand over my mouth.

"Shhhhhh. Don't wake Mike."

I nodded. Allen lifted his hand and kissed me on the lips like boys and girls did—and like Tom did to me in Kentucky.

"I like you," he whispered. "Do you like me?"

"Yes. You're my friend."

"I'm goin' to make you feel good, but you have to be quiet." Allen put his hands in the waist of my pajama bottoms and tugged. I grabbed his hands.

"Stop," I said. "What are you doin'?"

"Shhhhhh. You're my friend, aren't you? Don't you trust me?"

I didn't know whether to or not. What if he doesn't want to be my friend if I stop him? Tom did this, so it must be okay. When I relaxed and nodded, he removed my pajamas and underwear.

"Turn over," he whispered. "This is our little secret."

After I got on my stomach, he put something cold and wet on my butt—and stuck his finger inside me. The sharp sting made me grunt. Allen slapped his hand over my mouth and pressed hard.

"Hush. Relax and enjoy it."

Even though I could breathe through my nose, he pushed down on me with his body, trapping me on the bed. I squirmed to get out from under him but didn't have the strength.

My head started spinning like I was on a Tilt-A-Whirl. Everything got fuzzy.

Next thing I knew, I awoke, the sun shining through the curtains. Had I dreamed Allen kissing me and doing those other things? I reached down to discover I was naked. When I lifted the covers, I found my pajamas and underwear at the foot of the bed. My butt also hurt, and the sheet and pillowcase had dark red stains on them.

It hadn't been a dream.

Once I got dressed, I put my sheets under the dirty clothes in the hamper. We still had no electricity. That meant I'd have to wash my bed clothes by hand.

I found Allen eating cereal at the kitchen table. After filling a bowl and getting milk from the ice chest, I sat across from him. He had a rag wrapped around his right hand. Should I ask him what happened to it? As I ate my Cap'n Crunch, he pushed his bowl aside and leaned over the table.

"I had fun last night. Try not to bite me next time." He sat back in the chair. "Wanna go hikin' on the other side of the quarry today?"

He still wanted to do sex stuff with me. I didn't know what to think about that. Although Tom and I had done things, it never hurt—not like it did last night. But Allen was a friend, and he didn't treat me like a little kid. He made me feel special.

"Uh, sure. Hikin' sounds fun."

Allen had sex with me every night after that, sometimes during the day in our rock fort. I didn't always space out like I did the first night, and it got easier and hurt less the more he did it.

A month later, he and his family moved to Fort Smith. I managed not to cry while their car pulled away, but I went into our rock fort and bawled for a long time.

I'd lost my only friend.

Chapter 10

Not Just a Dog

June 1977
Fort Smith, Arkansas
Age 17

Mom took off work one June afternoon and picked me up in Greenwood. I had to be admitted to Sparks Hospital in Fort Smith the day before my surgery to have pre-op tests.

For the past ten months—ever since she met Harry—Mom rarely stayed at the house. Mike went to college that same month, leaving me mostly alone in Greenwood

Fortunately, Mike had moved back for the summer to work the third shift at Whirlpool. He'd be able to look after Major for the forty-eight hours I'd be away.

The doctor said the operation went well. He removed two large veins from my left calf and gave me twenty-eight stitches. I had to stay an extra night for "observation," he called it.

The next day, at ten minutes before noon, a nurse pushed me in a wheelchair to the front entrance where Mom waited with the car. Before sliding into the front seat, I tossed the crutches in the back. My throbbing leg had been wrapped in gauze and elastic bandages.

Mom drove me to Greenwood, although she wanted me to stay with them at the apartment—as if I would do that.

"I can't be in Greenwood to look after you," she said.

Given she worked all day, I didn't know how she planned to "look after" me. Besides, I'd rather be alone with Major than anywhere near Harry.

"That's okay. I can manage. Besides, Major will keep me company." My brother would be there, too, but I didn't want to rely on him.

"Major isn't there anymore."

"Is he at the apartment?"

"I had your Daddy give him away."

I must have heard her wrong. "Did you say Dad gave him away?"

Wake up, Steve. Wake up. This has to be a dream—or a sick joke. I can't lose Major. He's mine. I rely on him. I need him.

"Now that I'm married, we have to sell the house."

"*Liar*. You and Dad agreed to keep the house until Mike and I graduated." I'd read the divorce papers when she left them on the kitchen counter one day.

"We're gonna buy a house and need the money. Bobby agreed to sell it."

"I don't give a rat's ass. You and Dad agreed—"

"Steven Wayne Simmons, watch your language. You can't keep Major because dogs aren't allowed in the apartment."

"*Screw you. You gave Major away. Where is he?*" I'd go get him and bring him back to the house. We'd live in my car if we had to.

"I ain't tellin' you."

"I'll ask Dad, then." I couldn't catch my breath. The car seemed to close in on me. How could they take Major from me?

"Bobby isn't gonna tell you, either."

"How could you do this? Major will be scared and worried."

"He's just a dog."

"*Just a dog?*" We were two miles from home, but I couldn't stay in that car for another minute. It was suffocating me. *She* was suffocating me. "Stop the car. I'm gettin' out."

"I'm not stoppin' the car."

When I opened the car door, Mom slammed on the brakes, sending me into the dashboard and flinging the door wide open with a loud creak. She pulled to the side of the road. Once I crawled out of the car, I reached into the back seat for my crutches.

"Have fun walkin'. I gotta get back to work anyway."

"I'll never forgive you for this." I slammed the door shut and hopped away from it, balancing myself with the crutches. She made a U-turn and headed back toward Fort Smith.

What kind of parent gives away their child's dog while they're in the hospital?

It took me two hours to reach the house, but I'd do it all over again—despite the crutches rubbing my underarms raw and the shorts chaffing my thighs in the heat. If she had come back and offered to drive me home, I might have broken her windshield with a crutch.

Major had been there for me through so much crap. Sharon found him as a puppy and brought him home. He had rickets and needed veterinary care. Two months later, we found the owner, but they told us to keep him. Sharon eventually lost interest, and Major latched onto me. He became my trusted companion. No matter what I went through, that silly dog always brought me comfort. I had to find him.

My car was the only one at the house. Once the carport door closed behind me, I leaned against the washing machine and let the tears flow. Normally, Major would greet me at the door or be going crazy in the backyard when he saw me.

What am I going to do?

The telephone ringing snapped me out of my self-pity. I tossed the crutches aside and hopped on my good leg to the phone on the wall in the kitchen.

"Simmons residence," I answered.

"Steven Wayne—"

"Are you tellin' me where he is?"

"No, I—"

"Go to hell." I hung up on her. Did she call to see if I made it home safely?

If she cared about your well-being, she wouldn't have given Major away.

Did she call to apologize?

Good one. Mom has never apologized in her life.

If she wasn't going to get Major back, it didn't matter why she telephoned. I took the receiver off the hook and dialed the number for Dad's office.

"I'd like to speak to Bobby Simmons."

"He's out in the field. Can I take a message?"

"This is his son Steve. Have him call me at home as soon as possible. He has the number."

After hanging up, I peeled off my sweat-soaked clothes and tossed them in the washer. I stunk. As I hopped to the bathroom, I got a cold Gatorade from the refrigerator. The liquid hit the spot after my arduous walk home in the heat.

Only this isn't home anymore. I don't have one.

Getting clean proved to be difficult. If I got in the tub, I might not be able to get out. A shower was out of the question because I had nothing to keep my left leg dry. I compromised by washing from the bathroom sink. At least this time I didn't have to worry about a stranger walking in on me.

When the phone rang, I hopped back to the kitchen and sat on a stool next to the counter.

"Simmons residence."

"It's your daddy."

"Where's Major?" Silence. For a moment, I assumed we'd been disconnected. "Are you there? I want to know where he is. What did you do with him?"

"He, uh, he's gone."

"I *know* he's gone. Where the hell did you take him?" I got hot all over. My temper bubbled below the surface, ready to explode. This already had been the longest conversation I'd had with Dad since he bought the car for me.

"He's gone, and you ain't findin' him."

"How could you do that to me? To *him*?"

Dad hung up. I slammed the receiver down and left it off the hook. No more calls would interrupt me.

They gave Major away like he was nothing—like *I* was nothing. My stomach rolled and twisted. Everything hit me at once. Major, my blackouts, my attraction to men, the missed trip to France, the prostitution, all the guys I had sex with—

I'm so tired. I can't do this anymore.

The doctor said not to put pressure on my left leg for forty-eight hours, but I didn't give a shit anymore. I got off the stool and walked to the bathroom. With every step, twenty metaphorical ice picks stabbed my leg as damaged nerves sent pain signals to my brain. I pushed through.

I sat on the toilet and turned on the tub faucet. Once the water got to a comfortable temperature, I leaned over to put the stopper in the drain. The tub filled as I retrieved a razor blade from one of the vanity drawers.

The water stung my leg like a son-of-a-bitch when I slid into the tub. I turned off the faucet once the water reached the rim.

After lying in the hot water for a couple of minutes, I pressed the razor blade against the inside of my left wrist. With a little push, blood trickled into the tub.

You didn't leave a note.

Nobody cares about me.

What about Aunt Estelle and Uncle Cliff? How can you do this to them?

It'd be worse if they found out about the other stuff I did. My death will keep them from ever knowing.

The sharpness of the blade stung when I pressed harder. My vision blurred as the dizziness signaled an impending blackout. I tried to pull the blade up my forearm, but my hand froze. Blackout Steve was stopping me.

No. Please, let me do it.

Chapter 11

As the Wind Blows

Some might be thankful they were alive, but not me. Life wasn't worth it anymore. Blackout Steve shouldn't have saved me. With Major gone, I had a big hole inside me. Nothing in the house made me want to be there anymore. I'd been certain for a while that my parents didn't love me, but I'd never had solid proof until now. If Mom and Dad cared at all for me, they never would have given Major away behind my back.

Giving up on getting Major back proved difficult, but I had to move on. Mom and Dad would never tell me where he went. Arguing with them would be futile. As usual, tennis served as an outlet for my frustrations.

One Saturday afternoon in mid-July, I drove to Creekmore Park after work. None of my friends were playing, so I sat on the retaining wall to watch. A girl and two guys around my age began warming up on the court in front of me. They looked like pros the way their ground strokes zipped over the net. The girl returned the guys' shots without any effort. I couldn't believe how fast she moved. After picking up balls lying against the fence, she looked in my direction.

"Wanna play? Our fourth couldn't make it."

I turned, but nobody stood behind me.

"I'm talkin' to you, cutie pie," she said. "Wanna join us?"

The thought of trying to play with them made me laugh, but she took it the wrong way.

"What, you think you're too good for us?"

"Uh, just the opposite." Oh, my God, they'll roll right over me. It'll be the Wilkinson tennis court incident all over again. Nothing but embarrassment and humiliation.

"Oh, come on. Give it a try. You can be my partner."

She sounded so cheerful. How could I refuse? I jumped down and carried my tennis bag to the bench. While I removed my rackets and wristbands, the three players walked over.

"I'm Leslie. This is Will and Tony. We go to Southside."

That made sense. Fort Smith Southside had one of the top tennis programs in the state. We never competed against them because their school was much larger than mine.

"I'm Steve from Greenwood."

I couldn't take my eyes off Leslie, whose beauty made me smile. With her hair in a ponytail through the back of her white tennis visor, her face glowed in the sun. It wasn't sexual attraction because girls didn't have that effect on me. It didn't strike me until then that she was as tall as me.

For the next four hours, I barely paid attention to the train wreck known as my life. I didn't even flinch at seeing the men's restroom fifty yards away. Instead, I thoroughly enjoyed being with my three new acquaintances. None of them teased my play, which was sub-par compared to theirs. Although I had moments of greatness, Will and Tony seemed to enjoy using me as a human target when I played the net.

In the end, I mostly held my own, but Leslie's superior skills made me look good. We quit at 10:15 p.m. after she and I won the best of five sets, 3-2.

"You'll have to come hit with me at Hardscrabble," she said, referring to the country club near Southside. "That's where we usually play."

"Oh, so you were slummin' it today," I said, making everyone laugh.

Leslie and I exchanged numbers. They drove away in a Mercedes convertible, which left my car as the only remaining one on the lot.

A gust of wind kicked up dust as I threw my bag in the back seat. I started the car and rolled up the windows. What a great evening. I turned the radio to KISR 93 and leaned back in my seat. Maxine Nightingale's "Right Back Where You Started From" played. I closed my eyes and almost fell asleep listening to the catchy chorus. When the song ended, someone tapped on my window, causing me to jump. A slender man in shorts and a T-shirt stood next to my car. He smiled at me with hands planted on his hips, so I rolled down the window.

"Can I help you?"

"Just checking to see if you're okay."

He didn't have a southern accent. Either he'd lost it, or he wasn't from the area. Moisture on his arms glistened under the bright lights towering over the courts. He hadn't been playing tennis—I would have noticed him, without a doubt—but his rapid breathing pointed to some physical exertion, probably jogging. The lights shined on his pearly white teeth and twinkled in his emerald-green eyes. Why would someone that gorgeous be out running on a Saturday night instead of being on a date?

He shifted and—did he thrust his crotch a little? *Steve, stop imagining things.* He had a disarming, trusting smile.

"Thanks, but I'm fine."

"Cool. My name's Jamie. I was finishing my run and saw you here."

"I'm Steve. Wanna sit inside out of the dust?" *What the hell am I doing?* Jamie walked around the car and climbed into the passenger seat. The air suddenly seemed hotter. "Sorry, I don't have air conditionin'."

"No bother. At least I'm not getting covered in dirt."

My hands shook. Jamie's light brown hair hung in curls over his ears. His smile made me warm inside. I guessed him to be a few years older than me.

"I'm covered in it after playing tennis all evenin'. Do you go to WestArk?"

"The UofA. I'm on summer break."

"Same here. Well, not the university, but on break. I plan to go there after graduation next year."

"How old are you?"

At least he asked. "Seventeen. You?"

"Twenty-one."

Awkward silence descended on us. He reached over and slowly ran his fingers along my forearms, causing goosebumps to break out. When I didn't pull away, he put his hand on mine. I got excited instantly.

"I'm housesitting for my parents while they're on vacation. It's a couple of blocks from here. I was heading there when I saw your car."

"I could drive you." My voice cracked.

You offered a ride to a perfect stranger. Are you insane?

What if I'm reading Jamie wrong?

Dammit, Steve, why are you reading him at all? You're not gay!

A few minutes later, I pulled into the driveway of a darkened two-story house. Did I really want to go in? He could have others waiting inside to beat me up or worse. Neither of us spoke for a minute. *Is he waiting for me to say something?*

"Would you like to come in? There's nobody else home."

What am I doing? "Are...are you askin' me to—"

"Yes, if you're interested."

My brain said "no," but a certain part of my body said a firm "yes." "I need to shower first, but I have clean clothes."

Thank God I always kept a set in my car. The smile on his face accentuated dimples I hadn't noticed before. Why would a guy as good-looking as him be interested in me?

"I need one, too. Hope you don't mind sharing."

Jamie got out and motioned for me to follow.

Steve, seriously, what are you doing?

I should back out of the driveway and go home.

Disregarding my gut instinct, I grabbed the backpack and followed him up the driveway. He unlocked the door and held it open for me. With cautious abandon fueled by teenage hormones, I stepped inside.

The click of the door closing behind me signaled the finality of my decision.

Despite Jamie's mild-mannered personality, I half expected him or someone else to jump me. Being in the dark house with a total stranger seemed wrong and right at the same time. I flinched when he wrapped his arms around me from behind. He kissed the back of my dirty neck, sending chills down my spine. I dropped the backpack and turned to face him.

"Is this real?"

He answered by cupping my head in his hands and gently touching his lips to mine. This uncharted territory filled an emptiness, and I never wanted it to end. I tasted sweat and dirt but didn't care.

"Have you been with a guy before?" he asked.

I considered telling him about the others, the things they did, how they used me. Simple honesty won out. "Not like this."

We deposited our dirty clothes and shoes on the hardwood floor, and he led me upstairs to the shower. My watch read 10:43 p.m. when I placed it on the bathroom vanity. I had to be at work in a little over nine hours. That left plenty of time for fun.

At 3 a.m., I crawled into my own bed in Greenwood—exhausted and shamed. Guilt, sadness, anger, and disgust hammered at me. I crossed the line tonight because I *wanted* to have sex with a guy. Nobody forced, coerced, or threatened me. For the first time, I did it of my own free will—and enjoyed it.

But it was wrong. I couldn't be a homo, queer, faggot, sissy, cocksucker—all the names I'd been called over the years. Did I have sex with Jamie because I was gay or because the others made it seem normal?

What have they turned me into?

Over the next two weeks, Leslie and I played several times, either at Creekmore, Hardscrabble Country Club, or Ben Geren Park—where local tennis-great Lorene Barry ran the tennis complex and pro shop. Her husband, Lou, was the area's expert on racket stringing. I didn't often play at Ben Geren because you had to plan ahead and reserve courts. At Creekmore, I could show up almost anytime and find someone to hit with.

I continued taking lessons from Farrell, but Leslie also helped my game. Of all the times we played, I never won a set off her—and very few games. That might bruise the egos of many male players, but it didn't bother me. My ground strokes and service returns improved. More important, I relished being around someone who didn't look down on me or tease me.

She took me to her home a few times. I got to meet her mother—a nice lady. Many of my friends had families who made me jealous.

One day in July, I had to rest after Leslie trounced me one more time.

"Don't be hard on yourself, Steve. It's all in your head." She pulled a towel from her bag and sat next to me. "Your strokes are good."

I handed her a jar of Gatorade from my ice chest and opened one for myself. Her deep southern drawl and bright smile camouflaged an intense competitor with a killer instinct on the court.

"It's frustratin'. I hit well in warm-up, but then I choke durin' play."

"As I said: it's in your head. How long have you been playin'?"

"Two years."

When she laughed, I covered my head with a towel and put my head on my knees. Was I deluding myself by continuing to play?

"Sorry, I'm not laughin' at you. Steve, darlin', I've been playin' since I was five. You should be proud of yourself."

"I lose all the big matches."

"Look, you just need experience. The club's hosting a USTA boys' tournament next month. You should enter."

Right. Me in a USTA tournament. I'd get massacred. "I'm not ready for that."

"Of course you are. We'll keep practicin', and you'll do just fine. It's a consolation event, so you're guaranteed two matches."

She talked me into it. I submitted the membership form at the Hardscrabble clubhouse and paid the entry fee. Lou Barry restrung my rackets with new catgut—a fiber made from animal intestines, not real cats. The natural strings gave me more control of my ground strokes and volleys.

On the tournament day, I drove to Hardscrabble and parked my old Mustang among the Mercedes, Cadillacs, and Lincoln Continentals. Some of the best amateur players aged eighteen-and-under from Arkansas and surrounding states would be playing. How could I compete against them? I put my car in reverse and prepared to leave, but Leslie walked around the red Jaguar parked next to me.

Crap. I'll have to play now. After shifting into park, I got out and grabbed my tennis bag.

She escorted me to the check-in table where they told me about my first-round opponent. I'd be playing my arch nemesis, the top player at another school in our district. He had a serve with so much topspin that it would bounce over my head if I stood at the baseline. To have *any* chance of returning the serve, I had to stand just behind the service line and hit the ball right after it bounced.

In the four times we'd played each other during school matches, I never won a set off the guy.

To make things worse, the tournament officials scheduled our match on one of the courts below the clubhouse—where a large crowd of spectators assembled to watch us from the gallery. I cringed when Leslie sat front and center.

Now she can see you choke.

An hour later, I found myself up a service break at 5-4, 40-0, on my serve. All I had to do was win one of the next three points to take the first set.

With the sun directly overhead in a clear sky, the temperature on the court had to be at least a hundred degrees. I wanted to get this set over with so I could guzzle a Gatorade and rest for a minute. The packed gallery became silent as I prepared to serve. I bounced the ball and went into my service motion. As the racket made contact with the ball over my head, I did the unthinkable.

I farted.

It wasn't a dainty, low-sounding passage of wind—or a silent-but-deadly escape of gas. I ripped a wet one so loud it startled me. My aluminum Head Professional racket—the "Red Head"—flew from my hand. It hit my side of the court, bounced over the net, and landed near my opponent. Even though I automatically lost the point, my nemesis returned the ball. All I could do was watch as his irrelevant ground stroke zipped past me.

The sound of my foghorn-level emission reached the gallery. Giggles, belly laughs, and chuckles erupted. The players on the court next to us bent over in laughter.

I tried to ignore the guffaws as I walked to the other side to retrieve my racket—which had a big dent on one side and a cracked frame. Although I had another one, it and two more set points couldn't save me. I lost the next nine games along with the match, 7-5, 6-0.

Leslie and I got a good laugh out of the incident. I didn't get the outcome I'd hoped for, but at least I gave the spectators something to remember. As for my consolation match, I lost that 6-0, 6-0—and I couldn't even blame that loss on wind.

Chapter 12

Eating Crow

Mom **closed down the Greenwood** house in August and forced me to move into a three-bedroom apartment with her and Harry. My room barely held a twin bed and a dresser. The closet, no wider than the door and barely deep enough to hang clothes, quickly filled. Several boxes of my property—winter clothes, knick-knacks, tennis trophies, school awards, things Aunt Estelle had given me, yearbooks, and other stuff—went into the small storage unit provided by the apartment complex.

As I settled into my room, Harry opened the door and walked in without knocking.

"This is my apartment," he said, "and I have rules you *will* follow."

Oh, God. Here we go. I shut the closet door and leaned against it. My eyes met his, and I crossed my arms.

"Curfew is nine o'clock, so you *will* be here by then. If your mother cooks dinner, you *will* be here to eat it. You *will* keep your room clean. You *will* make your bed every day. The rules start today."

He stared at me for a few seconds, smirking.

"Are you done?"

"For now."

"I'll make my bed, but those other rules"—I put air quotes around the word—"don't work for me. Between work, school, and tennis, I'll rarely be here."

Harry took two steps toward me, so I backed up. "I don't care if you have something else to do. Your ass had better be in this apartment by 9 p.m. When your mama cooks, your ass will be at the table."

"I don't get off work until nine-thirty some nights. I often play tennis until ten-thirty or eleven—sometimes *after* I work late. I eat what I can, when I can. I barely have time to do schoolwork. Besides, Mom hasn't cooked me a meal in at least a year. Why should she start now?"

I also have no control over what Blackout Steve might do.

"Listen, smartass, your mouth is gonna get you in trouble some day."

I laughed, which made his face turn red. "What are you going to do? Lock me out? Drag me here to eat dinner?"

"Just test me, and you'll find out. You live under my roof, you do as I say."

Was he serious? "Look, *Harold*, I've lived by myself for more than a year. I've taken care of myself longer than that. I didn't have parents when I needed them, and I don't want another parent now—especially you."

In response, he made a fist with his right hand and pulled his arm back like a boxer. A low guttural sound came from him as he clenched his fist. I didn't flinch or move back.

"Go ahead. Hit me. I dare you."

If he killed me, that would give me two gifts: my death and his imprisonment. After a few seconds of staring me down, he grumbled and left my room, probably to seethe in his BarcaLounger.

For some unexplained reason, my blackouts intensified. Blackout Steve did most of the driving. He also attended most of my classes, played most of my tennis, took most of my tests, and worked most of my shifts. Rather than fight it, I went with the flow—playing dumb when necessary. It was like sleeping through life, which was fine by me.

Coincidentally, Sean and his family had moved to Van Buren over the summer. His new home was just across the Arkansas River from

Fort Smith, a few miles from Mom and Harry's apartment. He and I decided to carpool to Greenwood when our schedules allowed it. Because Blackout Steve did most of the driving, I was sure he and Sean had interesting conversations.

When the junior class sponsored a dance at the Greenwood fairground building one Saturday in October, I decided to skip it. Instead, I got off work at four, went to the apartment, and hibernated in my room. Before Mom and Dad gave away Major, I could always lie next to his warm body as he lightly snored. Now I had nobody, so I put my head on the pillow and nodded off.

I awoke, not on my comfortable bed but on a solid surface that chilled my back. In an effort to sit up, my head spun so much I had to brace myself. In front of me, metal bars ran from ceiling to floor just like a—

"Simmons. You made bail."

—jail.

Dammit, Blackout Steve, what did you do this time?

A slightly overweight man in a uniform unlocked the door. The floor seemed to move, and I could barely walk. The guard took my arm and helped me down the hallway. When we got to the lobby, I wanted to turn tail and run back to the jail cell.

Mom and Harry stood in the center of the room, their arms crossed and lips pursed. I didn't know what happened but was sure I'd soon be eating crow. Blackout Steve must have done something and called them from jail. As they took me to the apartment, neither of them said a word to me—or, if they did, I tuned it out.

When we walked into the apartment—I refused to call it "home"—I went straight to bed. I awoke later that morning to the sound of someone pounding on my door with a sledgehammer. At least that's how my brain processed the knocking.

"Come in."

A blurry Mom opened the door and stuck her head in. I grabbed my eyeglasses off the nightstand.

"Is your car in Greenwood?" she asked.

Car? Greenwood? Dammit, how was I supposed to answer the question? "Why was I arrested?"

"Public drunkenness. Tommy Tincher picked you up at the dance."

Way to go, Blackout Steve. At least you weren't drinking and driving—but how did you plan to get home?

"I guess my car's at the fairgrounds then." *Where else could it be?*

"You guess?"

"It's there." *God, I hope it's there.*

"Get dressed. I'll take you down."

Oh, Lord. Just take me back to jail.

I put on clothes and found Tylenol in the medicine cabinet. When I stopped in the kitchen to get a packet of Pop-Tarts, Harry mumbled something under his breath from the living room. My mouth once again took over despite my brain telling it not to.

"Hey, stepdaddy. I guess I didn't fall too far from the step-tree, did I?"

"Fuck off, smartass."

"Steven, shut up and go to the car," Mom said.

"I hafta call work first." I'd never just not shown up for a shift. Even when Blackout Steve prostituted himself, he called in sick. I was already two hours late. My boss answered on the third ring.

"Hey, Frank. I'm so sorry. I got food poisonin' and was pukin' most of the night. I meant to call earlier but fell asleep."

I expected him to yell, but he finally spoke after a few seconds. "Understandable. Feel better."

With that bullet dodged, I now had to deal with a worse problem: Mom. We maintained silence all the way to the parking lot, but I knew what was coming—and she pounced before we got out of the apartment complex.

"Steven Wayne, I'm very disappointed in you."

"I'm crushed." I had bigger fish to fry in my own screwed-up world.

"You could go to jail for this."

"I don't care." In the overall scheme of things, this was minor.

"After everything I've done for you—"

"Whoa. Everything you've done for *me*? Like walkin' in while Tom was molestin' me?"

"You were too young to remember anything like that."

"Bullshit."

"Steven Wayne, watch your language." She turned onto the interstate.

"I remember the submarine races at the river, sleepin' on the floorboard of your car, and pullin' the trailer behind us. If I can recall those things, why wouldn't I remember you walkin' in while I'm givin' my babysitter a blowjob?"

"That never happened."

"Sure, it didn't. How about your spendin' the money for my trip to France because your new husband got *another* DWI?" I couldn't sit still or keep my mouth shut. It all came pourin' out without any filter.

"Stop it."

"Or how about making me move out of our house before my senior year?"

"*Steven Wayne Simmons, I said stop it.*"

"*No, I won't stop it. You gave Major to a fuckin' stranger.*"

"That's in the past. Why can't you let it go? He was just—"

"So help me God, if you say, 'He was just a dog,' I'll grab the steerin' wheel and kill us both. That *dog* gave me more love than anyone in this family ever did. I've *never* been in trouble before. I make perfect grades, but you reward Mike when he gets a C. So what if I got caught drunk? You got a DWI, destroyed your car, and almost died. How many DWIs has Harry had? Six? Seven? Send me to jail because I. Don't. Give. A. Shit."

Steve, calm down. You've said too much already. Just let it go.

"Mom, if you'd paid *any* attention to me over the past, what, twelve or thirteen years, you might have noticed I have bigger things to deal with. Oh, silly me. You *did* notice but walked out of the room."

Neither of us said a word the rest of the way to Greenwood. We found my car in the fairground parking lot. The moment I shut her car door behind me, she drove away.

At school the next day, Mr. Coats, the school principal, called me into his office. Two of my coaches—Sadler for football and Hargis for basketball—stood next to the desk. On the desk, smoke from a cigarette in an ashtray swirled toward the ceiling.

"Mr. Simmons, have a seat," Mr. Coats said.

After pushing the door closed, I remained standing with my arms crossed.

"We've heard some disturbin' news," he said. "Were you arrested at the school dance on Saturday evenin'?"

"You already know I was. That's why you called me in here, right?"

"What were you arrested for?" Coach Sadler asked.

"Being drunk in public."

"That's a serious offense," Mr. Coats said. "*And* you were at a school function."

"It's not like I had an abortion, smoked pot, or, I don't know, *raped* someone." *If they only knew.*

"This is about you," Mr. Coats said. "Your fate is in the coaches' hands."

"You're no longer the basketball team manager," Coach Hargis said. "I can't have you representin' the school."

"Neither can I," Coach Sadler said.

After taking a drag off his cigarette, Mr. Coats leaned back in his chair. "You'll be transferred to PE class immediately."

"I'm still on the tennis team."

"We'll see about that." Mr. Coats smiled and took another drag off his cigarette.

I burst out laughing. They hadn't done or said anything particularly funny, but I couldn't help myself.

"Do you find this amusin'?" Mr. Coats asked. "Maybe I should suspend you for a few days to give yourself time to think about what you did."

"Do what you gotta do. I don't care." I opened the door a little too aggressively and slammed it against the wall.

"*Mr. Simmons, get back here in my office.*"

Despite his hollering for me to return, I kept walking. I hated this school, this town, and almost everyone in it.

At the Thursday arraignment, the attorney my mom hired said I *would* be sentenced to jail for thirty-to-sixty days if convicted. Who knew a state full of hillbillies getting drunk off moonshine took public intoxication so seriously?

"Mr. Simmons how do you plead?" Judge Parker asked. He lived a few blocks from our Greenwood home.

Judge Parker had been the true owner of Major when Sharon found him as a puppy. The judge didn't have the heart to make us give Major back after we'd gotten so attached to him.

Despite how I'd considered this offense to be minor, I had to be realistic about serving jail time. If I missed a month or more of school, I'd have to repeat my senior year in this backwater town. I had no choice but to fight the charges.

"Not guilty," I said.

Chapter 13

A Cheesy Situation

January 1978
Greenwood, Arkansas
Age 18

I went on trial in January for Blackout Steve's drinking behavior. Not the best way to start off a year. It could have been worse. He might have killed someone—including us, not that I would have minded the latter.

Two girls from my class offered to testify on my behalf. They'd always been nice to me, so I trusted they didn't plan to sabotage my trial. The attorney Mom hired seemed skeptical, but he put them on the stand anyway. My two classmates swore I wasn't "falling down drunk" like Officer Tincher had testified. Hell, they had *me* convinced, but I suspected they were lying to protect me. Nobody had ever stood up for me like that before.

After both sides rested their cases, the judge found me not guilty on the charge of public intoxication. However, he convicted me of minor in possession—something I hadn't even been charged with. He gave me a suspended sentence and would expunge my record in a year if I kept out of trouble. Surprisingly, he didn't restrict my driver's license—I guess because the offense had nothing to do with driving.

With that out of the way, I got to continue with my senior year. Blackout Steve had faded to the background since my arrest in October. That left me having to do everything, which exhausted me.

The only funny aspect of this ordeal was that Mom spent more money hiring an attorney than she would have on my trip to France. Oh, the irony.

On a Saturday in February, I'd been working at WINTON's since 8 a.m. Two older women—who always requested me to bag their groceries—came through one of the checkout lanes. They shopped once a month, and I long ago learned the picky ways they liked their groceries separated. Because I took care of them, they always tipped me ten dollars when I got to their car.

Before I could finish sacking their groceries, Mrs. Winton—all eighty pounds of her—came out of the office, her arms swinging while she held her head perfectly still and level. Rose and Edwin Winton owned three of the busiest grocery stores in the city. She would make surprise visits to make sure Frank managed the store to her satisfaction. In doing so, she would be condescending, rude, and downright mean to all the employees—think Catherine the Great, but without the charm and niceties.

"Do what she says while she's here," Frank had warned me on my first day at the store.

How can I do that when my mouth has a mind of its own? Mrs. Winton stopped near me as I placed the last bag into the grocery cart.

"Steve, go to lunch."

Had she lost her mind? The lines in all six checkout lanes were ten shoppers deep. If I went to lunch, we'd be down a sacker—plus, I'd lose my big tip.

"Yes, Mrs. Winton. Right after I take these to the car." Maybe a compromise would work.

"Go to lunch now. Luke can finish that."

When she spoke, only her lips moved. Everything else—the smooth, alabaster-white skin with smears of red rouge on each cheek—remained less animated than the *Venus de Milo*. Her silver hair had been teased and sprayed into a round bouffant resembling a football helmet.

"Mrs. Winton, with all due respect, it's too busy for me to go now. We'll be shorthanded." Why did my mouth keep making words? This would not end well for me.

"Go now, or you're fired." She pivoted and stomped back to the office, her red pumps sounding like clogs on the linoleum tile. I wanted to grab the tomato rolling down the conveyor belt and splatter the back of her pastel-peach skirt suit.

In the twenty-six months I'd worked at the store, I'd never gotten into trouble. When Frank wanted something extra done, I did it. If he needed me to work on a school night, I worked. I'd never argued with anyone—not Mrs. Winton, Frank, the department managers, coworkers, or customers.

As much as I loved my job, I hated bullies—and Mrs. Winton was a white, wealthy bully who didn't like *anyone* standing up to her, even when she was wrong.

Luke pushed the basket out the door along with my big tip. As my temper neared its bursting point, I clocked out, put on my coat, and left the store.

When my alarm went off at 7 a.m. on Sunday, I pulled the covers over my head. Incinerator day. The monthly job involved shoveling ashes out of the WINTON'S IGA incinerator and into plastic bags. It took me two hours to empty the thing and another hour to wash it out with a water hose. Then I had to turn the hose on myself. Frank paid me double-time for my efforts, so I sucked it up and did it.

After parking next to my boss's white Chevrolet Impala, I grabbed the backpack containing a towel, extra clothes, and an old pair of tennis shoes. I waited at the entrance while Frank busied himself hanging ropes in front of items the store couldn't sell on Sunday. In the name of "religion," stupid laws prohibited the sale of mops, brooms, cleaners, and anything else that could be used to perform "work."

Once he placed the last rope, Frank went to the office and lit a cigarette instead of letting me in. Didn't he see me? I waved my arms to get his attention. When he finally came and flipped the switch on the automatic door, I stepped aside as it swung out.

"What the hell are you doin' here?" he asked.

"It's incinerator day." I stepped toward the open door, but he blocked my way.

"No, no, no, no, no, no." He waved his arms for me to back away from the entrance. "You don't get another fuckin' chance. You crossed the line yesterday. And if you hadn't quit, she would have fired your ass."

I'd never seen Frank that pissed. He yelled at times, but he didn't use the F word.

"I don't understand." *Oh, no.* After Mrs. Winton ordered me to take my lunch break yesterday, I didn't remember anything until I awoke this morning. How did I not realize that?

God, I'm stupid. What did you do, Blackout Steve? Should I tell Frank I don't remember any of it? Should I tell him about my blackouts?

That would be foolish.

I didn't even get dizzy before switching to an alter.

"You are banned from all Winton's stores. If you don't leave, I'll call the police."

This isn't happening. It can't be. Although I tried to swallow the baseball-sized lump in my throat, it wouldn't budge.

"What about my check?" *Hold the tears back. Don't cry.*

"I'll mail it. Don't come back."

The walk across the parking lot to my car seemed like a bad dream. Despite the freezing-cold breeze, I leaned back against the driver-side door.

What am I going to do?

You can't let Mom and Harry find out.

I had to find another job—and fast—but I had no idea where to look. Why would Blackout Steve sabotage me like that?

A Ford Pinto pulled up beside me. Luke. I'd miss him. Of the four baggers who worked with me, he was by far the cutest and easiest to talk to. The blond hair and innocent-looking smile won me over. He rolled down the window.

"Get in."

When I slid into the passenger seat, the hot air blowing from the vent thawed my face.

"What's up?" I asked.

"Dude, are you crazy? You'd better leave before Frank knows you're here."

"Too late for that. Did you see what happened yesterday?"

"Man, that was freaky deaky. The whole store heard. When you hollered at Mrs. Winton 'I hope your face lift falls off,' dude, we all laughed."

Oh, Lord, it's worse than I imagined. No wonder I'm banned.

"I guess she won't be givin' me a job recommendation."

Luke laughed. Not a giggle, but an all-out guffaw—and he looked adorable doing it.

"Man, I gotta go. It's incinerator time."

We hopped out of his car. "Yeah, sorry about that."

"It's cool. Double time, you know? Peace out."

As he walked away, my insides twisted. Two years of fun times with coworkers—friends—gone in an instant. I could never explain to them what happened. Was my entire life going to be like that?

On the way to the apartment, I stopped at the new McDonald's on Rogers Avenue. I stood back from the counter and studied the menu hanging above the counter.

"Good morning, Steve."

One of my classmates from Greenwood walked past me carrying trays from the lobby.

"Hey, Kim. Didn't know you worked here."

She rounded the end of the counter and stepped up to the cash register. "I'll take your order when you're ready."

I ordered hotcakes and sausage along with a large Coke. Caffeine might help my somber mood. As Kim got my breakfast together, I noticed how spotless the store was. The five workers smiled and busied themselves. Kim put the last item on my tray.

"Do you enjoy workin' here?" I asked.

"I have no complaints."

After eating, I returned to the counter and asked Kim for a job application. She disappeared around the corner for a few seconds and returned empty handed. "The manager will be right with you."

A stern-looking woman with short blond hair showed up. The pin on her blouse said, "Glenda, Manager." She set an application and a pen on the counter.

"Find a seat in a booth around the corner. I'll be there in a minute."

She had no southern drawl whatsoever. "Oh, I was just gonna take it with me."

"Are you looking for a job?"

"Yes, I am." Silly question. Why else would I ask for an application?

"Then amuse me and complete it out now."

I found a booth and began filling out the application. While I worked on it, Glenda slid into the seat across from me. I soon finished and handed it to her.

She asked me about Greenwood High School, my plans for college, and my last job.

"Why did you leave Winton's?"

How the hell was I supposed to answer? I couldn't exactly say Blackout Steve—my other personality—quit. Maybe a partial truth would work. "The owner was an asshole."

Glenda laughed. "When can you start?"

"Uh, whenever you need me."

"How fast can you clock in?"

"Now?" I never expected to be offered a job so quickly. Did I really want to hover over greasy burgers all day?

"I could always call your previous employer for a recommendation just to make sure you're reliable and easy to work with."

The sarcasm in her voice made me chuckle. She and I would get along fine.

After finding a uniform in my size—ugly brown polyester pants and a pullover shirt—I changed clothes in a restroom stall. Glenda gave me good news I didn't expect: I'd be working the counter instead of cooking the food, although I'd still be trained to do both jobs.

She began my training by having me watch videos in the break room. Then she put me on a cash register at the counter. I worked a full shift without messing up too many times. When I finished, Glenda put me on the schedule for the following weekend.

My hourly wage turned out to be more than I got paid at WINTON'S.

On Tuesday, I got a packet from the UNIVERSITY OF ARKANSAS in the mail. They offered me admission for fall 1978. The week turned out okay despite all the shit that happened. I went to my room and put the packet on my dresser—next to an envelope I hadn't noticed that morning. It was a good thing I got home before Mom or Harry. Neither respected my privacy.

Someone printed my name on the envelope in handwriting I didn't recognize. I opened it to find a handwritten note.

> *Steve,*
>
> *We are Mark and Wayne. We've been watching over you for years. Sorry Mark lost his temper with Mrs. Winton and quit your job. We're glad you found another one you like.*
>
> *Wayne*

Holy shit. I couldn't believe I'd guessed correctly: I *do* have MPD. No longer did I have to call my other personality "Blackout Steve." They were Mark and Wayne.

What do I do now? If I tell anyone, they'll surely put me in a nuthouse.

Confirmation that I had MPD both relieved and worried me. I couldn't focus on academics or tennis. Although I knew my alters' names, how would I know which one took over during a blackout?

Shortly after starting my McDONALD's job, I began finding money in my pocket after a shift. None of the managers ever confronted me about my register being short, so I didn't know where the money came from. One morning, I found another note in my room.

I take orders, clear the register, and pocket the cash. It's a
game I like to play. Don't worry, I won't get caught.
Mark

Wonderful. All I needed was to get arrested for theft. I had no idea how to stop my alter, and I couldn't give the money back without raising questions I wasn't prepared to answer.

You know how to stop him. Tell someone what's going on.

That's not an option.

The extra money came in handy, so I ignored its origin. Besides, I remained focused on tennis where I did well at the district tournament. Even though I lost in the finals, I qualified for the state tournament—the first tennis player from Greenwood ever to do so.

At school, the accomplishment mirrored the party for my eighth birthday—lofty expectations with no follow-through. Other school athletes who qualified for the state tournament got congratulatory banners and cheers at assemblies. I didn't even rate getting an announcement over the intercom.

To hell with them.

The state held the tennis tournament in Conway, two hours away. I had to drive my own car and pay for the hotel room. The only thing the school did was let me fill up my car at the bus depot—and I had to fight for that. Typically, I choked and lost in the first round, 2-1 in sets.

I returned to Greenwood that afternoon. Nobody asked about the tournament except Coach Davidson. Talk about a letdown.

Back at school, Mrs. Johnson and the French II class became my downfall. She unfairly gave me a B for the semester. On the oral exam, she said I didn't enunciate the words clearly. I had no problem understanding what I said. Because that grade was subjective, I had no way of challenging it—as if that would have worked anyway.

One of my alters went nuts. He convinced Sean to buy a slab of Havarti cheese—which stunk to high heaven. My alter and Charlie spread it all over Mrs. Johnson's car engine. For unknown reasons, they also smeared it on the girl's restroom wall. Naturally, Charlie and my other personality got caught. Mr. Coats suspended us for two days. Did I mind? Not really.

Thanks to Mrs. Johnson's grade, my class rank dropped. As a result, I graduated as co-salutatorian. Aunt Estelle, Uncle Cliff, Mom, and Dad attended the ceremony, which the school held on the new football field. Harry didn't come, thank goodness. Afterward, I drove away from Greenwood with a sense of relief. I closed a chapter of my life—escaping a town full of people who had tormented me since I was seven years old.

At the end of August, I'd be at the UNIVERSITY OF ARKANSAS in Fayetteville. Would it give me the fresh start I desperately wanted and needed? It depended on Mark and Wayne. Soon they would be in a different town with new people and a million ways to get into trouble.

God help us all.

Chapter 14

A Year in the Life

July 1970
Greenwood, Arkansas
Age 10

G reenwood hadn't been the same since the tornado hit us two years earlier. A lot of people built storm cellars like in The Wizard of Oz. Mama and Daddy talked about putting one in the back yard, but they said it cost too much.

Mama brought two new lawn mowers home in March. I helped her unload them from the back of the station wagon. Boy, they were heavy.

"Why do we need these?" I asked. "We already have one."

"You're gonna use these to mow lawns for money. We'll use the old one to mow Granny's lawn because of all the rocks. Just go knockin' on doors to find customers. We'll buy the oil and gas. This way, you'll earn money instead of askin' us for it."

We found six customers in a day. I did the talking because Mike was shy. Until summer break, we mowed after school and on Saturdays until summer break. I wanted to work on Sundays, but Mama said it was against the law.

It had been too darn hot all week to mow, but our customers didn't care. We finished two yards in the morning and stopped for the day. After lunch, I told Mama I was going downtown to the candy store. I could go wherever I wanted as long as she knew where I was. Ever since the tornado, she didn't want us disappearing.

I was saving for a new bicycle, so I only took a quarter with me. That was enough to get what I wanted. By the time I got to the store, my underarms were soaked. Mama would make me take another bath before I went to bed.

The candy store had air conditioning. I stood under a vent just inside the entrance and let the air blow on me. Mr. Franklin, the owner, smiled at me.

I knew exactly what I could get with my twenty-five cents. After grabbing a Snickers and a pack of red licorice, I got a cold Coke from the refrigerator in the back. I made my way to the register and put my quarter on the counter.

"Will that be all, Steve?"

I smiled. "You got somethin' behind the counter for me?"

Some days he'd give me candy from a busted container. He laughed and dropped a handful of something into my bag. Then he gave me my change and a bottle opener.

"Thank you, Mr. Franklin."

I popped the metal cap off my Coke and walked outside where the sun tried to melt me. If I didn't eat my Snickers now, it would be a mess by the time I got home. The store's awning gave me shade when I leaned against the wall, but it was still hotter than Hades.

Before I could tear the wrapper off my Snickers, a car horn almost made me drop it. It was Mr. Jones, a tall skinny man from the church I attended. He rolled down the car window.

"Steve, you're a hard person to find. Come get in the car and cool off. I'll give you a ride home."

No way was I going to turn down a ride in an air-conditioned car. I got in the passenger seat and pointed the vent straight at me. The cold air gave me goosebumps. Mr. Jones drove toward home, but he pulled over and parked in front of Dr. Bailey's office.

"Why are we stoppin'?" I asked.

"I have a business proposition for you. I'm lookin' for someone to mow my yard, and you came highly recommended. Your mama said you went to the candy store."

"Yes, sir. I had a cravin' for a Snickers and Coke."

"Would you be interested in some extra cash? If you mow my yard, I'll pay you five dollars. You can even use my mower and gas."

All our customers were little old ladies. Why didn't Mr. Jones mow his own lawn? "You must have a big lawn if you're gonna pay that much."

"No, it's small. I just want it done right."

When he smiled, his bushy mustache looked like a caterpillar crawling on his face. Some of his hair is gray, so he must be older than Daddy.

"We'll mow it. If Mike's home, we can do it today." Even if it meant mowing in the heat, Mike wouldn't turn down that much money.

"Why don't you just do it yourself? It won't take very long."

"Okay, I'll do it." All the money could go into my bicycle fund. "When do you want it done?"

"How about now? I know it's hot, but I have lots of cold drinks."

I'd hate to turn him down and lose the job. "You got a deal, Mr. Jones, but I need to let Mama know."

"You can call her from my house."

He didn't live far from us, but I'd never noticed his house before. At least he told the truth about his yard. He had so many flower beds that there wasn't much room for grass. After calling home, I finished my Coke before it got warm and flat. Then I got his lawn mower out of the garage and filled it with gas.

"Mr. Jones, are you sure it needs mowin'?" The entire yard was smooth, like someone had just cut it.

"I don't like it to get very high. If you get hot just mosey in the back door."

The heat almost made me stop halfway through, but I kept going. It took me twenty minutes. When I finished, I went in the back door and found Mr. Jones sitting at the table drinking a Mountain Dew.

"Are you finished already?" he asked.

"Yes, sir. It was easy."

He tossed me a towel and got a Coke from the refrigerator for me. I used an opener he had on the edge of his kitchen counter. We sat at the table. The Coke was so cold it burned my throat when I swallowed it.

"My nephew Allen says you'll be in the fifth-grade next year."

"You're Allen's uncle? That's so cool. How is he?"

"He'll be a senior next year. In fact, he should be here any minute. He's spendin' the weekend with me while my wife's in Little Rock visitin' her sister."

I couldn't believe my luck. Ever since Allen moved, I wanted to talk to him. He didn't tease or make fun of me like other guys did. Even though he wanted sex all the time, he explained how friends did that for each other. I eventually got used to it.

A car honked as I drained the last drop of Coke from the bottle.

"That should be him now. I'll be upstairs. You two get reacquainted."

Sure enough, Allen came in the back door carrying a duffel bag. I ran over and threw my arms around him in a hug.

"You're wet," he said.

"I was mowin' the lawn. Hey, why didn't he pay you to do it?"

"Because I hate mowin'. Plus, I wanted you over here."

We sat at the table and talked for a long time. He told me all about Fort Smith, Southside High School, and movies he'd been to see.

"They're buildin' somethin' in Fort Smith called a 'mall.' It's gonna have about a hundred stores inside it."

"Wow. I'll bet it's air-conditioned too."

He leaned toward me and grinned.

"I'm gonna take a shower. Wanna join me?"

Shower with another person? That seemed weird, especially with his uncle in the house. We never even did that after the tornado.

"I was just gonna take a bath at home."

"A shower is much better. We're still friends, aren't we?"

"My clothes are dirty." These icky clothes would just make me stink again if I wore them after showering.

"Don't worry about that," Mr. Jones said as he walked into the room. "Some of Allen's old clothes are here. Somethin' will fit you."

"Okay, I'll do it." I followed Allen upstairs. We went into a bedroom that had its own bathroom. There was no bathtub, though—only a shower that took up the entire wall.

Allen opened a dresser drawer and found some clothes for me—a pair of shorts, underwear, socks, and a T-shirt. He put them on a chair next to the door.

"We need to clean before we shower."

I didn't understand what Allen meant. He held up a bag with a hose on it like we had in the bathroom at home. Mama called it an enema bag.

"Why do we gotta do that?" I'd never used one before.

"It makes sure we're clean. When we play, we won't get poop on us."

That sounds nasty. I'm not surprised he wants sex again. Did he get his thing dirty when we had sex after the tornado? He never said anything. After Allen used the enema bag to clean out, he showed me how. I'd never had water up there before. It tickled coming out.

We got in the shower and soaped each other up. Nobody had washed me since Mama did when I was little. The warm water sprayed on us for a long time. Once we'd rinsed, Allen turned off the shower and handed me a towel.

I put on Allen's old underwear and was bending over to slip the shorts over my feet when he grabbed me from behind. He tossed me onto the bed, causing me to laugh—and I didn't stop until he crawled on top and kissed me.

"Missed you," he said.

"I didn't think I'd ever see you again."

The bedroom door opened and closed. I turned my head to see Mr. Jones standing there.

"You guys didn't start without me, did you?" He unbuttoned his shirt.

"What's he doin' here?"

"My uncle and I play together when we can. That's why I cleaned up, too. Now he can have fun with both of us."

"You told him about us? How could you do that?" Allen told our secret. He's my friend, not Mr. Jones. "Get off me. I'm gonna go home." When I tried to wiggle out from under Allen, he held me down. Mr. Jones—now naked—lay beside me and started rubbing my chest.

"No. Let me go. Please."

As Allen kissed me again, his uncle pulled off my underwear. I didn't want to cry in front of them, so I squeezed my eyes real tight.

The room spun, and I fell into the abyss.

The smell of pine trees and bacon got my attention. I immediately recognized the campsites on the hill above Blue Mountain Lake. We came here to camp on most summer weekends. Mama would have everything packed by Friday afternoon. She'd back up the station wagon and hook it to our boat in the carport. When Daddy got off work, we'd drive two hours to the park and set up camp before it got dark. Then we'd water ski, swim, and fish until Sunday afternoon.

But I didn't' remember coming up here this weekend. The last I knew, Allen and Mr. Jones were naked and holding me down on a bed. *You know what they did to you, even if you don't remember it.*

With Mama cooking breakfast, it had to be Saturday or Sunday. My brother and sister were sitting across from me at the picnic table. This was much too realistic to be a dream. The odd thing had to do with Sharon.

"When did you cut your hair?" I hadn't seen it like that since she was a baby. The short curls made her look like Little Orphan Annie. She even looked bigger.

"You're silly," she said. "Mama cut it for school. I'll be in first grade."

"That's next year."

"No, it's not. It's *this* year."

"Mama, tell Sharon when she starts school."

"Oh, it's back to 'Mama' now, is it? What happened to 'Mom'?"

That's weird. I'd considered calling her that ever since Mike started doing it last year.

"Sharon thinks she's goin' to school this fall."

"She is, and you know that. Mrs. Zachary will be her teacher and Mrs. Webster will be yours."

Aha, now I know it's a dream. "Mrs. Webster teaches the sixth grade, not the fifth."

"Steven Wayne, stop arguin' about silly stuff. I think I know what grade you'll be in."

This has to be a dream, right? What happened to the fifth grade? How could I forget an entire year?

Chapter 15

Easy Money

August 1978
Fayetteville, Arkansas
Age 18

I arrived at the University of Arkansas at the end of August, a few days before classes started. That gave me a chance to settle into my room in Reid Hall and learn my way around campus. Orientation a few weeks earlier helped, but we didn't have time to see everything.

Reid Hall and Hotz Hall—two high-rise dormitories that housed about 1,000 students total—stood at the top of the hill overlooking Razorback Stadium. Even though I had a permit for my car, the closest lot turned out to be at the stadium. I grabbed my student folder, locked the door behind me, and headed to the elevator. When it opened on the ground floor, I smiled at the sight of Paul, who played on the McDonald's softball team with me. He stepped aside to let me out.

As they used to say in old movies, Paul made me swoon. I had a crush on him from the moment we met. When I learned he played a mean left field, he became even sexier.

Dammit, Steve, you're not gay. Stop thinking that way.

"What are you doing here?" I asked. "Aren't you living off campus with Bradley?" The elevator closed without Paul getting on.

"The bastards wouldn't let us. They said all freshmen have to live in student housing. Where are you off to?"

I looked at him a little too long. He snapped his fingers in front of my face.

"Earth to Steve."

"Oh, sorry. Registration. They stuck me in an early mornin' class. I'm gonna try to change it."

When he laughed, my confidence waned.

"What's so funny?"

"Registration is in front of the student union. Good luck, 'cause you're gonna need it."

And he was right. At least two hundred students formed lines in front of the student union, a new building made of glass and white stone. A dozen tables—each with a sign containing letters of the alphabet—stretched across the entrance. I went to the back of the R–S line where I tried not to die from boredom. Two hours later, my turn came.

"ID, please." The woman, who looked about Mom's age, held out her hand. I gave her my driver's license, which she promptly handed back. "*Student* ID."

If first impressions played any role in cutting through university red tape, I screwed the pooch.

I didn't have many things in my wallet, but it seemed like an hour passed as I searched for the white laminated University of Arkansas ID. I had my driver's license, fake ID, library card, car registration, and pieces of paper with phone numbers I didn't recognize. My shirt began absorbing the sweat coming from every pore.

"It's probably in your folder," said a male voice to my right.

Someone tugged at the glossy presentation folder I held under my armpit. I turned to face a student with a rounded face, green eyes, and dimples. His brown hair—no longer than a half inch—was so thick I couldn't see his scalp. He wore a white knitted shirt with the university logo on the upper left part of his chest.

"Your folder," he repeated. "The student ID should be in there."

"Oh, right. Thank you."

I found it paper-clipped to one of the inside pockets and handed it to the woman. She opened one of the three-inch binders on the table and turned several pages.

"Mr. Simmons, you're already registered."

"I need to change my sociology class. They didn't give me the time I signed up for."

Who in their right mind scheduled a class at 7:30 a.m.? The syllabus on the professor's door said he wanted us in our seats fifteen minutes before it started. Insane.

"You'll have to go through drop/add to do that."

"What's drop/add?"

She rolled her eyes. That was never good.

"You have to complete paperwork to drop the class you *don't* want, then fill out paperwork for the class you *do* want and have the professor of that class approve it."

"That sounds like a lot of trouble."

"Welcome to college, honey. *Next.*"

Steve, you're screwed.

I strolled around the tables toward the entrance when the gorgeous guy who helped me walked up.

"Did you get your problem solved?" he asked.

"She said I had to do something called drop/add."

"Ouch. That can be painful," he said before glancing toward the student union. "Look, this heat is killing me. Would you like to get a cold drink inside?"

"Uh, yeah, sure." *What are you doing?* "I'm Steve, by the way."

"I'm Derrick, but my friends call me DC."

When I shook his hand, he gently rubbed mine with his thumb. I pulled the glass door open and let him go ahead of me.

You're getting lost in his perfect lips, perfect teeth, perfect nose, and perfect dimples.

Just stop it, Steve.

We each bought a Diet Pepsi and sat at a table near one of the large windows overlooking the stadium.

"What's with the shirt?" I asked.

"Campus guide. Did you do summer orientation?"

For the first time, I detected the hint of a lisp. Almost imperceptible.

"Yeah, I didn't want to wait. What year are you?"

"I graduate in May," he said, holding my gaze.

I could stare into his green eyes all day—and night, if necessary. They practically glowed. If I didn't leave now, I might not be able to.

"I'm sorry, but I need to get back," I said, gathering my folder.

"To what? School hasn't started yet."

My head spun when I stood to leave. I plopped back into my chair and tried to shake off the lightheadedness.

Oh, no. Please, not now.

The taste in my mouth made me long for a toothbrush and toothpaste. Sunlight lit the room through cracks in the curtains. I had my right arm draped over the guy in front of me. The man snuggling behind me had an unmistakable case of morning wood.

Dammit, Wayne, what the hell did you get me into?

It became apparent over the summer that of my two alters, Wayne was the whore. He left me notes about his cruising park bathrooms throughout Fort Smith looking for sex. On several occasions, I "awoke" in compromising positions with other men. One note was quite clear.

I like lots of sex even if you don't. I won't apologize for it.

Wayne

My bladder screamed to be emptied, yet I formed the middle of a Steve sandwich. Unfortunately, I couldn't get out of bed without waking one or both pieces of bread. When I gently removed my arm from the redhead, I disturbed the man behind me. He put his arm around my chest and pulled me closer. So much for peeing.

"Good morning, sexy."

I knew the voice from the way he said the letter "s." I turned my head in his direction as much as possible. "Good morning, DC."

He pushed himself up and rubbed his lips against mine before giving me a slow open-mouth kiss. The other piece of bread turned toward us. His triangular face, cleft chin, and dimples reminded me of Kent McCord from *Adam-12*. Several years earlier, I'd gotten the actor's autograph when he appeared at a car dealership in Fort Smith. How did I end up in bed with two men *way* better looking than me?

After we finished "round four," as DC called it, I found my clothes and shoes. I still had no idea where I was. The room had one full-sized bed flanked by nightstands. Built-in bookshelves comprised one wall, and the opposite one had a roll-top wooden desk and love seat. Definitely not a motel or dorm.

My trusty Seiko proclaimed it to be Wednesday, so I lost only a day.

"Well, guys, I'd better get back to the dorm."

I got the door open about a foot when DC rushed over in all his nakedness and pushed it closed. "I'll have to escort you out. Or Dean can."

Ah, so that was the redhead's name. Derrick and Dean sounded like a vocal duo. Once they got dressed, DC pulled me into a hug and slipped something in my back pocket.

"That has our numbers on it. We'll have to do this again."

They walked me down the stairs, out the front door, and past the Greek-style columns holding up a balcony. Good lord, a frat house.

"Let me know if you want to pledge," Dean said.

"Thanks, but I could never afford it."

"A man with your talent always has options," DC said with a wink. "Keep in touch."

They turned and headed back inside.

The walk up the hill to Reid Hall took me past the stadium and parking area. When I got to my dorm, I pushed my way through a crowd of students moving in. There was a lot of activity for it to be eight o'clock in the morning.

My roommate, Ben, looked like he just woke up. His hair stuck out in several directions, and he wore nothing but his tighty-whities. We met during orientation and hit it off. Neither of us smoked, and he seemed nice, so we went to the housing office and got assigned to the same room. I could tell already that he would be a challenge. He left dirty clothes on the floor and didn't count hygiene as a daily requirement.

"I know the walk of shame when I see it," he said.

"Not really." Lying had become my superpower, especially when I stayed as close to the truth as possible. "I had too much to drink and crashed at a fraternity."

One thing I forgot to ask when vetting Ben had to do with his religion. He turned out to be a Bible thumper who didn't drink, curse, or do anything else fun. I was sure his virginity remained intact. If he learned of my indiscretion with DC and Dean, he wouldn't think twice about requesting new accommodations.

Why do I keep having sex with men?

Although I could blame Wayne for getting me into the situation, I sure didn't turn down the opportunity this morning.

Am I in denial? Am I gay?

After showering, I put on something clean and tossed my dirty clothes in a small basket I kept under the bed. That's when I remembered DC putting something in my back pocket. I pulled out the folded paper and opened it.

Dammit.

Five twenty-dollar bills fell out. How humiliating. Why would good-looking guys like that *ever* pay someone for sex, especially me? And why so much?

"Wayne, I know this is more than you asked but well worth it," one of them had scrawled.

They put their first names and phone numbers at the bottom. With the money I already had, a hundred bucks should be enough for all my books. That would eliminate the need to visit the financial aid office first. I put the money in my wallet and headed to the university bookstore.

I'm a whore. What if Wayne gets arrested for prostitution? I need the money, but selling myself isn't a way to get it. Why doesn't Wayne understand that? He and Mark are going to get me killed.

Chapter 16

Debate Is an Oral Activity

October 1978
Fayetteville, Arkansas
Age 18

A s the first semester progressed, DC and Dean tracked me down a few times and encouraged me to pledge their fraternity. Unfortunately, the champagne cost far exceeded my tap-water pocketbook. My refusal didn't stop us from getting together when our mutual schedules opened up.

I regularly attended all my classes except for one: sociology. As I feared, making it to the 7:30 a.m. class proved difficult. Mark and Wayne continued spending nights doing God-knows-what, which left me exhausted and prone to oversleeping. My professor allowed five unexcused absences—and two tardies counted as one absence—after which we automatically failed the class. I suspect he enforced the rule so he'd have fewer tests to grade.

By late October, I couldn't miss another class, and it was too late to add a new one. I was stupid for not going through drop/add when I had the chance. Losing sociology would leave me with eleven credit hours, but my financial aid required me to carry at least twelve the first semester.

I regularly had lunch with Rob—my tennis buddy from Fort Smith —who's also at the university. He and I had been talking about my shitty sociology schedule for weeks. As my inevitable demise in the class loomed, I brought up the issue again.

"I'm going to fail sociology." I said it nonchalantly while stirring gravy into the mashed potatoes.

"Man, I told you to just drop the class."

"If I do, I'll lose my financial aid." The brown gravy had a beefy, smoky taste like Aunt Estelle made. The Salisbury steak nauseated me.

"How many credits do you need?"

"I'll be one short." How humiliating. Rob didn't need loans and grants for college. He wanted to attend an Ivy League school but didn't have the grades to get in.

"Man, I have the solution," he said excitedly.

"Bank robbery?"

"No. Debate. Mrs. Ingalls will let you in. It's two credit hours."

Debate didn't sound appealing to me, especially given how much I hated to argue with someone.

"I don't know. Is it a lot of work?"

"Nah. I'm headin' over there now. Come talk to her."

Steve, you have no other options. You might as well try it.

Rob led me to the fourth floor of the Communications Center. He opened the door to a room filled with large tables covered in newspapers, folders, and note cards like the ones Aunt Estelle wrote recipes on. A skinny, red-haired man and a woman with long black hair looked up as we walked in.

"This is the debate room," Rob said. "And *this* is our top team, Doug and Jo."

"Nice to meet you," I said. They said hello and went back to work. To the left, six equally spaced doors with windows lined the wall. They looked like individual offices.

"Is Mrs. Ingalls in?" Rob asked.

The two debaters nodded toward the wall of doors. In the back office, an older woman sat at a desk. With her dark hair and narrow face, she reminded me of Mrs. Webster, my sixth-grade teacher. Rob knocked. When she turned toward us, her eyes brightened through black horn-rimmed eyeglasses. She jumped from her chair and opened the door.

"Rob, what can I do for you?" She smiled so wide I could see her front teeth.

"Mrs. Ingalls, this is Steve Simmons. He would like to join the debate team, but the time to add a class has passed."

"I don't pay any mind to those silly deadlines." She tilted her head toward me. "Why do you want to be a debater, Mr. Simmons?"

Oh, Lord. I had to come up with a good reason—and fast.

"It would be good trainin' for law school."

"If that were true, you would have signed up for the class during registration. What's the real reason?"

Busted. I hated getting caught lying. If I did it again, I had a feeling she wouldn't let me add the class.

"I need another credit hour to stay in school. They put me in an early mornin' class, and I keep oversleepin'. If I don't drop it, I'll fail. If I do drop it, I could lose my financial aid."

"How early?"

"Seven thirty, and he wants us there fifteen minutes before that."

"Damn. I'd flunk it too." She pulled paper from her desk drawer, wrote something on it, and handed it to me. "Fill this out. Take it to the registrar's office. Forensics meets daily and we travel two-to-three weekends a month."

"Travel?"

"Will that be a problem?"

How could I travel when I have two alters who like to do crazy shit? What would they do in other cities? I could feel the sweat under my arms soaking my shirt.

"I'm not sure I can afford to—"

"Don't be silly," she said. "The school pays for lodging and two meals a day. Do you own a suit?"

"No, but I can get one."

"Good. Debaters must participate in two individual events if the tournament has them. Things like extemporaneous speaking, dramatic interpretation, or even poetry. Go turn this in and come back here—unless you have class."

"My afternoon is free, so I'll come right back. Thank you."

Although I wanted to scream as we walked down the hallway to the elevator, I waited until we got inside.

"What the hell did you get me into?"

"I'm not sure what you mean," Rob said.

The little weasel wouldn't even make eye contact.

"You said this wouldn't be much work. You never said it meets every day, that we'd travel on weekends, or that I needed a suit."

"Man, you were desperate. Now you're not."

I hated it when he was right.

Debate turned out to be nothing like I expected. We had to research a national topic, photocopy pages supporting our arguments, and cut up those pages to put on index cards as evidence. Then we had to turn that evidence into briefs to support our arguments.

After watching a practice debate, I wanted to quit. They spoke fast, used terms I'd never heard of, and followed a confusing format. Mrs. Ingalls had me practice giving arguments. I stumbled over words and said things that didn't make sense.

No matter how hard I tried, I was worse than horrible. One afternoon before Thanksgiving, Mrs. Ingalls got very blunt.

"I'm not sure you're cut out for debate. You can stay in the class this semester. If you want to do just individual events, you can come back next term."

"You mean events like poetry."

"Exactly."

Hell no. This was tennis all over again—someone telling me I'd never be good at something.

"No poetry. I want to be a debater."

Mrs. Ingalls leaned back in the chair and crossed her arms. As she stared at me, I wondered if staying in school was worth being humiliated every day.

"I understand your determination, but I'm not sure you can do it."

"Mrs. Ingalls, with all due respect, you don't know me. Someone once put a tennis racket in my hand and embarrassed me on purpose. 'You'll never be a tennis player,' he said. Within a year, I was number one on the team. Two years after that, I became the first ever tennis player from our school to qualify for the state tournament. If someone tells me I can't do something, I'll prove them wrong."

Steve, when you started playing tennis, you also blew off your other responsibilities. You became obsessed.

"Fine, Steve. I'll pair you with another novice."

That person happened to be a handsome frat boy. The first time I saw him, the phrase that came to mind was "cute but stupid." He and I attended three tournaments, winning only one out of eighteen debates.

My inner voice was right. As I focused on debate, I stopped attending classes altogether—except on exam days. Studying comprised reading the material and getting notes from others in the class.

In April, Mrs. Ingalls posted a flier advertising the Arizona Debate Institute. It would take place in August at the University of Arizona in Tucson.

"The budget can't afford to pay for this," she told the squad, "but I encourage you to attend if possible. I have registration forms in my office."

In high school, I ascended to the top of the tennis team with the help of lessons. Wouldn't going to a debate workshop help me accomplish the same thing? I was determined to find out. Now I had to save enough money to go.

Hey, Mark and Wayne, don't even think about it. I'll get the money on my own. I don't want to be arrested for stealing or prostitution. That's something I never expected to worry about.

Chapter 17

A Harry Encounter

June 1979
Fort Smith, Arkansas
Age 19

When my freshman year at the university ended, I packed my car and made the hour drive from Fayetteville to Fort Smith. In April, Mom and Harry had purchased a three-bedroom house on the city's north side. She sent me a letter a few weeks earlier with directions and an offer to let me stay there for the summer. If I had any doubt of my sanity before, my decision to live in their house settled the matter.

I easily found their ranch-style home on the city's north side a half mile from I-540. Once I parked on the street, I froze behind the wheel.

Aunt Estelle and Uncle Cliff will let you stay with them for the summer. Turn around and go there.

I can't do that. Who knows what Mark and Wayne would do?

Accepting my fate, I walked up to the carport where Mom was stripping the paint and varnish off an old sideboard. We exchanged pleasantries but no hug. Ever since she gave Major away, we had a cordial relationship but nothing more.

"Your room is down the hallway, first door on the left. I put a key on the dresser."

"Thanks. Where's Harry?"

"Still asleep, so be quiet."

An alcoholic still in bed at noon. Shocking.

I unloaded the contents of my car into the ten-foot-square furnished bedroom. Once I filled the dresser and closet, I went in search of my things from the Greenwood house. Eighteen years of my life had filled four boxes.

Mom was still working on the sideboard when I stepped onto the carport.

"Do you know where my boxes are?"

"What boxes?"

She kept scraping the wooden top without looking up at me.

"*My* boxes—from the Greenwood house. There are four of them. They have my summer clothin' and other things in them."

"Your yearbooks are in the attic somewhere. I sold the rest of the stuff."

She continued removing what looked like many coats of varnish off the piece of furniture.

"Good joke. Seriously, where are the boxes?"

"I told you. We had a garage sale. There wasn't enough room for the boxes here."

Her face never changed expression. You'd think she described pulling weeds instead of selling my personal possessions—items that meant a lot to me.

"You *really* sold my shit?"

"Don't be so upset. They're just things."

"Like Major was 'just a dog'? Those boxes would have fit in the corner of my room. You keep pullin' the same shit. Why do I ever think things will be different between us? I keep trustin' you, and you keep screwin' me over."

Just my luck, Harry stepped out of the house.

"Son, don't you be speaking—"

"I am *not* your son, so you can stop that bullshit right now." My mouth had a mind of its own. This time, I was rooting for it to win.

"As long as you live in *my* house, you'll follow *my* rules."

"I'm gonna go check my work schedule and then play tennis. I don't know what time I'll be back."

"Curfew is at nine," Harry said.

"Not happenin'." I pushed past Harry and went into the house to get my wallet and keys.

You knew this wasn't a good idea.

I hated it when my subconscious was right.

Over the years, Aunt Estelle had given me things I cherished, such as seashells she collected off the beaches of California in the 1940s and a small replica of Rodin's The Thinker. She even gave me a little plastic donkey—which I had taken to Fayetteville with me—and said, "Don't ever vote for that other party."

Losing the seashells and statuette nauseated me. *Why do I keep subjecting myself to Mom's bullshit? What's wrong with me?*

I drove straight to McDonald's to get on the work schedule. Seeing Cheryl and Glenda—two of the McDonald's managers I loved working for—lifted my spirits. They put me on as many shifts as I could work starting the following day, Sunday.

After shooting the shit with them for a half hour, I headed to Creekmore for the first time in months. I played tennis with random people until late in the evening. When I walked into the house well past Harry's curfew, he gave me the evil eye—a smoldering cigarette in one hand, and a beer in the other. I went to my bedroom without saying a word.

Throughout that first week, I worked the opening shift daily, which started at 5:45 a.m. And every day when I got to Mom and Harry's house, I discovered money in my pocket that shouldn't be there. The amount ranged from $10 to $20 a day. Mark continued his thievery, and I had no idea how to stop him.

Yes, you do, but you just won't do it.

The thing was, I neither had dizzy spells to indicate that an alter was taking over, nor did I notice any missing time. None of the registers came up short for that much money, which would have been a red flag and resulted in my termination. Mark had me befuddled.

The opening shift usually ended at 2 p.m., but an afternoon worker failed to show. That put Glenda in a bind. She asked if I wanted to work through the dinner rush, and I readily agreed. Besides, I didn't want to be around Harry, whose angry stares continued to make me uncomfortable.

The afternoon passed quickly. Dinner rush usually ended by 6 p.m., even on Friday, but a tourist bus pulled in as I was clocking out.

"Do you mind staying?" Glenda displayed her "please" pout which always worked on me.

I didn't get to the house until 7 p.m. The moment I walked into the living room, Harry jumped up from the sofa.

"Where have you been? You missed dinner."

"Sorry, I had to work late."

His red eyes reflected those of an alcoholic several drinks into a night of drunkenness. "That's no excuse. Your mother worked hard on dinner. You disrespected her by not being here."

"Dammit, Harry, I have a *job*. When my boss asks me to stay late, *I stay late*. If you'll excuse me, I need a shower."

Before I could get past him, Harry grabbed my shoulder and tripped me backwards. I landed hard on my back, my head bouncing off the thinly carpeted floor. Harry pulled back his leg, and I rolled into a ball to minimize the area he could kick. The first blow landed just below my shoulder blade. When I tried to roll away, he kicked me in the side and then below my armpit. Something inside me cracked—probably a rib.

"Stop. Harry, stop. Someone help me."

He kept landing blows wherever he could make contact. I felt another crack in my chest. *Where's Mom? Will she find me dead on the living room floor?*

When he stopped and laughed, I got to my knees and tried to stand. *"You fuckin' drunk, leave me alone."*

That's when he wrapped his arms around my waist and tossed me over the sofa like a rag doll. I slammed against the wall and rolled onto the floor where he resumed kicking me.

Mark, Wayne, will one of you please help me? Please.

One of my alters had to step in, to do something I couldn't. The dizziness hit me, and I hoped it was one of them switching with me, not neurological damaged from the kicks to my head.

———————

"Boogie Wonderland" by Earth, Wind & Fire and The Emotions blared through the radio. Disorientation often followed a blackout. This time, though, my situation became clear almost at once. The MCDONALD's parking lot held several cars and more waited in the drive-thru line. My torso burned and ached from Harry's assault. I wasn't sure why my alter took me to work, but that was better than staying at the house with someone who tried to kill me.

My watch said 8:30 p.m. It sure didn't take Mark or Wayne long to pack my shit. Gym bags, boxes, and a suitcase filled my car's backseat.

The first time I met Harry, I somehow knew he was dangerous. What made me think I could live in that house?

Where will I stay now? A motel will quickly drain my bank account.

The fact I couldn't process information on an empty stomach didn't help. I hadn't eaten since my break after the lunch rush. That seemed like days ago.

The air-conditioned MCDONALD's lobby refreshened me somewhat. When I stood at the counter, two of my coworkers gave me strange looks. After getting some food, I found an empty booth around the corner in the side section where we held the kids' birthday parties. It hurt to swallow, but I forced the food down. I'd just finished when Glenda came around the corner.

"Didn't I send you home?"

"I decided to come back and eat."

She sat across from me and leaned forward.

"Steve, what's wrong? You're still wearing your dirty uniform, and you're moving like someone ran over you. Are you okay?"

I didn't mean to cry. When it started, I couldn't stop.

"Come with me," she said. "We can't have you scaring away the customers."

While Glenda turned away from me to dump the trash off my tray. I tried to stand, but I fell back into the booth. The jarring motion caused me to see white as my torso exploded in fire. Harry must have cracked some ribs. Putting my hands on the table, I helped push myself into a standing position. I followed her to the break room and slowly lowered myself into a seat, unable to hide my grimace from the pain. Glenda pulled a chair over and sat, facing me.

"Who did this to you?"

What do I say? Will she call the police if I tell her the truth?

"Don't tell anyone, but my stepfather did it. He was...unhappy...that I worked late and missed dinner." When Glenda's eyes widened and jaw dropped, I could tell she must be blaming herself.

"It's not your fault. I agreed to stay. Harry's the one who did this."

"Where was your mother?"

I wish I knew. Between my screaming and hitting the wall, she had to have heard it. Did she hide while he was beating the crap out of me?

"I think she was in the other room. I'm not sure."

"You can't go back there."

There's no way I'm ever going back there—at least not to live. "I'm not. My car's packed."

"I have an extra bedroom. You'll come stay with me and my son, William, for the summer."

People never help me unless there's something in it for them. *What's her angle?*

"Thanks, but I can't afford—"

"Did I ask for money? I'm closing tonight, but William's home. You can go over there right now. I'll call to let him know you're coming."

What should I do?

As much as I needed a place to stay, it could be self-destructive living with my boss. I didn't trust my alters. What were they capable of doing?

"I don't know. It's not that—"

"You can either stay with me or live in your car. Which is it?"

Maybe I should report the assault. It would be my word against his, but I had bruising and possibly broken bones.

You can't do that. It would devastate Mom.

Why do I keep worrying about her?

"Thanks. I appreciate this."

"You're scheduled to open tomorrow. I'll leave a note for Mitch saying that you won't be in. Rest."

Glenda wrote directions to her house. On the way, I stopped at a drugstore and bought two large elastic bandages. William let me in and helped wrap my chest. Then we moved my things into the spare bedroom. Sleeping proved difficult, but I managed to stay in bed until noon on Saturday.

The following week, I stopped by the house when Mom and Harry were at work. After getting my yearbooks from the attic, I went to leave my house key on the dining room table. There I found a sealed envelope with my name on it in Mom's handwriting. From the weight and stiffness, I could tell it was a card of some sort.

Does it contain an apology, something Mom never gives to anyone? Maybe money? For a brief moment, I considered opening it. Instead, I placed the key on top of the envelope and left.

I can't keep doing this, Mom.

Chapter 18

Opening a Wound

I finished the second apple Danish and swallowed the rest of my Tab. My feet throbbed, chest hurt, and head pounded. Weekend breakfast shifts could be brutal, especially during summertime with the Motel 6 next door—but I didn't mind. It made the workday fly by.

Six weeks after the assault, the damage from Harry's steel-toed boots lingered. Normally I'd be looking forward to an afternoon of tennis once my shift ended. Reaching, stretching, and twisting aggravated the healing ribs that had taken the brunt of his attack. My bruises had mostly faded, leaving a little discoloration in places. I still kept my upper torso wrapped with Ace bandages and avoided strenuous activities.

Extra Strength Tylenol had become my close friend.

There had been a time when I would never consider working at a fast-food place, but I loved my job at McDonald's. The managers scheduled me to open Wednesday through Sunday. At first, I didn't know if I'd be able to make it at 5:45 a.m. every day. Mark and Wayne's nightly gallivanting at the university caused me to oversleep too many mornings. But, since living at Glenda's house, they had behaved themselves.

I moved slower than before, but I still got the job done. My coworkers seemed to enjoy me not running over them every day like I did before.

Glenda and I agreed not to let Mom know where I was living. Part of me hoped she would call the restaurant or stop by to check on me. Of course, I had no idea if Mark or Wayne confronted her when they moved us out.

I returned from my morning break and started another pot of coffee. When I heard the side door open and close, I turned to see four adults approach the counter. They looked like they'd barely survived a night of drinking—unkempt hair, wrinkled clothing, and "I hate mornings" facial expressions. I'd seen the look in the mirror many times.

The last of the four customers stepped up to the counter to order—and time stopped. All the noise around me ceased to exist. How had I not noticed him? Allen looked much the same as the horny fifteen-year-old who shared my bed when I was eight—my friend, my confidante, my rapist. He was an older version of the handsome seventeen-year-old who fell back into my life two years later and picked up where he left off. I both despised and missed him at the same time.

How could you miss him? Even after nine years, you must remember what he did to you.

"May I take your order?"

My words seemed robotic, forced. Seeing him brought back memories I'd tried to bury—and pledged never to forget.

He looked right at me. For a moment, his eyes glimmered with distant recognition, but then it faded from them.

How dare he not know me. Did I mean so little to him? Does he no longer remember the eight-year-old boy—desperate for affection—who allowed him to commit rape every night for weeks? Did he forget the ten-year-old boy—still longing for friendship—who somehow lost a year of his life after being manipulated and lied to?

I expected us to be friends forever, that he'd never leave my side. Now, standing four feet away and looking into my nineteen-year-old eyes, he didn't see the boy he abandoned—the boy he repeatedly sexually assaulted.

Yet, you still miss him.

After taking Allen's order, I put their items on trays and thanked them. The four got a booth in the far corner where they talked, laughed, and touched each other. Every affectionate gesture he made to the woman next to him wounded me like Harry's reinforced shoe kicking my heart.

Go over to his table and tell him how much you hate and despise him. Yell at him for telling others about us. It almost destroyed you. He took your innocence. Your self-respect.

I can't do that. I miss the way he spent time with me and talked to me and held me and stroked my cheek and looked into my eyes and kissed me and—

He raped you!

"Fuck this."

"Do what?" a coworker asked.

Ignoring her, I walked back to the manager's desk.

"Glenda, I need a fifteen-minute break." I squeezed my eyes, trying to keep the tears at bay. "Maybe more."

She said something as I dashed out the back door, but I couldn't make out the words. I sat on the grass next to the trash bin, tears streaming down my face.

Why did I come back to Fort Smith? I'd put all of this behind me, and now I've ripped open the wound. He was breaking my heart all over again.

Steve, you're sick. He raped you and told others so they could, too.

Yes, but he also made me feel wanted, loved.

I didn't know how long I stayed outside. When Allen and the other three climbed into a sedan and left, I wiped my eyes and went back inside. Glenda stared at me, her jaws rigid and eyes heavy with concern, but she didn't say a word.

She knows, Steve.

Chapter 19

Paradise

It took me a few weeks to accept that I'd lost an entire year of my life. Would I ever remember what happened in the fifth grade? I had so many questions and couldn't ask a damned one of them without looking crazy. What would I do when school started? I'd be a year behind in all my subjects.

Mom and Dad decided we'd spend our weeklong summer vacation at Aunt Estelle and Uncle Cliff's in Lawton, Oklahoma, instead of going camping. I missed my aunt and uncle so much. Plus, I'd rather visit them instead of sleeping in a tent with the family.

They used to live in Fort Smith but moved four hours away because of my uncle's job. Since then, we spent every Thanksgiving with them. Aunt Estelle and Mom would prepare a big dinner for us with turkey, stuffing, and a variety of side dishes—plus Aunt Estelle's homemade apple pie for dessert. The smell of cinnamon always spread throughout the house trailer as the pies cooked. This would be our first summer trip there to see them.

We left early on Saturday. Mom made a bed in the back of the station wagon for us kids. To give us room, Dad strapped our suitcases to the top of the car in the luggage rack. We still had to share the back with an ice chest full of food and a grocery bag with bread.

When we finally got there, Dad parked the car behind Aunt Estelle's white Impala and honked the horn. Rather than wait for Mom or Dad to open the car's rear door, I squeezed past the ice chest and went out the side.

Aunt Estelle came out of the small house trailer and stood on the deck, waving at us. I ran up the wooden steps and threw my arms around her.

Why doesn't Mom ever hug me like this?

I smiled and cried at the same time because she made me feel safe. The last I remembered, my head came up to her shoulders, but I had grown a lot in the past two years.

Was I as tall as her last Thanksgiving? I lost last year's visit with them, and I don't know why or how. What did we talk about? Where did we go?

"Steven, you're as tall as me now," Aunt Estelle said.

"I missed you." With her arms wrapped around me, I didn't care about all the other crap. I refused to let my worries destroy this moment.

Uncle Cliff—wearing a wide-brimmed hat and a blue mask because of bad allergies—came around the corner of the trailer. Even with his mouth and nose covered, I could tell he was smiling.

I wish they were my parents.

Their one-bedroom, single-wide mobile home—ten feet wide and forty-five feet long—barely had enough room for us all. Every night, getting ready for bed involved moving furniture around like a complicated puzzle. Before pulling down the Murphy bed in the dining room, the table had to be put into the kitchen and the chairs stacked on top—which left barely enough room for anyone to squeeze by.

Two cots fit down the middle of the living room. To get by them, you had to climb over the easy chair. Mom and Dad got the Murphy bed. Mike and I took the cots. Sharon got the couch. Everyone made sure to use the bathroom before bedtime or suffer the consequences of completing the obstacle course. I had plastic under my sheet in case I wet the bed.

With the temperatures more than a hundred degrees by noon, we didn't go outside much. If not for the new central air conditioning, we would have been miserable. *How did they stand it here in summer before they got central air?*

We found lots of things to do—from going to the top of Mount Scott to seeing buffalo to watching prairie dogs. Of course, we did most of it from the comfort of cars with the air conditioning running full blast. I didn't care what we did as long as I got to spend time with my aunt and uncle.

On Wednesday, Uncle Cliff took everyone fishing except me and Aunt Estelle. We all got up at 4 a.m. They went to Lake Ellsworth while I stayed behind to help my aunt make apple pies. The sun hadn't come up yet, and we already had the pie crusts finished. Then we started peeling apples.

"I don't wanna go home," I blurted out. *Steve, what are you thinking? She's gonna ask why—and you can't tell her.*

"What? Don't be silly. You get to go back to your friends and have fun the rest of the summer."

I dropped the peeled apple in the bowl and picked up another one. *She thinks you have friends.*

"How many of these do we hafta peel?"

"We need seven for each pie, so fourteen."

She finished two for every apple I peeled. The faster I tried to go, the worse I did.

Steve, you can't tell her you don't have any friends, that you don't remember attending the fifth grade, that guys force you to have sex including your own relative—and you can't tell her you want to kill yourself. She can't know any of that.

"What if I stayed for two more weeks? I brought my mowing money. I'll buy my own food and do chores and buy a bus ticket home. I promise I won't be any trouble." My money box at home had more cash than I'd ever seen. I must not have spent any money during the year I couldn't remember.

If I looked her in the eyes, I'd start crying—and then I might say too much. I grabbed another apple and started peeling it.

"Steven, you really don't wanna go home, do you?"

"Can you and Uncle Cliff adopt me?" I'd love to have them as my mom and dad, even if it meant living in Lawton.

"Sweetie, what's wrong? I've never heard you talk like that before."

"I'm happy being here. Wouldn't you like to be my mom?"

When she put down her peeler and apple, I didn't know what she was going to do. Aunt Estelle wrapped her arms around me and squeezed.

"We'd love for you to be our son, but Bobby and Shirley would miss you."

"No, they wouldn't."

With all the apples peeled, she cut them in quarters, and we sliced out the cores. Then she showed me how to arrange the apples in the pie crusts. Once the sugary liquid on the stove started boiling, she poured it over the apples. Then she rolled out more dough, sliced it into strips, and showed me how to make a lattice on top. We somehow got both pies in her small oven. As they cooked, the smell of cinnamon filled the trailer.

Everyone else returned before noon with a mess of catfish and largemouth bass. They cleaned their catch outside in the heat while Aunt Estelle and I made fried bologna sandwiches for lunch. That evening, we had fried fish, hush puppies, and potato salad—with apple pie for dessert.

That night, I didn't say anything to Mom and Dad about wanting to stay behind when they went home. The next day, Uncle Cliff showed me the fish net he made. It was cool. He'd weaved it from scratch using nylon twine.

"I talked to your mom and dad," he said. "You can stay two more weeks here if you want to."

"I can?"

"Of course. Is everything okay at home?"

Steve, if you tell him the truth, they won't let you stay. They won't want someone like you around.

"I just wanna spend more time here."

Thursday and Friday passed slowly as I waited for the rest of the family to leave. When Saturday morning arrived, I couldn't stop smiling as Mom and Dad checked all the suitcases except mine before carrying them to the car.

"You better mind Estelle and Cliff while you're here," she said as Dad tied the suitcases to the luggage rack on the car roof.

"I will." Although I wanted to ask her if I could stay for good, I knew better. She'd get mad at home when I wanted to mail a letter or card to Aunt Estelle. If I asked to live with them for good, she might not let me stay for two more weeks.

As the station wagon pulled away, I waved good-bye. Mike was upset he'd have to mow lawns by himself, but the summer heat had already burned up most of the yards.

For the next fourteen days, I was in paradise. Most mornings, Aunt Estelle and I went fishing at Lake Helen, located in Lawton. She and Cliff even took me night fishing at Lake Ellsworth. Some days we did nothing. I tried to spend money on food, but they wouldn't let me.

Those fourteen days made me feel at home for the first time since they moved away. Mom used to leave me and Mike all day at their house in Fort Smith. When she would return to pick us up, I never wanted to leave because their home made me happy. Lawton turned out to be no different. Nobody teased me, called me names, or forced me to have sex.

When the time came for me to go home, they drove me to the bus station and bought my ticket.

"Please don't make me go back," I said to my aunt and uncle as I struggled to hold back tears.

Why didn't I feel upset like this when my family drove away? I'd give anything in the world to stay forever with Aunt Estelle and Uncle Cliff. When he walked through the door after work, Uncle Cliff always smiled and asked me how my day was. Aunt Estelle showed me how to cook and spent time doing things with me every day. They showed an interest in me nobody else ever had.

The suitcase pulled my arm as I held it next to the bus. They had filled it with gifts to take back to Greenwood: seashells from San Francisco, a photo album of pictures they'd taken of us, a fishing net, and a small plastic donkey I always liked.

"Sweetie, you have to go back," Aunt Estelle said. "They're your family."

"You're my family too. I wanna live here with you."

"You'll be back for Thanksgiving," Uncle Cliff said.

I hope to remember it this year.

After getting big hugs from them, I put my suitcase in the storage area under the bus and got on board. My stomach cramped as the bus pulled away. I waved until I couldn't see them anymore.

Would they have made me return to Arkansas if they knew what those guys did to me?

You can never tell them, Steve. They'll be ashamed of you—afraid of you.

Chapter 20

Crossing the Line

June 1981
Fayetteville, Arkansas
Age 21

For the second summer in a row, I stayed in Fayetteville. I hadn't been to Fort Smith since August 1979—two months after my stepfather beat the crap out of me. Since the assault, I've had no contact with Mom. My chaotic life had enough drama in it without hers adding to it.

The past two years had been a total shit-show, thanks to Mark and Wayne. Before Christmas of my sophomore year, a Montgomery Ward security guard caught Mark shoplifting an expensive camera lens. I spent five consecutive weekends in jail for that offense. He got caught *again* last December while stealing knickknacks from a store in the mall. The manager didn't call the police, choosing instead to make me pay for the items.

Mark's penchant for theft would be the end of me. Every time he got caught, he'd switch back to me—leaving me disoriented and confused—expecting me to clean up his mess.

Being on the university debate team had murdered my grade point average because I became obsessed with succeeding. I rarely went to class, choosing instead to show up for tests after very little studying.

Although I didn't know what to do after graduation—become a collegiate debate coach or go to law school—I needed better grades regardless.

My first debate coach, Mrs. Ingalls, retired at the end of my freshman year. The university replaced her with Candy Clark, a local woman only three years older than me. Though a southerner, she'd gotten rid of her accent through voice-and-diction classes. She and I became fast friends, something I needed.

But, with three years of college behind me, I had a big problem.

This past year, I had the best debate partner anyone could ask for. Carol and I got along well and had a great win-loss record at regional tournaments. The fact she was ten times smarter than me also played a big role in our success.

Although Carol and I didn't qualify for the National Debate Tournament, we most likely would have if we'd applied for what they called a "second round bid." Unfortunately, our forensics budget had no remaining money to pay for the trip—which Candy didn't tell us until it came time to send in the application. Carol graduated in May and was off to law school. That left me as a debate team of one, a not-very-useful scenario in the world of two-person debate.

"Someone is transferring to be your partner, so be patient," Candy had said a week after graduation. She gave me no details, which made me nervous, but I didn't have any other options.

So, with summer upon me, and my life in its usual maelstrom, I found an apartment located a minute away from my job at the Fayetteville McDonald's. I'd been working there for almost two years.

When classes ended in May, I found an apartment a minute away from my job. My roommate—Jeff—needed a summer tenant. He had no problem with my being gay, a part of myself I *finally* accepted.

One day in June, I woke up at 6 a.m. in a cold sweat, my mind racing. I'd closed the store the night before and didn't get home until after 1 a.m. No matter how tired I was anymore, I couldn't sleep for more than a few hours at a time.

My round-the-clock whirlwind of worries preoccupied my days and dominated my dreams. I never knew what Mark and Wayne had in store for me until it bit me in the ass—sometimes literally given Wayne's taste for kinky sex.

I quietly made my way to the bathroom, trying not to wake Jeff. Thanks to Wayne's nocturnal sexual adventures, I often brushed my teeth twice in the morning to eliminate the taste of alcohol, smoky bars, and men.

After refreshing my mouth and emptying my bladder, I tiptoed back to the bedroom. My shift didn't start for another two hours. If I went in early, I could have a leisurely breakfast and read the paper. The manager might let me clock in ahead of time. The extra pay would help fund my trip to Tucson for the Arizona Debate Institute in August. I'd attended the workshop twice before, and it had been instrumental in my becoming a competitive debater.

When I closed the bedroom door behind me, I froze. A stack of cash and checks on my dresser grabbed my attention.

Oh, shit. What now?

A Post-It Note on top made me shudder.

This should help.

Mark

At the bottom of the note, he added the same smiley face with horns I'd seen several times before.

Mark, what the fuck did you do?

I stopped breathing for a few seconds when I picked up one of the personal checks. It had been made payable to McDONALD'S #1363.

Oh, my God. He stole it from work.

So much for petty crimes I could hide or serve short jail time for. The bastard had graduated to felonies.

Are you surprised? You've let him get away with almost everything.

The stack had $200 in checks dated yesterday along with $1,800 in cash. That didn't make sense. Jake—the assistant manager—closed the store the night before with me, Shar, and Bev. The closing manager always put everything in the safe and locked it.

If the money had been taken while we were all there, Jake would have noticed it missing last night. That meant Mark must have gone back after I went to sleep. How did he do it? Only managers had store keys and the safe's combination.

God, what am I gonna do? I can take it back and tell them I found it in my car.

Steve, who the hell would believe that? Plus, your fingerprints are all over it, and you didn't even work a register last night.

I can't keep evidence of the crime in my apartment. What if I hide it in the debate room at school? I have plenty of time to do it before work.

After getting dressed, I shoved the robbery proceeds in a manila envelope and sat on the edge of the bed.

Am I doing the right thing? Maybe I should destroy it. No, that's just stupid. I can use the money. My car needs brakes, tires, and an oil change.

Steve, do you hear yourself? How can you keep it? You're the reason Mark does this.

Yeah, I always condone his thefts.

Bullshit. Condone? By covering up his crimes, you're as guilty as he is. You have to stop.

Fuck it.

I had to park three blocks from the Communications Center. When I got to my office in the debate room, I stood on a table to reach the ceiling. I lifted one of the drop-ceiling tiles and slipped the envelope on top of the adjacent tile. Tiny foam pieces fell on me. After cleaning up, I headed back to my car.

My hands shook during the five-minute drive to work. My car had no air conditioner, so, in this humidity, my sweating appeared normal.

Oh, crap.

Two cop cars sat in the McDonald's parking lot.

Act calm, Steve.

I went inside and stood behind four people in line. When it came my turn, I leaned across the counter.

"What's goin' on?" I asked.

"No idea," my coworker said. "It's all hush-hush. Barry's in the break room with Tom, Randy, Jake, and the cops."

Our manager had called in the big gun: Barry, the regional supervisor who also managed the Springdale store. He originally hired me to work there but moved me to Fayetteville after a few weeks.

I placed my order and found a seat. A few minutes later, Sam and Randy—the two top managers—came through the tiny lobby. Tom spewed curse words as they walked out the door to the parking lot. Five minutes later, the cops emerged from the back room and drove off.

"Did you get called in, too?" a female voice behind me asked.

Shar walked up to my table with Bev a few steps behind.

"No, I just came in to eat breakfast. Why were you brought in?"

"You got me," Bev said. "Barry called and said, 'Get your ass down here.' He said to go to the break room."

Steve, you're gonna get caught.

No longer hungry, I dumped my hotcakes in the trash bin and followed Shar and Bev to the back of the store. We found Barry and Jake sitting at the table.

"Have a seat," Barry said. He got up and slammed the door but remained standing with his arms crossed. The three of us grabbed chairs.

"Someone cleaned out the safe overnight," Barry said. "There were no signs of forced entry, and the safe had no tool marks on it. Five people had keys and the combination. Me, Sam, Randy, and Jake. Sam and Randy have been terminated, effective immediately."

Mark, you son-of-a-bitch. You cost two people their careers. Two people whose livelihoods depend on their jobs. No McDonald's will ever hire them.

Steve, get off your soapbox. You can save them right now by confessing.

I...I can't do that.

"Why didn't you fire *me*?" Jake asked.

"Because you're gonna be the store manager. Shar, Bev, and Steve, you'll be assistant managers. Don't let me down."

Barry handed us each a slip of paper containing the new combination to the safe. Then he walked out, leaving the four of us staring at each other.

"Holy shit, what just happened?" Jake asked.

*I can answer that. My mental disorder screwed over two innocent people.
Are you kidding, Steve? You're the one screwing them over by keeping quiet.
I know.*

We left the break room, and I followed Jake to the manager's desk.
He sat and pulled a little black book from his shirt pocket. On the first
page inside, he crossed out a number and wrote the new combination
below it. Then he rolled his chair to the black, three-foot-tall safe. With
the booklet open in one hand, he turned the dial with the other. Even
from four feet away, I could make out the numbers.

Oh, my God. That's how Mark did it. He had to have seen Jake hold the
booklet open while entering the combination.

Tension filled the air at work for the next few days. A week later, I
worked as closing manager. Before I and the three workers left, I walked
around to double check that the store had been thoroughly cleaned
and the doors had been locked. I almost forgot to check the drive-thru
window. When I tugged on it and found it locked, I had an epiphany.

That had to be how Mark got in. The fucker somehow unlocked it
before we left the store that night.

When I got to the apartment, I showered and crawled into bed—but
I couldn't sleep. It didn't bother me *how* Mark burglarized the store.
What troubled me was that he could take over control without me
becoming dizzy. He'd been doing it for years—that was how he skimmed
money from cash registers—but it took on greater significance with
the escalation of his criminal behavior to felonies.

Steve, you're fucked.

Chapter 21

On the Run

The Arizona Debate Institute went very well. For the second year in a row, I made it to the finals with a randomly assigned partner from another school. This time we won. I also received a top speaker award. If Mrs. Ingalls could see me now.

Candy's promise of a new debate partner never came to fruition, although she kept dangling the mysterious transfer. From the moment I arrived in Tucson two weeks ago, I let coaches know of my desire to transfer schools. After the awards ceremony, Bill Henderson—the University of Northern Iowa coach—pulled me aside.

"Mike Pfau, the coach at Augustana College in Sioux Falls, South Dakota, is looking for someone to be on his top team. I highly recommended you. It's a top tier program that competes nationally."

"Thanks. I appreciate the vote of confidence." I'd always liked Bill, who often had judged me in debate rounds.

He handed me a slip of paper with the coach's name and number on it. On the way to the dorm, I stopped at a pay phone and called collect. Coach Pfau and I had a productive conversation that lasted fifteen minutes.

"If you're interested, I have a place for you on our top team with Liz," he said. "She's an excellent debater and will be a sophomore."

I couldn't believe my luck. Going to Augustana would get me out of Arkansas, thus solving two problems at once. I'd get out of the state before law enforcement came after me, and I'd have an experienced debate partner. Leaving Candy would be hard, though. She had become a good friend.

Steve, put yourself first.

"I can't do it without financial aid," I said to Coach Pfau.

"Just get here and we'll find the money."

"I'll be there Monday."

My flight left Tucson International Airport at 8 a.m. on Friday, the next day. After changing planes in Dallas and Atlanta, I landed at Drake Field in Fayetteville at 6 p.m. With the time difference, I had spent eight hours worrying if I'd made the right decision to transfer schools. I would have fewer than three days to get my affairs in order, pack, and drive to South Dakota.

You can do it. Stop second-guessing yourself.

I set off to Candy's house, located just a few minutes from the airport. The drive seemed to take hours as I dreaded breaking the news to her. She greeted me at the door with a hug and a smile.

This is wrong, Steve. You can't do this to her.

"Did you just get in?" she asked.

"Yeah, we landed thirty minutes ago."

We sat at the sectional that took up half her living room. The soft furniture felt good after being in uncomfortable seats all day. The enormous brown cat that hated everyone rested next to Candy. Her dog, excited to have company, spun in one direction and then the other.

"What brings you by? Want a Coke?"

"No thanks, I'm good." I hated taking a beverage from her before delivering the news. "Uh, we need to talk."

Candy had always been intuitive. Her toothy smile turned into a frown, a look I'd seen just before she yelled at someone.

"Go on."

"I don't have anyone to debate with here."

"I'm working on that."

"Candy, school starts in two weeks." Go ahead. Get it over with. "I'm transferrin'."

"No, you're not," she said.

"Yes, I am. I've been offered a spot on Augustana's top team." My stomach cramped. "You know I won't be happy here without an experienced partner."

My mouth dried out, making me wish I'd gotten the Coke.

"After all I've done for your ungrateful ass, you're pulling this shit?"

"Do you expect me to debate with someone who doesn't know what they're doin'?" I asked. "I've worked my butt off to get where I am."

"Wow, you think highly of yourself, Mr. Hot Shit Debater."

No matter how good of a friend she was, I didn't have to put up with abuse from her.

"Please don't insult me. I'm here out of—"

"It's too late to transfer."

Then why is she leading you to believe she's gonna get someone here?

"Thanks for admittin' that you won't be getting a partner for me. It makes this easier. I'm leavin' on Sunday."

When she stood, I flinched. *She's not Harry.*

"Bring me all the debate shit you got in Arizona because the program paid for it. Then get the fuck out of here."

"My pleasure."

Even though I expected her to react the way she did, it still hurt. I got a catalog case from my trunk and carried it to the front door where I emptied it.

"This is everything. I've put some evidence on cards while the rest is still in booklets. Good-bye, Candy. I'm sorry."

It's a good thing I had another complete set of evidence books and briefs. Sleeping with a debate coach at the workshop paid off.

As I drove away, Candy stood in the yard looking in my direction. I'd miss her. She talked me off the proverbial ledge many times over the previous two years when things got to be too much. Another lost friendship.

Steve, you're gonna regret this.

I had to be in Sioux Falls, South Dakota, by Monday morning. That gave me one day to pick up my last paycheck, quit my job, tell my roommate, pack, and rent a small trailer. How could I possibly do all that?

Jeff had a poker game going when I walked into the apartment. The last time I played Texas hold 'em with him and his friends, I walked away fifty bucks richer. I knew two of the three other guys at the table. Zack had been a starting forward for the university basketball team. Brian—a cheerleader—slept with me after two of their poker nights. I didn't know the third guy.

"Steve-o, grab your wallet and join in," Jeff said.

"I gotta shower first. It's been a long day."

After unpacking and showering, I was energized enough to play a few hands. I grabbed a beer from the fridge and pulled a chair up to the table.

"Steve, this is Bruce," Jeff said. "He's your replacement at the end of the month."

What the hell? I had no idea he expected me to move out at the end of the month. With no other housing lined up, what would I have done?

"Cool. You can move in early if you want. I'll be out Sunday."

Four hours later, I was ahead by twenty bucks and falling asleep.

"Guys, I'm calling it a night," I announced.

"I think it's time we all quit," Jeff said.

Once he cashed us all out, I went to my room and crawled into bed. I wanted to sleep for several days but didn't have that luxury. A few minutes later, Brian came in and slipped under the covers. He kissed me on my chest and ran his hand up my thigh.

So much for getting to sleep right away—but I didn't mind at all.

The line of cars in the drive-thru wrapped around the building. I slipped past them and walked into the busy lobby where customers stood five deep behind each register. Shar stood at the bins wrapping Egg McMuffins.

"Good mornin'," I said.

She finished the last breakfast sandwich and turned toward me. "Hey, Steve. How was Arizona?"

"Hot. Is my check here?" I needed the money from my last work period, and my bank closed at noon.

"It should be in the safe."

I entered the combination and found my check on the top shelf, next to a deposit bag. "Is Jake workin' today?"

"He'll be here at noon. Is there something I can help you with?"

Shar and I held equal positions as assistant managers, so telling her "I quit" would be inappropriate. The schedule above the desk showed me working the closing shift. Shit. Jake won't be happy with me not working tonight, but there's no way.

"Nah, I'll catch him later. Don't work too hard."

I drove to my bank down the street where I cashed the paycheck and closed my account. That gave me about $500 to last until Pfau came through with his promise of financial aid.

My next stop—the U-Haul center—proved to be fruitful. That location didn't have a trailer to rent one-way to South Dakota, but the one in Springdale did. I could pick it up at noon Sunday.

When I got back to McDonald's, customers again packed the drive-thru and lobby. I jumped on a register to help through the rush while Jake expedited food. When it slowed down a few minutes after 1 p.m., I closed out the register and carried it back to the desk.

"Hey, Jake. Here's register four." I set the drawer and printout on the desk next to a deposit bag.

"Thanks."

This wasn't going to be easy. I liked Jake, and quitting would put him in a significant bind. Shar and Bev would have to cover my shifts until someone else could be trained and promoted. Their overtime would kill his payroll numbers.

"I have a big problem," I said.

"What's that?" Jake answered.

He counted the last of the paper money and entered the amount in the calculator. Then he removed the quarters and began sliding them off the desk into his left hand. If I didn't give it the Band-Aid removal treatment, I might not be able to do it.

"I'm quittin'."

"Uh-huh."

Finished with the quarters, he started on the dimes.

"I'm transferrin' to a school out of state, so I have no choice."

"Okay." He grabbed the nickels next.

"Please stop for a minute."

"I'm almost done."

After he finished the pennies, Jake added the checks and compared the total amounts to the printout for the drawer.

"You haven't heard a word I said. I know this is a bad time, but I have things—"

"Sure."

When he pulled the other drawer in front of him, I put my hand on the top.

"Jake, listen to me."

"I heard every word," he said. "We talked about this when you called me on Thursday, don't you remember?"

Actually, I don't. Mark or Wayne had to have called. That must be how Jeff knew to have Bruce to move in. Dammit, I have no fucking idea what's going on anymore.

"Of course, I remember. I just wanted to apologize in person for doing this at the last minute. Then you know I can't work tonight's shift."

"Don't worry. I've got it covered."

Dizziness caught me off-guard. *No, not now. Please, let me say bye to my friend.*

The alarm clock pulled me awake. I reached to hit the snooze button and bumped into someone.

Are you kidding me, Wayne?

If I had sex half as much as he did, maybe I'd be in a better mood most of the time. The guy had hair long enough to pull back into a ponytail. I got him up, dressed, and out of the apartment quickly so I could get packed. Checking my watch confirmed it was Sunday morning of the right month and year.

A stack of moving boxes, tape, and markers in the corner of the bedroom surprised me. On top were maps that one of my alters had used a yellow highlighter to mark a route to Sioux Falls. Too bad they didn't pack for me.

I filled a suitcase with items I'd need right away. Next, I assembled a few of the boxes and began filling them. It took me two hours to pack everything I owned. I didn't have a lot, but all of it would never fit in my car.

At 11 a.m., I headed to Springdale. The U-Haul company had better have my trailer, otherwise I'd have to leave most of my shit behind. I parked in front of the office and opened the glove compartment to get my car registration.

A deposit bag fell to the floorboard.

I jumped back and instinctively checked to see if anybody was standing near my car. The bag hadn't been there Saturday morning.

Shit. The blackout I had at work. Mark, what the hell did you do?

Stupid question. He did what he wanted to do, regardless of whom he hurt or how much danger he put me in. I slid the bag under the passenger seat and got the car registration.

The manager didn't work today, so I had to deal with a different person. My hand visibly shook as I handed him my information.

The dot matrix printer spat out the paperwork, which I signed. My scribbled signature looked worse than ever and didn't resemble the one on my driver's license. The clerk attached the temporary hitch to the back of my car and had me back up to the small trailer. He connected the wiring to my taillights, and I left the office by 12:30 p.m.

With the threat of arrest looming, I filled my car and the small trailer with my property, not overly concerned with damaging anything. My wooden magazine rack —five feet tall and six feet long—wouldn't fit, so I called Paul to see if he wanted it. He pulled up in his small pickup truck an hour later.

"You're really leavin'?" he asked.

"Afraid so. It's an opportunity I can't pass up." This would likely be the last time I see him.

"Too bad. I'll miss seein' you around."

"Same here."

I helped him carry the magazine rack to his truck. Once we secured it, awkward silence followed. He was such a nice guy, someone I enjoyed being around.

"Take care of yourself, wherever it is you're goin'."

"Thanks. I might be back someday." *When hell freezes over.*

He waved as he pulled away. It took me another ten minutes to prepare the car and trailer for my journey. On the way out of town, I parked next to the road in an IGA parking lot—far away from peering eyes. After taking three deep breaths, I grabbed the deposit bag from under the seat and unzipped it. Inside I found a note wrapped around a bundle of cash—more than $600.

Don't worry. I swapped an empty deposit bag for this one.

Mark

Oh, hell. Steve, that asshole's gonna put you in prison someday.

How stupid could my alter be? At least he didn't keep the deposit slip or any checks payable to McDonald's. If the police questioned me about the missing deposit bag, the cash itself would prove nothing. I had to get the hell out of Arkansas.

At 3:30 p.m., with the highlighted maps on the passenger seat next to bags of Doritos and M&Ms, I pulled into traffic and headed north. This would be the farthest I'd ever driven. The previous record was the trip to Conway for the high school state tennis tournament. The drive to Sioux Falls would be at least ten hours—maybe more with a trailer in tow. I prayed my sixteen-year-old Mustang would survive the trip. At least it had new tires and a tune-up, courtesy of Mark.

Don't you mean "courtesy of McDONALD's"?

All the way to the Missouri state line, I kept glancing in my side mirrors for flashing lights. The trailer made my rear-view mirror useless. Once I crossed into the "Show Me State," I counted to ten, and the tension left my body.

For someone with at least two other personalities inhabiting his brain, I sure was alone.

Chapter 22

Road to Hell

Driving overnight had its disadvantages. I fell asleep behind the wheel a couple of times—briefly. Whoever highlighted the maps did an excellent job. I did keep my eye on the engine temperature. Although the car hadn't overheated since I changed the thermostat in June, I brought antifreeze and put in a new thermostat just in case.

I stopped every hour or so to rest, pee, and get caffeinated. The more diet pop I drank, the shorter the time between breaks. At 7:45 a.m., I finally arrived in Sioux Falls. I had time to grab an Egg McMuffin and hash browns before meeting my new debate coach.

The city impressed me. Clean, modern, and inviting. I had no trouble finding Augustana College. Some of the buildings appeared to be fifty or sixty years old while others looked new. The administration building on South Summit Avenue must be one of the oldest.

I'd never met the Augustana coach, so I had no idea what he looked like. Bill said he had a scruffy beard, so I went with that. When I entered the lobby, I spotted him right away. He wore a tweed sports jacket and gray pants but not a tie. I guessed his age to be late thirties to early forties.

We exchanged pleasantries and shook hands. The unmistakable smell of cigarettes surrounded him like an aura. I hoped he didn't smoke in the debate room.

He led me to the registrar's office where I completed several forms, including a transcript request. Next was the financial aid office. Since I'd already been approved for it at ARKANSAS, the woman said it would be easy to transfer it to AUGUSTANA—with increases, of course. I filled out more forms. Once she handed paperwork to me showing how much the tuition and boarding would be, I understood what she meant by "increases." I hoped they didn't hear me gasp. Private colleges cost a lot more than state universities.

"They'll find you the money," Coach Pfau said.

One year of tuition at the college would cover four years at the UNIVERSITY OF ARKANSAS. I opened the brochure and got another shocker. AUGUSTANA was a college of the Lutheran Church.

You've got to be kidding. A religious college? Bill left that little detail out. Steve, you're a dumb ass for not asking questions when you spoke with Coach Pfau last Thursday. What the hell have you done?

An hour later, I had in my possession a class schedule, dorm key, meal card, and parking permit. My financial aid was pending, so the money in my pocket would be all I had for weeks. If Mark hadn't taken the deposit bag, I would have been in trouble.

From the administration building, Coach Pfau escorted me to the library building next door. We went through the front entrance and down some stairs.

"Down here is our squad room. At the end of this hallway is the back entrance."

He unlocked a plain door with no sign on it. "We call this 'The Pit.'"

The twenty-by-forty-foot area had eight folding tables like the ones we had at ARKANSAS. An IBM Selectric typewriter sat atop six of them. Their cords, covered by duct tape, stretched across the floor to electrical outlets.

"Through that door are rooms you'll use for practice rounds." He gave me a key. "This works on all the doors. Be back at one for a team meeting."

After putting my property in the dorm and returning the trailer to a U-Haul rental place, I made it to The Pit with five minutes to spare. Coach Pfau showed up a few minutes later and had us all introduce ourselves. I learned everyone called him Pfau—not coach or professor. When he announced who would be debating together, I discovered I'd made a huge mistake.

The asshole lied to me.

Instead of being on the top team with Liz—as promised—he assigned me to debate with Ryan, a cute freshman I soon began dating. He paired Liz with Blake, an excellent debater I knew from a Missouri university. Carol and I often ran him across at tournaments the previous year. His transfer to Augustana surprised me—especially because Pfau neglected to mention it.

"You're goin' to regret this," I told Pfau the next day.

"I doubt it."

As I predicted, Ryan and I had a better record in the fall tournaments than the "top" team—although they attended some stronger tournaments than we did. I enjoyed debating with Ryan and looked forward to the second semester tournaments. After watching Liz bully Blake around and try to control everything, I decided debating with her would be too stressful for my MPD.

Determined to prove himself right, Pfau sent Liz and Blake to the two "west coast swing" tournaments over the Christmas break. The day after they returned from what turned out to be a disastrous trip, Pfau found me working in The Pit along with some of the other debaters. He pointed at me and then the practice room.

"We need to talk."

If anything, Pfau was predictable. All he cared about was winning and didn't give a rat's ass if he trampled over someone to do it.

"I'm putting you and Liz together for the rest of the year," he said when we were alone.

"Nah, I'll pass. Ryan and I are good."

"I thought you wanted to be on the top team?"

"That's funny. I thought Ryan and I *were* the top team. At the same tournaments, we did as good as or better than they did. If Liz let Blake do what he's good at, they would win a lot more."

Pfau lit one of his Camel cigarettes and blew smoke toward me. He leaned back and stared at me, letting silence fill the room.

"Liz thinks you and she could be a national power, and I agree."

"Ah, so it's her idea. She's been yankin' your chain from day one. I don't wanna be paired with a bully."

"This is not a debate."

Oh, the irony.

"Blake transferred here before you offered me the top team. When I called you from Arizona, you flat out *lied* just to get me here. That's sad. Then you stuck me with a green freshman. Despite that, we kicked ass. We're happy debatin' together."

Mark and Wayne had also been dormant since I got to Sioux Falls. I didn't want to poke the sleeping sociopath and his doppelganger manslut.

Pfau could put you and Blake together. That would be the strongest team.

That would put Ryan and Liz together. I can't do that to him.

"The decision's been made," Pfau said. He took the last puff on the cigarette and lit another one.

Something else had to be at play that caused him to pair Liz and Blake—and I let my intuition lead me down the path.

"After we spoke, you found out I was gay, didn't you?" It was a guess, but it made sense with what happened. "You told Liz over the weekend, and she didn't want to debate with me. So you did what she wanted.

"I worked my butt off to get where I am. I sacrificed grades and friendships. People said I'd never be a debater. I proved them wrong. Ryan and I made a laughingstock out of you. Now Liz wants me as a partner, and you'll do anything she says. As I said, I'll pass."

"That's not at all what happened." He smirked and took another drag off his cigarette.

"Bullshit."

"Debate with her or I'll pull your scholarship."

That would be the same as kicking me out of school. *What will I do? Where will I go? What will Mark and Wayne do?*

"You asshole. I'm happy, and you don't know how critical that is for my mental health." *I'm not going to cry. I'm not.*

"Be here at two this afternoon," he stubbed the cigarette out in the ashtray. "Find a way to make this work."

He left me sitting in the dark, dreary practice room, not much larger than a bathroom. The walls closed in on me, and I had to get out of there. I grabbed my coat and headed out into the cold.

Now that I'd be on the official top team, I didn't want it. I had to tell Ryan what happened—and I dreaded it. After traipsing across the snow-covered campus to his dormitory, I shook the snow off my boots and made my way to his room. I stood at his door for at least twenty seconds trying to formulate a way to break the news. He opened it on the third knock.

"We need to talk." *Yikes. I said the words nobody ever wants to hear.*

"What's up?"

As he held open the door, I slipped into the room. My gut told me how this conversation would end, but stupid me decided to have it anyway.

"I need to tell you something," I said. "Just know, I had absolutely nothin' to do with it."

"Pfau fucking put you with Liz, didn't he?"

Ugh. It's that ability to read the situation that made him such a good debate partner for me. Why did I feel like this would be our break-up discussion?

"Yes, but we got in a huge argument over it. If I don't do it, he'll kick me out of school."

"Well, you got your wish. You never wanted to debate with me anyway. Get out."

"Ryan, don't do this. You and I are good together. That doesn't have to change."

I'd fallen in love with this crazy guy in the four months we'd been together. Being unhappy and single had never served me well. I stood next to his bed, hoping he'd calm down and see reason.

"I said get the fuck out. We're done."

I did as he asked and stepped into the hallway. He slammed the door behind me, a fitting end to a promising relationship.

Candy, I'm so sorry. I never should have come here.

———————

AUGUSTANA had a "mini semester" during January. They nicknamed it "Jan Term." A lot of students used the time to travel abroad for special credit. Debaters took a class from Pfau where we had to complete specific research assignments.

Working with Liz equated being in a never-ending nightmare. I had no idea why she wanted me as a debate partner. Because of her controlling nature, she wouldn't let me do what I knew how to do. The stress quickly got to me—and it sent my two alters into a frenzy, just as I feared.

Sioux Falls had one gay bar—the HITCH 'N POST—and Wayne began going in January. He dumped me there a few times, so I went with the flow and hung around to meet people. Along the way, I met a few tricks for meaningless sexual adventures, but Wayne prospered. Some mornings I woke up in strangers' beds and had to find my way back to the dorm. At other times, I discovered my clothes smelling of smoke.

Beginning in February, the debate squad traveled weekly. We usually drove to tournaments on Thursdays and returned on Mondays. That left us Tuesday and Wednesday to prepare for the next one. With that hectic schedule, I didn't attend classes. None—well, except for voice and diction. I was determined to get rid of my godforsaken hillbilly accent. For the other classes, I got notes from other students and I read—skimmed, actually—the books and handouts. Come exam time, I did the best I could. The semester ended with my worst grades ever: A-, B+, C, and C-.

My unhappiness made life hectic in my mangled mind. Mark filled my dorm closet with stolen things: candy bars, small knickknacks, and other worthless shit. I'd return from tournaments with a suitcase full of weird crap that Wayne got his hands on. After one tournament, I found three pairs of dirty tighty-whities shoved in the corner of my duffel bag. Another time I discovered a pair of handcuffs with a phone number taped to them.

I never knew where I'd be in the morning—and that included at tournaments. On more than one occasion, I awoke in a hotel room with another school's debater or—in some cases—coach. Wayne didn't seem to care who it was as long as they fit his "type." On the upside, having sex with coaches worked out for us when they judged one of our debate rounds.

Liz and I finished the season with a good run. We won the district tournament, which qualified us for the National Debate Tournament (NDT) held at Florida State University in Tallahassee. But our acrimonious relationship doomed us. When they announced which teams advanced to the elimination rounds, we didn't make it—and I no longer cared.

At least being at AUGUSTANA helped me get rid of my southern drawl. The voice and diction class I took gave me a neutral, midwest accent, so I no longer sounded like one of the Clampetts.

As mistakes went, moving to South Dakota turned out to be a big one. I had no friends, no support, and nothing to look forward to. The last time I found myself in this situation was after my varicose vein surgery when I was seventeen—and that's when I tried to kill myself.

Why do Mark and Wayne want to keep you alive? Maybe one of them can take over for good. If you don't want this life, one of them should have it.

I wish they would.

Chapter 23

Violated

November 1982
Sioux Falls, South Dakota
Age 22

For my senior year at Augustana College, I moved into a small apartment in an old, converted house near the school. It gave me and Wayne a place to bring guys whenever we wanted.

Two weeks before Thanksgiving, I met a guy named Gary at the Hitch 'n Post. He was clean-cut, polite, and fifteen years older. Although I didn't mind the age difference, we had nothing in common. He didn't do sports, hated sci-fi and fantasy, and listened to boring jazz music.

We had hot and heavy sex—an uninhibited interaction with no embarrassment or boundaries. It was a perfect one-night stand to fuck and get fucked—nothing more. The next morning, he drove me to my apartment.

"How about dinner next weekend?" he asked before I could escape the truck.

"Sorry, I'll be out of town until Monday. We're leaving early Thursday morning."

"How about Wednesday?"

Damn, I didn't see that coming.

"Sure, but I can't stay the night."

When Wednesday arrived, Gary took me to an expensive Italian restaurant where he spent a small fortune. Feeling somewhat obligated for my overpriced fettuccine Alfredo, I went home with him. We had a frenzied sex session—the kind where you feel immense temporary passion with the goal of having a satisfying orgasm.

Once we finished, I had the urge to get out of there. Something about him bothered me, but I couldn't identify what—he was just "off." When he went to the bathroom, I quickly dressed. I had my outerwear ready to put on by the time he returned.

"Why don't you spend the night?" he asked.

"We've been through this, Gary. I have to leave early tomorrow."

"Come on. Please stay. I'll get you there on time."

I wrapped a scarf around my neck and slipped on my coat.

"Look, I've had a good time, but I need to get home so I can pack and get some sleep."

He got under the covers, pulled them back, and patted the mattress in a "come hither" moment. The clinginess came off a little too creepy.

"Gary, if you don't want to drive me back, that's fine. I'll just walk."

If I couldn't find a cab, it would take me about an hour on foot to get home—but I preferred that to staying with Gary. As I headed for the door, I put my ski cap on.

Something hit the back of my head. My glasses flew off and I tumbled over. I tried—but failed—to keep my eyes open.

When I regained consciousness, I couldn't move my arms and legs. I lay face down on the bed. Gary had tied my ankles and wrists to his four-poster bed with nylon rope. He also stuffed some kind of cloth in my mouth—forcing my jaw wide open.

I don't know how long Gary poked, prodded, whipped, and violated me. I moved in and out of consciousness. The only one I could envision getting me out of this was Mark.

Please take over, Mark. Please. He's going to kill me. He's going to kill us. It can't end for me this way, not on his terms.

Steve, you don't want to die. You just want to be happy, to be loved.

Gary entered me again and lay on top. He put his hands around my neck and squeezed.

How did I not see this coming? Now I know what's wrong with him, what's off. The coldness in his eyes when he looked at me, the complete lack of emotion.

I somehow spit out the cloth in my mouth.

"Please stop."

My words barely made a sound as he choked me harder. Dizziness made the room spin as I welcomed my sociopathic alter's impending arrival.

You're so fucked.

I "awoke" standing next to the bed. My throat felt as if I'd hung myself—ironically, one method of suicide I hadn't contemplated. Streetlights shined through the curtains.

Please be the same night.

Mark had somehow pulled my hands out of the bindings. My wrists and hands had deep scratches, but the bleeding had stopped. The scene reminded me of a note Mark had left for me during my first year of college.

Steve, if anyone messes with you, I'll fuck them up good.

Mark

He kept his word. Mark had tied Gary to the bed with a shirt around his head as a gag. Blood covered the side of his face. The *pièce de resistance* was the wooden pee-wee baseball bat shoved up Gary's ass—knob end first. My hand instinctively went to the back of my head to find a knot the size of a lemon.

Way to go, Mark.

After dressing and finding my glasses, I felt Gary's pulse. The slight thump of his heartbeat told me he'd probably live, but what did I know? Watching *M*A*S*H* and *Trapper John, M.D.*, didn't make me a medical expert.

I liberated $200 from Gary's wallet and wiped my fingerprints off everything I might have touched—except the unseen end of the bat. Then I untied the ropes binding him.

If Gary called the police when he came to, they'd arrest me—but I doubted he would. I couldn't call them myself after what Mark did.

After finding a cab, I had it drive me home and wait ten minutes while I packed. I always left my car parked on the street at my apartment when we traveled. Along with the clothes I'd need for the weekend, I stuffed my makeup bag in the suitcase along with clothes I needed for the weekend. I'd need something to conceal the impending bruises from Gary's choking me.

With my suit bag over my shoulder and duffel bag in my right hand, I got in the cab and directed the driver to the library basement entrance where the debate squad van stood waiting for everyone. It was time to get the hell out of town—even if just for a few days.

We didn't do well at the tournament because I couldn't sleep or concentrate. If Gary died, the police would find me eventually. I'd been seen with him at the bar and in public. Maybe I should have called the police and an ambulance.

It's too late to think about that now.

The van dropped me off at my apartment. As I walked past my car, something on the windshield caught my attention. Someone had put a cut-up hot dog in a plastic bag along with a note.

Wait until I find you.

He didn't sign it, but I knew who put it there. Gary.

Thanks to Gary, my insomnia returned. Lack of sleep made it difficult to concentrate and perform simple tasks. As a result, my grades plunged. I made an A-, a B, a C+, and a D the fall semester—and Pfau gave me another A- in debate. If I had known he was such a prick, I never would have transferred.

But you had to get out of Fayetteville before you got arrested.

Nothing in the McDONALD's thefts could be traced back to me, so I didn't have to run.

Stop lying to yourself.

Over Christmas, Liz and I flew to participate in the two west-coast-swing tournaments. Pfau booked a three-day layover in Los Angeles in between the tournaments because she wanted to do research at the better libraries there.

"Where will we stay?" I asked.

"The school isn't paying for it, so stay wherever you want," Pfau said.

"What? I can't afford a hotel. I didn't ask for this. Liz did." With Wayne's constant partying and the debate team's weekly traveling, I barely had enough money for rent and food.

"Stay in the airport terminal if you want. It's only two nights."

He's out of his fucking mind.

Pressed for a solution, I remembered that Sean from high school lived in Huntington Beach, about an hour from LAX. I tracked down his phone number and called. After exchanging pleasantries, I got to the point.

"I need a big favor. I'm on a debate team. We're flying into LAX and have a three-day, two-night layover. Is there any way I can stay with you?"

The silence on the other end answered the question. It had been a long shot, after all.

"I'm sorry, but my stepdad has business associates staying here."

When the dizziness hit me, I tried to hang up—but I didn't make it in time. Wayne or Mark must have told Sean off with colorful language. *You can kiss that friendship good-bye.*

As I ran out of options, I telephoned the USC forensics department for suggestions. It turned out that Allan, a debate coach I knew from an east-coast university, had relocated to Los Angeles to pursue his PhD. He graciously let me stay at his place—or, more specifically, he let *Wayne* stay. The manslut—Wayne, not Allan—left me a note.

Thank you. West Hollywood gays are the best.

Wayne

Something told me I owed Allan lots of apologies.

Once the tournaments finished, Liz and I flew back to Sioux Falls. One of the other squad members picked us up at the airport in the team's van. We dropped our debate gear at the school before heading to our respective homes.

I closed the van door and walked past my car. Gary had left a present for me under a windshield wiper. This time, the plastic bag contained photos. The first few were of me on campus, apparently shot using a telephoto lens. When I thumbed through the remaining pictures, I recoiled.

Gary had taken photos of my apartment—from the inside.

Chapter 24

Undue Pressure

Mom and Dad became friends with a new family in town, the Winslows. I met them for the first time when our two families went camping together at Blue Mountain Lake. We had a new tri-hull ski boat powerful enough to pull two and three skiers at a time—depending on the size of the person. Our two families got campsites next to each other.

The Winslows had a son my age, Jeffrey. We hit it off and had a wonderful time waterskiing together. As we packed up on Sunday to return home, he invited me to spend the night at his house on Monday.

The sleepover at Jeffrey's was the only one I'd been to since the first grade when I wet my friend's bed. I prayed it wouldn't happen again. Mom drove me to the Winslow's place just before supper. Jeffrey's mom, Deborah, made delicious spaghetti and meatballs for dinner. I had thirds. We watched TV until ten and then went to bed.

Jeffrey and I chatted for an hour about school, sports, and anything else that came up. I finally had another friend I could talk to and have fun with. When he got a flashlight out and got under the covers, I joined him.

"Wanna see something cool?" he asked.

"Sure."

He removed his pajama bottoms and underwear. *Oh, no. I didn't come here to do sex things.*

"Here, look." Jeffrey shined a light on his crotch. "I have hair growin' down there."

"Feel it." He grabbed my hand and placed it on his crotch.

I pulled back like I'd touched a burning stove. "That's okay. I can see it."

"Come on, feel it. That's what friends do."

That's what Tom and Allen said. My stomach cramped, probably because I ate too much spaghetti.

"Show me yours," he said.

Before I could react, Jeffrey pulled my pajamas and underwear down to my knees. Then he grabbed my crotch and started rubbing.

"Please, stop. I wanna go to sleep."

"We will after some fun."

I stopped protesting and lay back. He seemed like a nice guy, and I did need friends at school, so I did everything he wanted.

The next morning, I woke before anyone else did. My watch said it was 5:30 a.m. I had difficulty climbing down from Jeffrey's bed without making any noise. After putting on my clothes, I snuck out the side door.

It took me only ten minutes to walk home because I cut across the creek. Unable to see the rocks very good in the dark, I almost fell in. Everybody at the house was still asleep, so I changed into clean pajamas and crawled into bed.

A few hours later, I stumbled to the kitchen for a bowl of cereal. Mom must have been working in the garden because she was washing dirt off her hands.

"What happened last night?" she asked. "Deborah called this mornin' to say you left."

Lord, I sure didn't think it through, did I? "My stomach hurt. I was afraid I'd throw up. I must've ate too much spaghetti."

"You worried her to death. Don't ever do that again."

Why *did* I leave? It's not like Jeffrey wanted me to do something I hadn't done before.

He came over the next day and asked if I wanted to go walking around in the rock quarry. If I said "no," I'd look stupid, especially since Mike and I had finished mowing for the day.

Jeffrey and I climbed down the side of the quarry to the bottom. We sat next to Crawdad Lake, throwing pebbles into the water.

"How come you snuck out last night?"

"I didn't feel good." What else was I supposed to say? If I told him the truth—that I didn't want to do those things with him—he'd be mad at me.

"Mama would've drove you home."

"Sorry. I won't do it again."

He stood and pulled up on my arm. "Come on. Let's go hikin'."

We walked across the quarry and climbed up the hill into the trees. On the other side of the hill, we came to two boulders leaning against each other. They formed a hiding place both of us could fit in. Jeffrey suggested we go inside and sit.

I didn't want to risk our friendship, so I crawled into the hiding spot with him—despite knowing what he wanted. Sure enough, he unzipped his pants. With the choice of going along or losing a friend, I gave in.

For the rest of June, we went camping with the Winslows every weekend. Jeffrey always found a way to get me alone so we could play, as he called it. He'd take me to the campground restrooms at night when nobody else was around.

When we swam, he'd dive under the water and pull my bathing suit down, then ask me to do the same with him. I couldn't bring myself to refuse, especially when he was one of the few people who didn't call me "Sissy Simmons."

During the week, he drove his minibike over to the house or called to have me meet him somewhere. I found myself giving into his sexual demands whenever he wanted.

Every day, I walked around ashamed and afraid that someone would find out.

How much more of this can I take? Do I need friends this badly?
I needed a way out.

Chapter 25

Escaping Sioux Falls

Liz and I qualified for the National Debate Tournament as one of the top sixteen teams in the country. We made it to the quarterfinals where we lost in a 3-2 decision by the judges. To finish fifth in the country was quite a feat for someone who never debated in high school. I was proud of myself for the first time in years.

Afterward, one of the judges approached me.

"Mr. Simmons, I'm George Ziegelmueller from Wayne State University. I understand you're a senior. What are your plans for next year?"

"Nothing at the moment." I wanted to coach debate while pursuing my master's degree. All the schools I'd sent my résumé to had turned me down.

"How would you like to come to Detroit?" George asked. "I need another graduate assistant."

If I could survive two years in South Dakota, Detroit couldn't be that bad.

"Debate killed my GPA," I said.

"What is it?"

"A little over three-point. It certainly doesn't reflect my abilities."

"Your GPA needs to be at least three-point-zero-five. If it meets that, we'd love to have you."

He promised to send an application to me as soon as he got back to his school. If Pfau would stop dogging me on grades for forensics, my GPA would be higher. I shouldn't be getting an A- or B for debate after all I'd done for the school. Maybe Detroit would do me good.

Stress piled up when I got back to school. I carried six classes—sixteen credits—the heaviest load I'd ever taken. The hardest was Pfau's Organizational Communication class. I got three students' notes, read the material, and studied—a lot. When the proctor handed me the exam, I read through all the questions first—and smiled. It took me an hour to complete the test, and I left the classroom knowing I'd aced it.

Two days later, Pfau called me into his office. He slid my exam paper across the desk. It had "100%" written at the top. I screamed in joy.

You did it, Steve.

"Not so fast," Pfau said. "You're getting a C minus."

"I'm what? I don't understand." What kind of bullshit was he up to?

"You cheated."

The accusation gut-punched me. I slammed the test onto his desk, knocking off his full in-box, scattering papers on the floor.

"Cheated? I don't *cheat* on tests. Besides, how could I have cheated? The proctor watched me the entire time."

Pfau leaned back and smiled.

Reach across the desk and choke him.

Steve, hush. Don't give Mark ideas.

"It's impossible to get a perfect score on one of my exams. Especially you. The questions are too hard."

"You arrogant SOB. If you don't think someone can get a perfect score on your tests, then you must be a lousy goddamned professor."

"It doesn't matter what you think. I've seen your other grades. You're just not smart enough to get this high of a score. You're lucky I didn't give you an F."

Calm down, Steve. How can someone be that conceited?

"You're a despicable person. You lie to and manipulate students, and then you threaten them if you don't get your way. You want everyone to think you're this big intelligent professor who's smarter than them.

I hate to break this to you, motherfucker, but you're not even the smartest person in this room."

I snatched my exam off the desk and left his office. If I had expected a C- would keep me out of WAYNE STATE UNIVERSITY, I might have lost my shit. Fortunately, my other grades for the semester kept my GPA high enough to get into the graduate program.

Transferring to AUGUSTANA had been a colossal mistake. I had a bully for a partner who made me miserable every day—and a prick of a coach who condoned her actions, tossing in a fair amount of bullying of his own.

And I could never forget *him*—Gary.

In the six months since he raped me, the man had tormented me daily. He called every night—moaning and hanging up. He kept placing bags of cut-up hot dog wieners on my windshield—and I still didn't know what it meant. Even though I missed going to the Hitch 'n Post, I didn't want to risk running into him again.

Why can't Gary just let it go? He started it. Mark acted in self-defense.

How is a baseball bat up the ass "self-defense"?

I need to get out of this state before Gary gets hold of me again.

George sent the graduate school application as promised. I received it the last week of school. After completing it, I stopped by the records office to see when a final transcript could be sent. My professors posted our grades within a week after the exams. As I predicted, the C- I received from Pfau didn't pull my grade down below the minimum I needed for WAYNE STATE UNIVERSITY.

I mailed the application with a copy of my transcript the day before graduation. When I telephoned George to let him know, he said the application was a mere formality.

"Welcome aboard," he said. "You need to be here the second week of August at the latest."

"What about financial aid?" Yet again, I steamrolled ahead without asking about costs. It's not like I had any other options, though.

"Your classes are paid for, and the school pays you a stipend for living expenses. You can apply for loans if you want, but you shouldn't need them."

"Thanks, George. When I get settled for the summer, I'll call with my new phone number."

The next day, I stopped by the records office and filled out an alumni form with a forwarding address. The simple act of writing down that woman's address nauseated me.

You've lost your fucking mind.

I packed my car with everything that would fit—which was about a third of the property I moved north with. If I could afford a trailer, I'd take it all home to Arkansas. Instead, I gave the rest of my property to other students.

Before leaving South Dakota, I called Glenda at the Fort Smith McDonald's.

"Of course you can work here," she said. "I'll give you all the hours you want."

Although I wanted to attend the graduation ceremony, I had to lie low. Gary most likely would be looking for me there.

A secretary in the administration building promised to mail my diploma to me. With all business completed, I filled my car with gas, checked the oil, and put air in the tires.

Stop delaying. Get in the car and go. You can do this. It's only three months. Maybe Mark and Wayne will let you "sleep" the entire time.

Against my better judgment, I turned the car south on Interstate 29 and headed for Arkansas. My plans would be screwed up if the police greeted me with an arrest warrant. The theft of the deposit bag the day I left Fayetteville two years previously surely made me the prime suspect.

At least you won't be working at that McDonald's.

Even though Mom had divorced Harry, I didn't want to be anywhere near her—but poverty prevailed. She and my brother lived in a two-bedroom apartment. With Aunt Estelle playing peacemaker, Mom wrote a letter telling me I could stay there for the summer.

Hell must have gotten an arctic blast because I was going back to Arkansas and staying with my mother—proof I'm fucking insane.

Chapter 26

Homo, Go Home

A fresh start in a new city. I kept telling myself that, hoping it would come true. After three months living with Mom and Mike in Arkansas, any city would be better for my mental health. Despite having every reason to say "I told you so" about Harry, I didn't. I worked at McDonald's, played tennis, and kept my head low.

Never planning to return, I gave my Mustang to Sharon and flew to the Motor City. One of Wayne State's forensics coaches picked me up. She dropped me off at student housing—the Helen L. DeRoy Apartments, a fifteen-story modern building on campus. It was conveniently located across the street from Manoogian Hall—with the debate room on the fifth floor. My roommate, Kris, arrived a few days before me.

"Hurry, Kris. We're gonna be late."

In under twenty-four hours together, I learned that Kris tended to run behind. She flew out of her bedroom with a monster-size purse on her shoulder.

"I'm ready."

We walked into the forensic offices to find staff and students congregating in the department's common area. George arrived a few minutes after we found seats. Once we all settled in, he had everyone introduce themselves. Wayne State University had about the same number of debaters as Augustana. The squad had three debate coaches: George, Kris, and me—a definite improvement over Arkansas and Augustana.

The squad had several very capable debaters, including first-year students. None went to any debate workshops over the summer, so all the research started from nothing. The debate topic had been released a month earlier. Even without prompting, most of the debaters had already done a significant amount of work.

The following day, one of the sophomore debaters—Nick—and I took a break in the student lounge across the hall. He had the makings of a great debater: intelligent, a fast talker, and a quick thinker. Standing about six-foot-one, he had a boisterous personality. His likability factor gave him an adorability that debate judges would love. We got around to the topic of my debate career.

"NDT quarterfinals," Nick said. "Quite impressive."

"Thanks. A lot of hard work. We would have done better if my partner and I liked each other."

"Did she have a problem with you being gay?"

Well, that loaded question shocked my shorts.

I hadn't discussed my sexual orientation with anyone other than Kris. That's why she agreed to share an apartment with me.

"Liz never said anything to me about it, but I think she and Pfau both had an issue with it."

"George had a meeting about it a week before you arrived," Nick said.

Please tell me I heard him wrong.

"What do you mean, he 'had a meeting'?"

"He told us you were homosexual and asked if anyone had a problem with it. If we did, he said he wouldn't bring you on."

"A week before? Are you kidding me?"

"It's true. None of us cared, which is why you're here."

Breathe deeply, Steve. If you get too upset, you know what will happen.

I couldn't have Wayne or Mark appear and screw things up. Should I confront George or let it go? If one of my alters went off on him, that would be the end of me here.

The next day, I caught George in his office. If I let the issue stew inside me, it risked a worse confrontation down the road.

"George, can we talk?"

"Sure, Steve, come in."

I closed the door behind me and took a chair next to his desk.

"I don't know who told you I'm gay, and I don't care. But did you have a meeting with the students about it before I arrived?"

As much as I tried to make eye contact with him, I couldn't because he looked down at his desk and fidgeted with some papers. I tried to control my emotions.

"Yes...uh...yes, I did," George said. But you...you have to under—"

"Why would you do such a thing?"

"I had to make sure none of them had a problem with it."

"A *problem*? What the fuck does that mean?"

"Steve, that kind of language—"

"Oh, I'm just getting started. What were you gonna do if someone had, as you said, 'a problem with it'?"

"Cancel your position here."

"Unfuckingbelievable. You're—"

"I asked you to watch your language." George kept moving papers around his desk, still avoiding looking at me.

"You're a real piece of work, you know that?"

"I have to protect my students."

The letter opener on his desk came into focus. I could grab it and shove it into his jugular.

Steve, why would you think such a thing? Is that Mark bleeding through?

"What exactly did you want to protect them from?"

"Well, there's...uh...the influence you could have—"

"Do you hear yourself? I can't *make* someone gay. Surely, you're not that ignorant."

"No, but you...uh...might coerce—"

"Coerce? To have sex? I'm not a rapist or an opportunist."

"Maybe not, but there's...uh...the issue of, you know, AIDS."

"Fuck you, George."

How can I stay here after this? I need to pack my shit and leave.

Slamming the door behind me didn't make me feel any better. I grabbed a Diet Coke in the lounge and collapsed in one of the ugly, orange, cushioned chairs. As much as I wanted to leave, I had no place to go and no money to get there. Giving my car to my sister before flying to Detroit had been a mistake.

If you had that piece of junk up here, you'd get in it and drive from Detroit just to get away—with no money or plan.

I finished my pop and went to one of the debate rooms where two students had papers strewn all over the tables. After a few deep breaths to steady my nerves, I examined what they were working on.

"Anything I can help with?"

Over the next week, I got to know the debaters. Most seemed driven, but I knew two or three who would never last. They didn't have the level of commitment necessary to be in a competitive program.

One Friday after spending a long day working on the teams' arguments, I and five of the debaters went to the local pizza joint. We blew off steam for two hours before going off in different directions.

"Steve, wanna ride?" someone yelled from a car stopped on the street. Nick.

"That's okay. I can use the exercise."

The few blocks to my apartment wouldn't kill me.

"Aw, come on. Hop in."

Against better judgment, I jumped in the passenger seat. It took less than a minute to reach my building. When I said goodnight, I had my hand on the console between the seats.

"Steve, I *like* you."

"I like you, too, Nick. I think we'll be good friends."

"No, I like you."

He put his hand on mine and squeezed. I yanked mine back. Attractive, yes. Off-limits, definitely.

"This isn't appropriate. I can't date students. Thanks for the ride."

I got out of the car and watched as he drove away. What the hell just happened? Nick and I had spent a lot of time together since I arrived, but I never got a gay or bisexual vibe from him. Shit, if any of this got back to George, he'd fire me in a hot second.

The incident kept me away from Manoogian Hall over the weekend. Instead of going there to work with the debaters, I stayed at the apartment to do classwork. Four classes demanded my attention—two of them taught by George. I had to assume he'd be a tough grader like Pfau, but I hoped not as unreasonable.

On Monday, I showed up at the debate room after my Psychology of Human Communication class ended at 11 a.m. Unlike in my undergraduate, I didn't plan on blowing off classes. I found Christina—a freshman debater as talented as Nick—working on her files.

"George is looking for you," she said.

"Thanks." *What the hell does he want?*

I meandered around desks in the forensics office and turned down a hallway. When I knocked on his door frame, he motioned me in.

"Please shut the door."

Oh, no. Nothing good ever came from your boss calling you to a closed-door meeting. I did as he asked and lowered myself onto the chair next to his desk.

"What's up?"

"I had a very disturbing visit this morning from Nick and his father."

Are you shitting me? Nick, what did you do?

"Go on."

"Nick has alleged you made a pass at him on Friday."

"A goddamned lie." How could he do that to me? Did he know how much trouble I would be in? I shifted in my chair. Should I just leave? This wasn't going to end well for me.

"Steve, I've asked you to watch your language in here."

"I don't give a rat's ass." *Really? My career is on the line, and he's worried about my language?* "I never made a pass at Nick. Never."

"Well, he seems quite adamant about it." George wouldn't look at me. "He says you asked him for a ride and—"

"That's his first lie. I wanted to walk, but he *insisted* that I get in his car." Why did I go with him? How could I be so stupid?

"He then alleges you groped him when he dropped you off."

"That's his second lie. I *know* why Nick told you that, but none of it's true." Outing the kid went against everything I believed in. "Absolutely *none* of it."

My graduate degree was about to crash and burn after only a few weeks. No other program would have me after this.

"Help me understand why he would fabricate such an allegation."

"I'm sure he has his reasons. Ask him." *Steve, don't tell him. It's not worth it.*

George sighed loudly and sat back. He rested his elbows on the arms of his chair and intertwined his fingers. Then he bent forward and moved some papers around on his desk. He picked up one and handed it to out for me to take.

"That is the department's sexual harassment policy. Violation of the policy is grounds for termina—"

"You can keep your fucking policy. I didn't make a pass at him. I didn't touch him. I didn't grope him." I stood to leave. This time, I didn't get a chance to slam the door—or even get it open.

"Steve, sit down."

I returned to my seat and counted slowly to ten.

"Professor Pfau said you were difficult to deal with," George said, "but I'm beginning to think his assessment was a bit understated."

"Pfau is an arrogant piece of shit. He lied when he recruited me for his top team. After my partner and I did *better* than the other team, he threatened to pull my financial aid if I didn't debate with Liz. Then when I got a perfect score on his final, he accused me of cheating. *Cheating.* I wish I'd never gone to that godforsaken school, just like I *now* wish I'd never come here. If you want to believe Nick, then so be it, but I didn't do *anything* to that kid. *Nothing.* In fact, when *he* made a pass at *me*, I turned him down and got out of the car. I'm sick and tired of people telling lies *to* me and *about* me."

My hands shook and voice quivered.

Dammit, Steve, why did you just out Nick? That's his story to tell, not yours. I didn't know what else to do.

"This morning, I spoke with Professor Pfau. He said you *did* cheat on the exam and then lied about it. He said you couldn't be trusted."

I shook my head. How had my life come to this? I spent so much time telling lies that nobody believed me when I told the truth.

"About that exam. Did you ask Professor Pfau to give you a different one?"

"It wouldn't have made a difference."

George picked up some pages and flipped through them. "I'm going to ask you a question. Do me a favor and think about it for a minute. Then give me an answer."

"Sure. Whatever."

If George wanted to humiliate me some more, why not let him? So, I leaned back in the chair and listened. He read a question on a familiar topic: organizational communication. Easy stuff. When he finished, I visualized my answer. It took a minute to organize what I wanted to say.

I told him the answer in one sentence, then justified my answer and gave a brief conclusion.

George sat still for a minute before laying the paper on his desk.

"That's a question from Professor Pfau's backup exam for that class. He said nobody ever answers the question correctly, and I believe him because this exam is *harder* than my graduate level final. He said students always leave out a small critical detail."

George remained silent for a minute before pulling a paper from a drawer. He read me another question, this time on a specific organizational communication topic not covered in Pfau's class. It took me a minute to formulate an answer, which I gave to him in detail.

"Interesting," he said.

"I guess you think I cheated, too."

"To the contrary. You answered Professor Pfau's question with the detail he said students usually left out. As for mine, your answer was almost verbatim to my key."

"George, I know the material inside and out. I wanted to prove to Pfau that I wasn't stupid, something another debater on the squad often called me. I even read footnotes and followed them to those sources. His arrogant ass refused to believe me."

My eyes watered as I unsuccessfully tried to hold back tears. How humiliating to be thought a cheater. That kind of accusation follows you through the rest of your academic career.

"You're dismissed," he said. "Just know: if I receive any more complaints or allegations regarding your sexual preference—"

"It's not a preference. It's an orientation we're born with."

"Whatever you want to call it, I don't care."

"Well, I do care. It's sexual orientation. The word 'preference' assumes I have a choice."

"If I get one more complaint or hear another allegation, I'll terminate your position here."

"Not without a hearing, you won't. I know the university policy." After I learned two weeks earlier about George's meeting to discuss my sexuality, I went to the library and read the university's policies on employment termination and sexual harassment.

George stared at me for a few seconds of silence.

"Fine. You can go."

I left the meeting with a larger target on my back. If anything, it built a wall between me and the male debaters. Because of Nick, I couldn't be alone with one of them in any capacity—a rule I should have implemented at the beginning.

We had debate practice scheduled for 2 p.m. That gave me time to drop Directed Study and Directing Forensics. I'd have to take a summer class to make up for it. When I handed the forms to George, he scrunched his forehead.

"You're dropping my classes? Why?"

"Because I don't trust you."

How do I keep getting myself into these situations?

Because you make decisions without thinking them through. First, South Dakota. Then Detroit.

I'm doing the best I can. I hope Mark doesn't decide to take things into his own hands.

Steve, would that be so bad?

Chapter 27

When Tricks Go Wrong

SEPTEMBER 1983
DETROIT, MICHIGAN
AGE 23

Wayne had no problem getting accustomed to Detroit. Given the number of condoms he went through, at least I knew he was being safe. It still terrified me that I might catch AIDS. I never got accustomed to waking in strangers' beds. Since Gary raped me a year earlier, Wayne hadn't switched back to me during a sexual encounter. Maybe my alter decided to be sensitive of my needs for once.

A month after moving in with Kris, I awoke on a Saturday morning to discover I wasn't alone. Cuddled next to me—in my twin bed—slept another guy who felt young and slim.

"Good morning," he said.

I knew Wayne's type all too well. Twinkish with a slight effeminate look, high cheekbones, and sandy blond hair.

"Morning. How old are you?"

Not the kind of conversation I liked having first thing. The question got a giggle out of him, which gave me a view of his perfectly white, straight teeth. The kid didn't look a day older than fifteen.

"Eighteen, silly. Don't you remember asking for my driver's license at MENJO'S? I'm a senior at Cranbrook."

Ugh. A high school student. *Thanks, Wayne, for making sure he's legal.* Although Michigan recognized sixteen as the age of consent, I preferred them to be out of high school, at a minimum.

"How did you get into the bar?"

"A good fake ID."

"Wait, how do I know you didn't show me a fake ID?"

"Nobody buys a fake ID to show they're eighteen."

Yeah, he had me there. He pouted when I didn't want to go another round, but I hadn't consciously been with anyone since Gary. How could I?

I escorted the sex kitten to his car. When I returned to the apartment, I found Kris on the sofa with her arms crossed. She didn't look happy.

"Steve, you can't just bring strangers to our apartment like that."

"Excuse me? As long as I pay my half of the rent, I can bring anyone I want here."

"It sounded like a gay porn coming from your room."

"I didn't know you were gay porn expert."

That got a laugh out of her. I couldn't tell her I had no control over Wayne bringing men back. He did whatever he wanted, regardless of the consequences—a characteristic he shared with Mark.

The Metro Detroit area had a lot of gay bars, but the popular ones had their busy nights. On Wednesdays, BACKSTREET ruled. I'd been going there since learning they played *Dynasty* on the bar's big screen at 9 p.m. After the closing credits, the bar became the busiest dance club in the area. I frequented the place to be part of something—to feel alive—not to get laid. Ever since Gary, I'd found it difficult to pursue one-night stands.

On Friday, December 16, I decided to go out—maybe get lucky. With Kris back home in Utah for the holidays, I had the apartment to myself for two weeks.

While living through two winters in South Dakota, I learned how to dress warmly. I put on my parka, gloves, and ski hat to brave the 23° Fahrenheit weather. A twenty-minute bus ride and five-minute walk took me to the hottest gay bar in the area on Friday—MENJO'S.

After checking my outerwear at the coat room, I walked around the place. The club had a strategic circular layout for customer movement. Just inside the entrance, stools lined the large L-shaped bar where you could sit, drink, and try to talk to someone over the loud music.

If you walked to the right, you entered a room with stadium-style seating. There you'd find lots of guys sucking face or talking. That room led out to the dance floor with its flashing lights and mirrored columns. After the dance floor came the bar again.

I bought a screwdriver and found a stool so I could observe people. Although I tried my luck at dancing, the two guys I asked turned me down. At midnight, with three strong screwdrivers in me and nobody on my dance card, I stood in line to get my coat. Someone tugged on my sleeve.

Behind me stood an adorable man a couple of inches shorter than me.

"Would you like to dance?" he asked.

Five songs later, we got drinks and sat in the snogging room.

"Wayne, I'm glad you danced with me this time."

Why would my doppelganger turn him down? I wouldn't kick him out of bed for eating crackers—or soup, for that matter.

"I obviously wasn't in my right mind before. Sorry, I don't remember your name."

"Kevin."

We talked for half an hour. A graduate student in the WAYNE STATE UNIVERSITY theatre department, Kevin wanted to be a Broadway actor.

"My dream is to play the lead in *Joseph and the Amazing Technicolor Dreamcoat.*"

"Ambitious. So, you can sing?"

"Quite well, actually."

It bothered me that Wayne wouldn't sleep with the guy—a five-foot-ten blond Adonis with blue eyes and dimples. The guy far exceeded our pay grade.

"Want to get out of here?" he asked, his right arm caressing my back.

Steve, you don't know this guy.

He looks harmless—and delicious.

Gary looked innocent too.

"Yeah, but I don't have a car."

Holding up his keys, Kevin smiled.

"That works," I said. "My place or yours?"

"I live with my parents."

He found a parking space close to my apartment. As soon as my door locked shut behind us, we started taking off each other's clothes.

Steve, what are you doing? What if he's another Gary?

I wished my inner voice would shut up and let me get laid. Once Kevin and I made it to the bedroom, my self-doubt evaporated. Ninety minutes and four condoms later, we rested and made small talk. I excused myself to pee. When I came out of the bathroom, Kevin was dressed.

"I'll walk you to the car." I quickly threw on some clothes, a skill I'd learned all those mornings I woke up fifteen minutes before my shift started at McDonald's.

"That's okay. I know the way."

"Nope. I insist. You want to swap numbers?"

"Uh, why not."

He sure didn't act like the man who threw himself at me a few hours earlier. We exchanged numbers and donned our coats. When I opened the front door, Kevin took off jogging toward the elevator.

"Wait up." I fumbled to get my key in the lock. Once it clicked, I ran toward the elevator. My trick wasn't there. The dizziness hit me by surprise and swept me away.

———————

"**Stop.** Please, stop."

His words came out muffled. Kevin lay in a pile of snow with me sitting on his stomach. My hands squeezed his neck, choking him.

Dammit, Mark.

I pulled my hands away but kept him pinned down.

"They're in my coat pocket. All the money's there."

I searched coat pockets until I found what he was talking about—my wallet and the envelope of cash I kept in my jewelry box on the dresser. The $75 in it had to last me a week. The little bastard had robbed me.

"You're a damned thief. Let's go call campus security—or the police."

"I'm sorry. Please, don't call anyone. I didn't mean to."

"Oh, you robbed me by accident?"

"Fuck it. My boyfriend said you'd be an easy mark. I liked you and didn't want to do it, but he told me I had to bring back something."

Somehow, Wayne and Mark knew he was shady. What were the odds? The first chance I had in a year to have sex, and I picked up a twink who rolled his tricks.

Great. Another blow to my ability to trust men. "How did your boyfriend know you could steal from me?"

"Because he got a hundred dollars off you a few weeks ago."

That solved two mysteries—how my cash had disappeared after Thanksgiving and how the little shit knew Wayne's name. I'd believed my alter had spent the money at the bars.

Sorry I blamed you, Wayne.

I wanted to beat the shit out of the punk and then locate his boyfriend. Instead, I found Kevin's wallet. The little thief had almost $200.

"You already robbed someone tonight, didn't you?"

"Yeah. Then I found you when I came back. I couldn't resist your smile."

"Nice try." Along with all his cash, I kept his driver's license and student ID. "I'm making photocopies of your IDs and giving them to bouncers at the bars. If you want them back, they'll be at MENJO'S."

When I let him up, he ran. I returned home and stood under a hot shower to wash his stench off me. Mark must have punched him because my right hand hurt like a son-of-a-bitch.

The next day, I ventured to the library and made copies of the driver's license and student ID. Instead of distributing them as promised, I put them through the shredder.

Have fun replacing these.

Chapter 28

Indignities

The steel door closed behind me when I stepped into the alleyway. If not for the faint yellow bulb above the exit, I wouldn't be able to see much. I tossed three bags of garbage in the dumpster and used my shirt as a towel to clean my hands.

Done. Finished.

This once-a-week cleaning job was tough, but I needed the extra money. It's the only reason I'd spend twelve hours in a smoke-filled claptrap like Tiffany's. For the first eight hours, I worked for tips waiting tables, walls, stools—hell, anywhere men could cram themselves. Many of the guys took liberties grabbing my goods as I squeezed by while balancing a drink tray. Once the bar closed at two, I scrubbed the place.

I leaned against the door and inhaled a lungful of the early morning air. None of the WWII-era homes behind the alley had their lights on. The kitchens likely overlooked the back yards, so I'd notice if someone got up early for coffee or breakfast. It was Sunday, though, and the sun wouldn't appear for another hour.

For a few peaceful minutes, the alley and fenced-in lawns belonged to me. I'd be long gone by the time the families headed downstairs toward the aroma of eggs fried in bacon grease, flaky buttermilk biscuits hot out of the oven, and sausage gravy on the stove. Once their stomachs had been filled, they'd put on their best Sunday dresses and suits before strolling a few blocks to their local church.

Had my home been like that, if my parents had tried to keep me safe, my life might have been different. Normal, even.

Steve, it doesn't do any good to play "what if."

I wiped the moisture from my eyes, getting a whiff of my shirt at the same time. The overpowering odor of cigarette smoke smacked me in the face. I'd kill for a shower. In June, I moved from our Helen L. DeRoy apartment into a two-bedroom, roach-infested place, located two blocks from campus. Instead of a shower, I had a claw-foot bathtub. Baths took way too long, and Bob expected me back at twelve for the busy afternoon crowd. Even if the bus ran on schedule, I'd be lucky to get three-and-a-half hours of sleep after scrubbing the stench away.

Playing Dodge-the-Horny-Men while slinging drinks didn't bother me. Hell, I encouraged the attention by wearing tight short-shorts and an undersized tee to emphasize my slim, athletic body. Being twenty-four had its advantages in a sea of middle-aged queens. The gratuities would fly today—especially after the patrons had a few drinks. As much as I hated working for tips only, I made enough to pay the bills and expenses my graduate teaching stipend didn't cover.

A slight breeze kicked up. I closed my eyes and fought the urge to nod off. Thanks to Mark and Wayne, sleep time hadn't been my own for years. I let the calm surroundings of the alley relax me. Other than an occasional car or bus on nearby Woodward Avenue or McNichols Road, not even the sound of a bird pierced the predawn air. Unfortunately, my serenity had to be short-lived if I intended to catch the bus.

After making sure the rear door locked when it closed, I dragged my feet into the darkness toward the bus stop at the Woodward-McNichols intersection. I got about ten feet down the alley when an arm whipped around my neck from behind and squeezed. Something sharp pressed against my lower back—a knife, most likely. Every muscle in my body seized, and I gasped for breath. The sound I made could be described as something between a grunt and a low scream.

Steve, you're about to die. Give him what he wants.

"I have money in my right pocket. Take it all."

The pressure on my throat made it difficult to speak and caused my voice to sound raspy, gravelly. Would about a hundred dollars be enough to ransom my life?

"Shut the fuck up. I don't want your money."

His sharp whisper into my right ear raised goosebumps on my neck. If he didn't want my money, then he planned to kill me. My bladder released, soaking the front of my shorts, and running down my legs.

How humiliating. Everyone will know I pissed myself before he killed me. Will anyone be able to identify my body? Who will bury me? Does Wayne County have a pauper's grave?

"Do as I say, or I'll fillet you like a fish. Now back up slowly."

The tip of the weapon penetrated my skin, causing a burning sting that spread up my back. Instead of calling for help, running, or fighting, I stood motionless—my muscles, tendons, and ligaments frozen.

You're a pathetic coward. You won't even fight for your life.

No matter the effort, I couldn't budge.

My attacker tightened his arm around my neck and pulled me under the familiar yellow light. Gasping for air and coughing, I hoped the sound would wake a good Samaritan who would look beyond their back yard and call the police.

"Open the door."

"I can't."

Despite not *wanting* to die—ironic given my suicidal tendencies—I couldn't do the impossible.

"Bullshit. Open the fucking door."

"Bob doesn't give me a key, okay? Once it shuts, I can't get back in." I waited for the sensation of a knife cutting deeper into the small of my back. At least his arm around my neck protected my carotid arteries—for now.

Hold it together, Steve.

"Fine, we'll do it over there." He pulled me away from the door to where light and darkness merged. "When I remove my arm from your neck, put your hands against the wall."

Somehow, I managed to stand and lean slightly against the painted concrete blocks. Every second seemed like an eternity.

Why does he delay killing me? How bad will it hurt? Maybe it'll sting for only a few seconds like a bad paper cut. Maybe I'll die quickly if he shoves it into my heart.

Colin—my roommate for the summer until Kris returned from Utah—would miss me first. Then the debate squad, but I didn't meet with them until Wednesday. If the bastard dumped me here, Bob would find my body later this morning. What if he tossed me in the dumpster? I might never be located.

I twitched when he pulled my urine-soaked shorts and underwear down to my ankles, then he lifted each foot out of them. Clarity set in.

Not again. Please, God, stop him.

He pushed me flat against the wall, knocking off my glasses. When he pressed his body against mine, the man rested his chin on my right shoulder. Spearmint-laced breath flooded my nostrils.

Fight back. Don't let him do this to you.

He nibbled on my ear while running a hand through the crevice of my ass, lingering to slowly rub the sensitive areas. Bile and the remnants of junk food filled the back of my throat. Before everything in my stomach came up, I swallowed, but the acidic taste remained.

Please ram the knife into my heart. Get it over with.

Dammit, stop thinking about how you're gonna die and figure out how you're gonna live.

"Please don't do this."

At least this time you're not tied to a bed with a towel stuffed in your mouth.

My legs wouldn't move, almost as if concrete encased them. This time cowardice, not rope, immobilized me.

Turn and hit him, then run.

I'd never defended myself in a fight, never punched anyone—not even the bullies who tormented me as a kid.

"Move your feet back and spread them apart. I wanna see that hot sexy ass."

Concentrating on the blurry light at the far end of the alley, I did as he demanded.

You're a fucking coward. You can lift your feet for him, but you can't run, can't fight back?

A cold liquid—lubricant, I imagined—ran down my backside before he pushed it inside with a finger.

"No. No." I tasted the saltiness of the tears streaming down my face. "Don't do this."

I need you, Mark. Please.

Would asking the rapist to use a condom be appropriate?

Stop thinking stupid shit. AIDS is the least of your worries.

After a few seconds, he added another finger—and another. The soft, sensual preparation confused me, almost as if he wanted me to enjoy it. The sicko got off by torturing me.

How can you feel euphoric? He's raping you. Then he's gonna kill you.

When he removed his digits, I exhaled, craving them to return. The efficiency with which he destroyed all my self-respect was too smooth, too practiced.

You're not the first he's done this to.

Undoubtedly, when my rapist finished, he would dispense of me. At this point, my death was *fait accompli*, and I was too big of a chicken shit to stop it—or even try.

With no warning, he pushed all of himself into me.

"*Ugh.*" The rapid stretching overloaded my nerves, shooting down my legs and causing my vision to white-out for a second. Unable to hold the bile at bay, I vomited on the concrete-block wall and kept heaving until nothing more came up.

"Yeah, bitch, take it all."

"For the love of God, please stop."

My stomach ached from the heaving. It reminded me of vomiting after Lonnie made me give him a blowjob in Granny's house.

Why does this keep happening to me?

"Please kill me now," I begged.

"Not yet. First, I'm gonna—"

A familiar—and welcomed—dizziness enveloped me as silence cut off his words.

When I emerged from the blackout, out of breath, I found myself holding a blood-covered switchblade, the kind where the blade pops out when you push a button. On the ground, my attacker writhed—moaning, with jeans around his ankles. His hands covered a spot above his right hip. Blood covered the bottom of his white short-sleeved Oxford shirt and seeped through his fingers.

Thank you, Mark. Thank you.

After finding my slightly bent glasses, I got a better look at my rapist. White, dark hair, thin, close to my age. He came in just before the last call but sat at the end of the bar. Under normal circumstances, I would hit on him—at least in my mind, that is. I wouldn't have the guts to do anything other than gape from afar and go home alone.

Steve, you're lusting after your rapist. Just stop.

The asshole mumbled something, but I ignored him. What now? Given the horrible experiences the gay community had with police, I couldn't call them. They likely wouldn't believe me anyway. They'd classify it as a lovers' feud and arrest me—or think I was a hustler knifing my john. Why else would the guy be meeting me at this time of the morning after I got off work?

"I hope you die," I said, taunting him.

Let the rats and stray dogs feast on him until Bob arrives.

I wiped both sides of the blade on his jeans, cleaned the prints off the handle with my underwear, and pushed a button to close the knife.

Steve, you have to get the fuck out of here before someone sees you.

The knife went into my pocket. I could dump it in a garbage can on the way to the bus stop. Keeping an eye on my rapist, I put on my urine-soaked underwear and shorts. I checked my shirt in the light. It had no noticeable traces of blood. Besides, the bus driver never paid attention to me at this ungodly hour, so I should be okay. I wouldn't be the first person smelling like a urinal who rode the bus.

The bastard continued to mumble, as if I'd do anything to help him. Nothing of mine had fallen on the ground except for the vomit the rapist rolled around in. Good. I sure didn't want to be connected to a stabbing. That would lead me down an unwanted path with the police.

Satisfied, I left no evidence behind, I backed away from the guy and ran down the alleyway toward the Woodward-McNichols intersection. I surely missed my bus, but another would be along about the time the sun peeked over the horizon.

Good-bye, TIFFANY'S. There's no way I can ever go back there.

What a shitty way to start a day. Raped and unemployed, all before breakfast.

I stopped going to bars, choosing instead to stay home. Wayne and Mark didn't get the memo. My bank account continued to be drained, and I could only assume Wayne spent it partying. Almost every morning, I'd find smoky-smelling clothes containing condom wrappers and pieces of paper with telephone numbers.

Mark didn't disappoint, either, by returning to his thieving ways. Once again, he got caught shoplifting—this time a camera lens at yet another MONTGOMERY WARD. Typical of him, he switched back to me when the security guard took us to the manager's office. I tried to pay for the lens to make the issue go away, but the store manager refused. When hauled before the judge the following day, I pled guilty and asked for lenience. He sentenced me to three days in jail plus court costs.

I hate my fucking alters.

Chapter 29

Kissin' Cousins

July 1972
Greenwood, Arkansas
Age 12

Last week, our cousin Lonnie came to stay with Granny for a
month. Mom said Aunt Kate and Uncle Jay were mad at him,
but nobody told me why. He hadn't been allowed out of Granny's house
yet, so he must have done something bad. My brother went over to see
him a few times, but Granny scared me. Every time I visited her, she
wouldn't let me touch anything.

One morning, Mike and I mowed our customers' yards early in the
day because it was supposed to get hot. We finished before lunch. We
were hosing off our dirty legs when Lonnie came out of Granny's house.

"Hey, you're outside." I gave Mike the hose and ran to the fence.

"Yeah, Granny locked me down good."

I hadn't seen him in two summers. Lonnie was sixteen years old
now and skinny like me. With his blond hair hanging all the way to his
shoulder, he looked like those guys on TV that Dad called hippies. Mom
and Dad would never let me grow my hair that long. I wouldn't do it
anyway because the other kids at school already made fun of me.

"Are y'all done mowin'?" Lonnie asked.

"Yep," Mike said. "Now I'm gonna go sit in front of the water cooler."
Good riddance.

He had been grumpy all morning because I woke him up to mow. Maybe Lonnie and I could do something fun without him around.

"Do you watch *Star Trek?*" Lonnie asked.

"I seen it lots of times."

"Come see what I brung with me."

Granny had an old house. The floors weren't level, and they creaked when you walked on them. We went through her back porch. She had a front door, but she didn't use the rooms in that part of the house.

"You're gonna love this." Lonnie handed me a box from the table.

"*It's the Starship Enterprise.*" I'd never put together a model before.

"Yeah, I'm gonna do it while I'm here."

"This is so cool."

"You wanna help?"

"Can I?" *Will he really let me put it together with him? Nobody has ever done anything like that.*

We pulled out chairs and sat at the table. That's when I noticed how quiet it was. "Hey, where's Granny?"

"She went downtown to get groceries."

Mom used to take her with us to stores in Fort Smith, but they argued a lot. Now Granny walked to Piggly Wiggly, pulling a metal basket for her groceries.

"Why were you grounded?" I asked.

"Dig it, they caught me smokin' grass."

Grass? Why in the world would anybody smoke grass? "Yuck. I don't even like mowin' it."

Lonnie laughed as he put me in a headlock and rubbed his knuckles on my head. Noogies always made me giggle. That's when he let me go and started tickling me. I slipped off the chair and couldn't stop laughing. I almost peed myself.

"*Stoooooop. Pleeeeeeze.*"

Lonnie sat cross-legged next to me and ran his fingers through my hair. As his fingers massaged my scalp, my body tingled in a weird way.

"Steve, you can help with the model if you do something for me."

"Sure. What is it?" *He'll make me do his chores.* Knowing Granny, she told him to clean the commode. "You want me to clean something?"

"Follow me." Lonnie led me to the back porch and opened the curtain to Granny's pantry. It was really just a small closet, but she kept cans and boxes of food in there. He pushed me inside and on my knees.

"Now, clean this." He yanked down the front of his shorts.

I tried to stand, but he was a lot stronger than me. "Let me go."

"You're my friend, ain't ya?"

How can he say something like that? This isn't right. "I'm also your relation."

"Come on. What does that matter? Do this and you can help me with the model. Hurry, before Granny gets back."

His hard thing hung right in front of my face. *If I don't do what he wants, he won't be my friend anymore.* My stomach hurt really bad, but I reached out and touched him.

"Please don't make me do this."

"I guess we're not friends after all."

How bad can it be? I did it with Allen to be his friend. Leaning forward, I put it in my mouth. After a few seconds, I got really dizzy.

The noise on the TV made me open my eyes. I didn't remember sitting down to watch anything. Did I have lunch? I had no idea what happened after I visited Lonnie at Granny's before lunch. Then he—

The bad taste in my mouth told me what he did. My stomach hurt again like someone kicked me there. Even though I couldn't remember eating lunch, something was coming up. I ran to the bathroom but didn't make it to the commode. Most of it went in the sink.

"Don't do that there." Mom pushed me out of the way and turned the faucet on to wash my throw-up down the drain. It was mostly small pieces of food. She grabbed a rag and cleaned the floor and counter.

"I work all day cleanin' this house. Sometimes I don't know what you're thinkin'."

When she finished wiping my mess up, I leaned over to rinse my mouth directly from the faucet. She put her hand on my forehead and pulled my head up.

"What happened? You're not runnin' a fever."

"My stomach started crampin'."

"You musta ate somethin' bad. Go finish your program."

I almost got to the living room when my stomach cramped again. This time I made it to the commode, but a lot splattered on the floor around the back of the toilet. Mom stood at the door with her hands on her hips like she was going to yell at me again.

"It didn't splash anywhere." I lied, and she must have believed me. After Mom left, I cleaned it up and rinsed my mouth again.

I avoided the mirror. How could Lonnie do that to me?

Steve, you allowed it to happen.

What am I supposed to do? It's not like I can refuse.

Why not?

He won't like me anymore.

Chapter 30

On the Run—Again

My life hadn't been the same since the assault behind TIFFANY'S. When I walked past random people at school, the mall, and debate tournaments, I saw his face. Simple things like career and love didn't have the same meaning they once did. The man destroyed something inside me—more than any of the other incidents ever had.

Incidents? Steve, call them what they all were. Rapes.

By some miracle, I finished my graduate classwork the next two semesters. I got a B in two classes but received an A in all the others. Definitely better than my undergraduate. The problem was my master's thesis. I never started it. Never even picked a topic for it. I gave up. Maybe if Mark had stepped in sooner.

Don't blame Mark. You should have fought back instead of being a coward.

Without a completed degree, I didn't qualify for any of the debate coach openings at universities and colleges. I never took the Law School Admissions Test (LSAT), so I couldn't apply to law school. The only thing I had going for me was a temporary public relations—or PR—job at Riverside Osteopathic Hospital in Trenton, just south of Detroit. The job didn't excite me, but it fit my educational qualifications.

In July, I landed a new PR job at the Michigan Hospital Association (MHA) in Lansing. The entry-level position paid terribly, but it got me out of Detroit.

I found a room for rent in an East Lansing house where two other gay men lived: Bob, the owner, and Tim, another tenant. Living with them helped me relax—but it didn't keep Wayne at bay.

Soon after the move, he began going to Trammps, a gay bar in Lansing. The only evidence I had of his activities were smoky-smelling clothes, empty condom wrappers in pockets, and Trammps business cards—with names and phone numbers written on the back.

Wayne's promiscuity terrified me. More gay men in the area died from AIDS each day. It had become a public health crisis that scared the shit out of me. Even though I couldn't stop Wayne from sleeping around, I at least kept condoms in stock. All I could do was pray he used them.

My job served as a means to pay my bills—and that became more difficult as Wayne spent the money as fast as I earned it. The job itself turned out to be a toxic nightmare. Some of the people I worked for set unreasonable deadlines, gave condescending critiques of my writing, and spoke to me like I was ten years old. I went to work exhausted from Wayne's nocturnal wandering only to be criticized at every turn. Not surprisingly, my blackouts increased in direct proportion to the amount of stress I faced.

I'd been in my job for a year when, one Monday morning, the phone rang in my office.

"I'd like to speak to Wayne," the caller said.

Holy hell. I didn't need this crap at work. Why the hell would Wayne give someone the number to my private line?

"Hold on."

How was I going to play this? The only way I could, I guess. I closed the door, hoping to avoid the attention of my coworkers.

I took a deep breath to calm myself—as if that ever worked.

"This is Wayne."

"It's James. My wife's hired a private detective to find you."

Oh, shit. You slept with a married man? Wayne, what pile of shit did you step in?

"Why would she do that?"

"A nosy neighbor saw you leaving the house. He didn't get your license plate, though."

"So what?" I quickly improvised. "You let a drunk friend sleep it off on the couch."

"He caught you leaving other times, too, which is why he got suspicious and told my wife."

I couldn't believe this crap. For once, could I have a week without drama wrecking my life?

Steve, you don't need a private investigator following you or snooping around work asking questions.

"Please tell me you're calling from a pay phone somewhere."

"Of course. Look, lie low for a few weeks. The PI will be watching Trammps."

It sounded like the wife already knew about her husband's proclivities. Otherwise, why would they be watching a gay bar?

"Thanks for the head's up. Please don't call this number again."

"What if I—"

"*Never* again. Understand?"

The line disconnected.

Even though I'd been at the MHA job for only a year, I had to leave, or James's wife might find me. I didn't want to get dragged into a divorce case.

On Sunday, the *Detroit Free Press* had a three classified ads for PR jobs in the city. I mailed résumés the next day. My phone rang a week later.

"Steve, this is Mike Marcotte at ANTHONY M. FRANCO PUBLIC RELATIONS in Detroit."

Yay. FRANCO was one of the companies I sent my résumé to. They had offices in the RENAISSANCE CENTER—or RENCEN, as we called it—next to the river in downtown Detroit.

"Hey, Mike, what can I do for you?"

"We'd like you to come in for an interview. What does your schedule look like?"

I hadn't even thought about having to take time off. My boss wouldn't be happy. The joke around the office was he wanted twenty-four-hour notice for anyone wanting to take a sick day.

"Can I call you back? I have to ask for time off."

"Sure, but please hurry. We have a lot of people vying for this position."

"I'll get back to you within an hour. What's the number?" I jotted it down and tried to figure out a way to get the day off. I found my boss's door open. He looked intense going through files on his desk.

"Vince, do you have a minute."

"A minute. What's up?"

"I need to take a personal day this week and was wondering which day works best."

"Why?"

"It's *personal.*"

"If you can't tell me why, the answer is 'no.' Is that all you needed?"

One thing I learned as a debater was to think on my feet.

"My doctor wants to run some tests."

Vince searched through the pile of files until he found a leather portfolio that I knew to be his calendar. After turning a few pages, he stopped.

"With Sharlene out, Monday's the soonest I can give you off. Close the door on your way out."

Calling in sick would have solved the problem better. I called Mike and set the interview for Monday.

––––––––––––––

On Saturday morning, I drove to Novi—just outside the Motor City—and got a room at a motel I could afford. I made a dry run into the city to find the ANTHONY M. FRANCO PUBLIC RELATIONS offices. I'd been to the RENCEN before but only to the movie theatre. The monstrous complex comprised seven skyscrapers.

Locating anything in the RENCEN was like finding a specific pinto bean in a six-foot-tall pile of pinto beans. I imagined people wandering here for eternity through the maze of corridors and stairs, their pictures on milk cartons.

After looking on my own for ten minutes, I finally asked for help. Of course, I had been on the wrong level to get to the elevator. Once I took escalators to the correct level, I found Tower 400 and rode the elevator up to suite 1000. A peek inside the glass doors revealed a tiny lobby with a reception desk on one wall.

Thank God I performed a test run because I would have been late for my interview.

Satisfied with the excursion into the city, I returned to my motel. I wanted to go out—to get laid. It had been two years since the rape. Ever since then, I couldn't stop seeing the man's face—so I stayed away from bars. Being in a relationship with my right hand wasn't as fulfilling as I'd like. Somehow, I needed to find a way to put the assault behind me.

Wayne had been prolific, but he'd also been considerate. It had been four years since I'd awakened in a bar, adult bookstore, or while having sex. He also hadn't switched back to me in the morning after spending the night with one of his tricks.

If I didn't try to hook up with someone, I might never have sex again. My best chance to meet someone on a Saturday would be BACKSTREET.

Steve, you've lost your fucking mind.

The internal struggle between my desire to have sex and my fear of strangers raised my anxiety. I took a long, hot shower to relax. Too bad it couldn't wash away all the moral turpitude I'd absorbed over the years.

After drying off, I collapsed on the bed. Since BACKSTREET wouldn't be busy until about ten, I had time to take a four-hour nap. I closed my eyes and drifted off.

I awoke before the alarm went off. Light peeking around the curtains told me my slumber didn't last long. I rolled on my back and spread my arms out.

"Ouch."

"What the hell?" My feet landed on the floor before I finished my sentence. A man on the other side of the bed sat up.

"I can think of better ways to wake me up," the guy said.

Dammit, Wayne. After all this time, why now?

The cute guy had spiked blond hair, high cheekbones, and a chiseled chin. He looked to be in his mid-twenties—Wayne's type. At least I awoke in my hotel room and not some strange house, apartment, or basement with a sex sling hanging from the ceiling. Still, I had the urge to flee or slash his throat.

"Sorry about that," I said.

"I'll live. I'm glad you came out. I didn't think I'd ever see you again."

Again? I don't remember this guy—and he had an unforgettable face and body. Well-defined pecs, muscled arms. Yummy.

He had this innocent charm about him, in juxtaposition to his punk look.

"What time is it?" he asked.

"Almost seven. Sorry I woke you."

When he smiled and pulled back the covers, my body reacted. Wow. Maybe this was Wayne's gift horse for me to get back on.

"Just a sec," I said. "Let me get a condom."

An arm pulled me into bed before I could move. He ran his hands over my body the way I liked it—the way someone remarkably familiar with my body would. *Wayne, how many times have you been with him?*

"Nah, bareback is more fun."

I couldn't get away from him fast enough. In the year I'd lived in Lansing, AIDS had killed three men I knew socially—one had been only nineteen years old. I couldn't expose myself to that.

"Please leave."

"You're kicking me out over a condom? It didn't stop you last night."

"Obviously, I wasn't in my right mind. Now please go."

Although he grumbled while getting dressed, the guy accepted his fate. He hugged and kissed me as he got ready to leave.

"Come find me at work the next time you're in town."

"I have no idea where that is."

"BANANA REPUBLIC at TWELVE OAKS MALL. Ask for Jack. You're acting odd this morning."

"I'm just not myself." That was an understatement. After Jack left, I scrubbed myself in the shower and douched several times.

Dammit, Wayne, I thought we had an understanding?

How can I reason with another part of myself who thinks he doesn't have to follow the rules? It's like living with a perpetually horny teenager.

On Monday morning, I showed up at FRANCO for the interview. After several questions from the interviewers—Mike Marcotte and Joe Giumette—I settled down and focused. When they finished, they offered me the job—and I accepted. Now I had to break it to my boss in Lansing.

Two weeks after Wayne's encounter with Jack, I developed an itchy rash on my palms. My doctor got me in to see her the next day.

"You have syphilis. Have you had unprotected sex in the past few weeks?"

I nodded, too ashamed to say anything. *Good job, Wayne.*

The doctor gave me a shot of penicillin and a prescription to be filled for another antibiotic.

"Go to the health department right now to have an HIV test," she said.

I did as she recommended. The health department called me a few days later with the news that my ELISA test had come back negative for HIV antibodies. They recommended that I have another test in six months—with no unprotected sex until then.

Wayne, please do as she asks. We dodged a bullet.

The following Saturday, I drove to Twelve Oaks Mall to find Jack. He started having symptoms two days after our tryst, but he didn't know how to reach me. At least that provided me with an answer as to where I got the STD.

Please, Wayne, try keeping your dick in your pants and your ass cheeks clenched. If you can do that, we might live to be thirty.

Chapter 31

Way Out of My League

O n August 21, I escaped Lansing and returned to Detroit. Everything I owned—except the waterbed—fit in my Dodge Turismo hatchback. Bob said he didn't mind holding onto my bed until I needed it.

I provided no forwarding address at the post office or work. I could change my address directly with my creditors and car insurance company once I found an apartment. Because I lived in Bob's house, I had no utilities in my name. My driver's license might trip me up because I'd have to change it eventually. Even though I couldn't disappear completely from the private detective's radar, I made it as difficult as possible for him to find me.

My job didn't start until September 8. That gave me two weeks to find an apartment. Cindy—a friend and former debater at WAYNE STATE—let me crash at her place a block from campus. I didn't want to stay with her very long because of Mark and Wayne.

Why did I come back to Detroit? Nothing good ever happened to me here. What if the rapist tracks me down? What if he sees Wayne at one of the bars and gets revenge?

Steve, let it go. You'll be fine.

On Friday morning, I met the apartment manager at Lafayette Pavilion Apartments. Her candy-red power suit looked like something Alexis Carrington would wear—a knee-high pencil skirt and single-breasted jacket with square shoulder pads and big silver buttons.

The glass-and-steel, twenty-two-story high-rise—located across the interstate from Greektown—had the perfect location. I could walk to work in fifteen minutes.

With only one efficiency available September 1, I had to decide quickly if I liked it. The elevator ride to the tenth floor didn't take too much time, although the manager kept fidgeting and looking at her watch.

Do you have somewhere better to be? This literally is your job.

When we got to the apartment door, she put the key in and turned.

"We're painting and replacing the carpet," she said.

I stepped inside and gasped. A floor-to-ceiling window comprised the entire far wall. The vertical blinds had been pulled to the side, giving me a view of the RenCen and most of the downtown architecture.

"Beautiful, isn't it?" she asked.

"I want it."

"Across the park is 1300 Lafayette East," she said. "Mies van der Rohe designed both buildings and the two Lafayette Towers to the left."

Who the fuck cares who designed the building? I just want the keys to the apartment and to be left alone.

When we got back to the manager's, she handed me the four-page application. It asked for everything except who circumcised me.

"We have a fifty-dollar nonrefundable application fee to cover a credit report and background check," she said. "You'll need to provide copies of your latest two pay stubs."

Oh, shit. So much for this place, thanks to Mark's shoplifting—which got me tossed in jail in Arkansas and Michigan. What if the Fayetteville McDonald's finally figured out who stole the money? There could be a warrant out for me.

I handed the application back to her and stood.

"I thought you wanted the apartment," she said.

"Oh, I do, but I have a criminal record and—"

"We check only for violent felonies, sex crimes, and outstanding warrants."

Fuck. Arkansas, South Dakota, and Michigan could have multiple warrants out for me. Burglary, embezzlement, assault with a deadly weapon.

Steve, they raped you. They deserved it.

The McDonald's thefts weren't justified.

"So, you going to apply or not?" she asked.

"Sorry, I spaced out. My new job doesn't start until September eighth."

"Not a problem. Just give me pay stubs for your last job and the information for your current employer."

I jumped through all the hoops and gave her $50 cash along with Cindy's phone number. The manager promised to call by Monday afternoon.

Instead of heading back to Cindy's place, I drove to the METRO TIMES office. The weekly magazine had a personals section. I hated being alone—and I was tired of fighting the internal demons born in Gary's bedroom and in the alleyway behind TIFFANY'S. After composing the ad, I paid for the phone mailbox option. All I had to do was call a number and enter a code to hear messages guys left for me—if any ever did. The ad would appear in the following Wednesday's edition.

The Pavilion manager called Cindy's phone Saturday afternoon with the news that I got the apartment. I signed the lease forty minutes later.

"We'll be closed Monday, September first—it being Labor Day and all," the manager said. "We aren't open on Sundays, so you can pick up the keys next Saturday."

"Do I have to wait until Monday to move in?"

I might as well ask, right? That would get me out of Cindy's hair.

She hesitated and looked down at her desk as if the answer would appear on her blotter. "What the hell. Move in that day if you want. You have to use the freight elevator, though."

I had a week to buy furniture. At JCPENNEY, I found a nice daybed with a trundle, two mattresses, and an entertainment center for my TV and stereo. They'd deliver everything next Saturday. At Hudson's downtown clearance center, I scored a two bright-red chairs shaped somewhat like baseball gloves. I also bought a brass-and-glass dining room set. Hudson's couldn't deliver until the Thursday after I moved in, but I'd make do until then.

The METRO TIMES came out on Wednesday, so I snagged a copy at the WAYNE STATE UNIVERSITY student union. A few guys recorded messages for my ad throughout the day, but only one intrigued me.

"Hi. My name is Ethan. I'm twenty-six and a graduate student at WAYNE STATE. I'm six feet tall, weigh one hundred fifty pounds, and have blue eyes and brown hair. You can call me any time on weekends and after six in the evening Monday through Thursday at...."

My hands shook as I wrote down his phone number. I listened to his message several times to make sure I remembered the details. Same age, height, hair color, and eye color as me. I weighed ten more pounds, but that was tennis muscle. My mind ran wild as I imagined how he looked. I didn't call that evening for fear I'd look too desperate. The following day, I dialed his number at 6:01 p.m.—still desperate-looking, but fashionably so.

After six rings, he answered. Awkwardness ensued for about a minute until we found topics to discuss. We both despised Ronald Reagan, loved spaghetti and meatballs, and thought Whitney Houston had the voice of an angel. Sure, we had differences—I loved playing sports whereas he enjoyed acting in community theatre—but we found compatibility in many areas.

"Would you be interested in getting together?" I asked.

Please say yes. Please say yes.

"I'd love to," he said. "I have plans this weekend, but I could meet for dinner next Wednesday."

"That works for me. Where and what time?"

"I get off work at four. We can have an early dinner in Greektown. Will four-thirty work?"

"It's perfect." Inside, I screamed, mentally jumping up and down. Ethan gave me the name of the restaurant for our first date.

On Wednesday, I arrived ten minutes early and secured one of the dozen tables in the small Greek restaurant that Ethan recommended. The place wasn't much larger than my studio apartment. Customers placed orders at the counter where a worker sliced meat from a vertical rotisserie holding an entire leg of lamb.

At precisely four-thirty, a gorgeous man entered the restaurant wearing a brown trench coat much like my own. He had thick brown hair and a neatly trimmed mustache. He fit Ethan's description.

If that's him, Steve, he's way out of your league.

The closer he got to me, the more jittery I became. My insecurities bubbled to the surface. He had a disarming smile that made my heart melt. When he stopped at the table, I swallowed hard.

It's him, so don't panic.

"Steve?"

I stood, trying not to do something embarrassing like knock over the table or fall on my face.

"You must be Ethan."

We shook hands, although I'd rather jump his bones on one of the restaurant's tables.

He doesn't look like a rapist.

What does a rapist look like?

We ate without any rush and exchanged views on a number of topics from the theatre to politics. Sure, he had good looks—and a smile that gave me goosebumps—but he also had an intelligence I understood.

"Want to see my place?" I said after we finished our meals. That classic pick-up line would normally be an invitation for sex, but not this time. This situation called for playing it slow. "It's just across the Chrysler."

Steve, you barely know the guy. What if he's dangerous?

I have to try sometime. Loneliness is killing me.

"Sure, my car's over there at the clinic. I can't stay long, though."

The stroll with Ethan at my side had no awkwardness or nervousness. We crossed the bridge spanning the Chrysler freeway. He pointed out the mental health clinic where he worked, just a short walk from The Pavilion. When we reached the high-rise building, my stomach twisted.

Why did I invite him over? I have a tiny one-room apartment filled with boxes, a daybed, and an entertainment center.

I watched Ethan's face as we entered, but his expression never changed.

"Sorry, I don't have any chairs. That's the best I can offer." I pointed to the white daybed enclosed on three sides by metal tubing bent into curved designs resembling handrails and banisters. A quilt covered the twin mattress, and four pillows rested against the back.

We sat and talked with our fingers often touching and intertwining. That had to be the first time I—or Wayne—had a guy on my bed without having sex. I found it to be intimate, refreshing, and wonderful—something I never wanted to end. Although more than an hour passed, it seemed like a few minutes. I could have talked to him all night.

"I'd better be going. It'll be getting dark soon."

"Want to come to dinner on Friday?" *Where the hell did that come from? You sound desperate.* The pause after my question lasted a few seconds.

"Sorry, I can't."

Dammit, I pushed too hard. Will he ever want to see me again? Maybe he wants to have sex, and I screwed up by not making a move.

My feet dragged as I escorted him the ten feet to the door. Before I could open it, Ethan backed up against the wall and pulled me to him. He gently pressed his soft lips against mine, a move that made my neck tingle. As our mouths moved against each other, everything seemed right. When Ethan finally broke contact, my knees wobbled. If Ethan hadn't been holding me, I would have fallen over.

"Could you make dinner for us tomorrow instead of Friday?" he asked.

The unexpected question bitch-slapped me awake. "Of course. What time?"

"Five? I have classes in the afternoon."

"Five it is."

As he walked down the hallway, I couldn't stop watching him. Twice he turned to look back, smiling both times. The elevator doors opened, and he disappeared.

Yep, he's way out of your league.

Chapter 32

Opportunities

Agreeing to cook dinner the next evening was evidence of my insanity. Hudson's delivered my dining room set and casual chairs at 1 p.m., which gave me very little time to shop for cookware and groceries—but Oakland Mall and Farmer Jack saved my ass.

My galley kitchen proved to be a challenge. A mere eight feet deep with a thirty-six-inch path, the kitchen held a full-sized refrigerator and range, a dishwasher, and cabinets on both sides. I had to stand by the side of the oven to open its door. Cooking required agility and flexibility.

At precisely 5 p.m.—just as dinner finished cooking—Ethan arrived carrying two bottles of wine.

"I didn't know whether to bring red or white, so I did both."

"We're having chicken." I figured that was the most important of the two meats in the dish.

"Chardonnay it is." Ethan opened the wine and poured two glasses while I assembled dinner.

Tonight has to be perfect. This is your one shot to impress him.

After filling our plates with chicken cordon bleu, roasted fingerling potatoes, and sauteed asparagus with almonds, I carried our two plates to the table.

He'll love this. He has to. It's my best dish.

With his brow furrowed, Ethan stared at something on his plate. He didn't smile, which got me worried.

"Is everything okay?" I asked.

"What did you make?"

"It's chicken cordon bleu and—"

"Is that cheese inside it?"

"Yes. Chicken breast stuffed with Swiss cheese and ham."

Oh, my God. He's frowning and biting his lower lip.

"Is something wrong? You didn't mention any food allergies." *Or did he? I sometimes daydream when I look at him. I can't help it.*

"Uh, I'm Jewish. No mixing meat and dairy, and definitely no pork."

You've gotta be fucking kidding me. What the hell did I do? Don't cry. Please don't cry.

Tears welled, but I fought to hold them back. Unable to make eye contact, I focused on the cheese oozing from the middle of the folded chicken breast.

"Ethan, I'm an idiot. I'm sorry."

"No, this is my fault. I should have told you what I don't eat."

My ignorance and stupidity embarrassed me. If he mentioned being Jewish any of the times we talked, I missed it. Greenwood had no synagogues, and I'd never been around any Jews that I knew of. I knew nothing about Judaism.

"I feel so stupid." *What can I salvage? The melted cheese ran all over his plate.* "I have more potatoes and asparagus in the kitchen. Can you eat them?"

"Sure."

I removed his plate and stepped into the kitchen. *You wanted the evening to be perfect, and you fucked it up.* As I reached into the cabinet for a clean plate, arms wrapped around me from behind—and I flinched, then froze.

I can't go through that again. Please don't hurt me.

It's not him, Steve. It's not him. Take a deep breath. It's Ethan.

"It's okay," Ethan whispered into my right ear. "You're the reason I'm here. Not the food."

Dinner got cold, but I didn't care. As Anita Baker sang "Sweet Love," Ethan and I removed each other's clothing by the daybed.

The warmth of his skin. The tenderness of his touch. I've wanted this for so long. He's looking into my eyes and smiling.

Take it slow, Steve. Enjoy this. There's no hurry.

Of all the times I had sex, I'd never truly made love until then. Not even with Ryan. Ethan and I intertwined to the point where I had no idea where mine ended and his began.

If he finds out what I am and what I've done, I'll lose him. He'll be disgusted by everything I let happen to me.

Steve, you can never tell him.

After that night, we got together two or three times a week. Either we would meet at a restaurant in Greektown, or I would cook dinner at my apartment. No matter the meal, we followed it with an intimate evening. Sometimes we skipped eating altogether. Ethan showed me the kindness and affection I'd always craved—and I fell in love with him quickly.

The week before Thanksgiving, Ethan telephoned just after 7 p.m. We spoke every night, and I always looked forward to it.

"I need to talk to you about something," he said, his voice strained and harsh.

"What's up?"

"Uh, I can't do this."

"Can't do what?"

"Us."

Us? Is he breaking up with me? Please, God, please, let it be something else. We've never had an argument. Not even a disagreement. We fit well together.

"I don't understand. What did I do?"

This can't be happening. I'm happy for the first time ever. I feel safe around him. Complete. These are the best ten weeks I've ever had.

"You didn't do anything," he said. "I'm not...this is just not me."

Don't believe him, Steve. You did something. You always do something.

"Please don't, Ethan. Please. We're so good for each other."

"I...I can't. Don't call me again."

The phone clicked, soon followed by a dial tone. Numb, I placed the receiver on the base. That beautiful man—someone I never should have had a shot with—ended the only real relationship I'd ever had.

Did I have a blackout and not know it? Did Mark or Wayne do something that freaked him out? They must have. That's it. One of them fucked it up.

I threw the phone as hard as I could. The cord popped out of the jack, and the telephone smashed against the far wall. In less than three months, I'd fallen hopelessly in love with Ethan.

How could I drop my guard like that? I'd let him lure me into a false sense of security—only to hurt me in the end. This was worse than being raped. Those guys took only my dignity and self-respect, but Ethan ripped away what mattered—my heart. He had made me believe someone else could care for me and want me. I'd thought for the first time that I could experience love and tenderness like normal people did, that maybe I deserved it.

How could he give me all I ever wanted and then take it away?

Steve, you're broken. Nobody wants to be with someone like that.

Chapter 33

Second Chances

Without **Ethan in my life**, I stopped eating, getting to work on time, speaking with clients, and completing assignments. Marcotte kept throwing projects at me, and I kept screwing them up. As a result, he wasn't happy, his boss wasn't happy, and the clients weren't happy.

After the first of the year, I realized Wayne hadn't been withdrawing money from my bank account. A check of my credit cards showed no unusual charges or cash advances. My job gave me no access to funds, so Mark couldn't have been stealing from there. If Wayne didn't need my money, whose did he use?

He must have money stashed somewhere. I tore my place apart looking for it. After finding nothing, I remembered reading about people hiding money and jewels in the freezer. I opened the door and noticed a container of Stroh's Mackinac Island Fudge Ice Cream behind the ice trays. I'd probably seen it a hundred times but never registered it as something that didn't belong. The problem was I didn't remember buying it.

Please be ice cream.

I set the container on the kitchen counter and pulled off the lid.

Shit.

Instead of a delicious frozen dairy treat, the container held rolls of cash with rubber bands around them—totaling more than $3,000. How? Either Mark had stolen it from somewhere, Wayne had earned it by returning to his old ways, or a combination of both. I returned the cash to its hiding place.

My life had turned into a ticking time bomb.

By the end of March—four months after Ethan dumped me—my weight had dropped from 170 to 150 pounds. Coworkers did subtle welfare checks on me as they walked past my cubicle.

"Are you okay?" Linda, the office manager, said almost every day.

"Wanna go to lunch?" Julie, another PR associate, inquired a few times a week.

I wanted none of it, so I declined all attempts to socialize. Each day after work, I'd shower, eat part of a sandwich, watch TV, and cry myself to sleep. During the period Ethan and I dated, neither Mark nor Wayne appeared—as far as I knew. But my manslut doppelganger made up for lost time after Ethan broke up with me.

Some days, I'd wake up alone in my apartment and find a pile of clothes reeking of cigarette smoke. Pockets would be filled with empty condom wrappers, pieces of paper containing names and phone numbers, and bottles of amyl nitrite—poppers. Wayne left me sore and my lungs polluted.

At other times, I'd wake up next to a stranger—some mornings in my bed, but more often in someone else's.

I wanted only *him* to be in bed with me, not some strange man. When I got home from work, I wanted *him* to call me, not some guy looking for casual sex.

Despite my chaotic, screwed-up existence, I still wanted to meet someone. Being with Ethan had helped lower my fear of being assaulted. Although I didn't place another personal ad in the *METRO TIMES*, I perused the magazine every Wednesday looking for Mr. Right. Nobody piqued my interest.

One Wednesday in April, I relaxed on my daybed and opened the latest edition of the Metro Times. As usual, the pages were filled with pleas from desperate, lonely guys looking for other desperate, lonely guys. They lied about their age, looks, weight—you name it.

Motherfucker.

I threw the magazine, its loose pages flying around my one-room apartment. The son-of-a-bitch had placed a personal ad. The age, height, and weight matched, plus the author called himself an NJB—which stood for Nice Jewish Boy, as Ethan once explained to me.

After I cooled off, I tried to approach it logically. Maybe he placed the ad knowing I'd respond. That would make sense if he was too embarrassed to call, right? The author had paid for the phone message option, so I called the number.

"This is Steve. I saw your ad. I'd like to meet. How about this Saturday at FOOTLIGHTS? Say, three p.m.? I'll be at a table in the courtyard. If you can't make it, or don't want to, call me—or just don't show up. You have my number." FOOTLIGHTS seemed like a good neutral location. The upscale gay bar was on Woodward Avenue next to—*aw, fuck.*

TIFFANY'S.

Cancel it if you don't want to drive past it.

No, I need to see him again.

When Saturday arrived, I drove up Woodward Avenue. Just past McNichols, I tried *not* to look at my old employer's establishment on the right, but I couldn't help it. I never went back to get the fifty dollars for cleaning the place that last time. Considering I should have been dead, it seemed a reasonable loss.

I used valet parking and walked to the FOOTLIGHTS courtyard. Ethan beat me there, having secured a table. The warm feeling inside reminded me how much I missed him. I couldn't avert my eyes from him no matter how hard I tried. He looked in my direction and smiled. As I meandered through tables filled with customers, I held my breath.

I can't do this.

"I'm so glad you answered my ad," he said as I sat across from him.

"Ethan, you could have just called me." *Do I want to do this with him?*

Yes, you do.

"I didn't think you'd ever want to see me again." He reached across the round glass tabletop to hold my hand. "I missed you."

"It's not that easy. You...you...I can't do this."

This won't work. I love him. I miss him. I can't go on without him. I can't be with him. I can't trust him. My brain is so jumbled right now.

I scooted the chair back and stood to leave.

"Please don't go," he said.

Go now. What if he suddenly decides to end it again? It will destroy you.

"I loved you," I said. "Did you know that?"

"Please, stay and talk to me."

Against my better judgment, I sat and ordered a drink. Silence dominated our conversation.

Tell him how much you miss him. How much you hate him for what he did. How much you want to be with him forever. How much you never want to see him again. How much you despise him. How he makes you whole.

"Can we please try again?" he asked. "Can we start over?"

How dare he ask me that.

"Under one condition."

Condition? Steve, what the fuck are you doing.

"What condition?"

"When's your apartment lease up?" You've lost your mind, Steve.

"I'm on a month-to-month."

"Mine is up the last day of August. If this works over the next four months, let's find a place and move in together." I can't believe I said it.

Ethan jerked his hand away and leaned back. "I don't know. It's just that—"

"This was a mistake. Have a nice life, Ethan."

Dammit, stop pushing him. He extended an olive branch and wants to start over. You're being too needy, too clingy, too controlling. You can't steamroll him into making a commitment like this.

I stood, downed my gin and tonic, and walked away. As I reached the exit, I stopped at the sound of his voice.

"Steve, wait. Okay, let's see how it goes. If it works, we'll live together."

I turned and put my arms around his neck. No matter what it took, I'd never let him go. Ethan was everything I ever wanted in a man. Handsome, intelligent, funny, sexy, loving.

We resumed dating—and it was good, just like before. When August rolled around, we found a great two-bedroom place at Amber House Apartments in Clawson, just north of Detroit. Because he hadn't come out to his family, we staged the second bedroom as a "beard" for anyone who didn't know our true living situation.

Getting back together with Ethan could be a mistake, but I couldn't walk away from him. Being with him helped identify the triggers for my MPD. During happy, relaxed times, I didn't switch—at least none that I detected.

How can you be sure? Remember the McDONALD's burglary? The cash skimming?

I have to believe in something.

In contrast, Mark and Wayne flourished when I became very unhappy or stressed. Once Ethan and I got back together, my alters went dormant.

The Clawson apartment as a family. Monday through Friday, we went to work, came home, had dinner, watched TV, and went to bed. I was in heaven.

How long will it last? You'll find some way to fuck it up. What then? You might not survive it next time.

Chapter 34

Coach Has My Back

I didn't look forward to the seventh grade because I'd have to switch classrooms several times a day. Other students would have more opportunities to make my life miserable as I walked the hallways. Would it ever end?

One day in July, Dad—whom I'd never told about my problems at school—came up with another one of his brilliant ideas.

"You should play on the football team," he said. "That will toughen you up and make a man out of you."

Lord, not this again. For years, Dad had pushed me to do things he considered "manly," such as squirrel hunting and playing pee-wee baseball. He didn't fool me. This had to do with the darned Easy-Bake Oven incident when I was six.

As Christmas approached six years ago, I kept seeing commercials where a girl mixed batter in a small pan and put it in a little oven for kids. The cake cooked in no time and looked delicious. *If I get that,* my naive six-year-old brain had thought, *I can make pies and cakes just like Mama does.*

The Easy-Bake Oven was the only gift I asked Santa to bring me. When Christmas morning rolled around, I found under the tree a big box with my name on it. In excitement, I ripped off the paper. *"Santa brought me the Easy-Bake Oven."* I jumped up and down.

"It's for a girl," Dad had said.

"No, it's not." The TV never said it was just for girls.

"If Santa thinks you're a girl, then you're a girl."

His words stung. After that, he made snide comments about how I needed to participate in "normal" activities for boys. Much to his disappointment, hunting and baseball each lasted the bare minimum amount of time necessary for me to fail, both in motivation and execution—much as with the Easy-Bake Oven. Putting a .22 caliber rifle or a baseball bat in my hands proved just as effective as trying to cook food using two light bulbs—but at least the latter interested me.

So, it didn't surprise me when Dad decided I would play football. After all, Mike hunted and participated in two sports—baseball and football. I decided Dad might be right, albeit for a different reason. If I got on the football team, others in school might stop calling me names and teasing me.

So began my quest.

I knew the coach—H.B.—because I gardened for his mom every spring and summer. A few weeks before school started, he stopped by while I was pulling weeds in her front yard. I ran up to him before he went into the house.

"Hey, H.B., can I ask you something?"

"Sure, Steve. What's up?"

"When are football tryouts?"

"Next week. Interested?"

"You bet I am. At least I'd like to try."

"Hold on right there." He ran back to where he parked and returned with a sheet of paper. "Have Bobby or Shirley fill this out and sign it. Tryouts start at eight o'clock Monday morning at the school baseball field. Don't forget to bring the form with you. It tells you how to dress and where to go."

"Yes sir."

On Monday morning, Mom drove me to the tryouts. At least fifty other kids had shown up—including Jeffrey. I caught him staring at me several times, but he didn't say a word to me. A few of the guys teased me, but I ignored them. Well, I tried to.

H.B. worked our butts off. He first had us run a mile. If we couldn't finish, he cut us. My side hurt like the dickens, but I didn't stop. Next, he had us do a bunch of silly drills. The hardest one was running through tires lying flat on the ground. I fell a few times, but I got up and kept going.

The others called him "Coach," so I did too. It would be weird calling him H.B. in school.

Coach gave us a water break, which I desperately needed. I filled a cup from the big jug on the back of his truck. When I stepped away to swallow it, someone patted my butt.

"Nice ass."

Breath tickled my ear. I rubbed it and turned to see Danny walking away, laughing. Ever since the second grade, Danny had teased me more than anyone.

"Break's over," Coach called out. "Line up."

He made us run the drills again. By the time we finished, I could barely walk. My left ankle throbbed.

"Y'all go home, eat a good meal, and get some rest. Same time tomorrow mornin'."

A bunch of us helped him put the equipment in the back of his truck. I took off across the field toward home. Every time I stepped on my left foot, my ankle throbbed. I reached the street that went past the school when Coach's truck pulled up beside.

"Hop in," he said.

"I don't mind walking."

"When the coach says get in, you get in."

I opened the door and climbed into the passenger seat.

"You worked hard out there today," he said. "Are you okay? I noticed you limpin'."

Maybe I shouldn't tell him about it. If I don't, though, he'll be pissed when he finds out it hurts when I exercise.

"It's my left ankle. It swells up."

Coach pulled to the side of the road. "Let me see."

I removed my shoe and sock. When I put my foot on the seat, he whistled.

"What did you do to it?"

"Nothing. Last summer, my veins started bulgin'."

He picked up my foot and twisted it a little.

"Does this hurt?"

"I'd be lyin' if I said no."

"Put your shoe and sock back on."

We talked about junior high on the rest of the way home. He parked in front of our house and climbed out of the truck. Mom sat on the porch, smoking a cigarette and shucking corn.

"That's a mess of corn you got goin' there."

"Hey, H.B. You gotta take some home. It's more than we'll ever eat. Steven, fetch a paper bag."

I ran to the kitchen and pulled a bag from under the sink. If I didn't hurry, I'd miss what they were talking about. The carport door slammed behind me as I dashed back outside.

"If Doc Bailey clears him, he can continue with the tryouts."

"What did I do wrong?" I handed the paper bag to Mom.

"Nothin'," Coach said. "I have to be sure your foot's okay. I don't want you gettin' a serious injury."

Mom put eight ears of corn in the bag and handed it to him. "I'll check if Doc Bailey can see him this afternoon."

"Much obliged for the corn. Call me at home later to let me know what the doc says."

After lunch, we drove down the street to Dr. Bailey's office. We didn't have to wait very long. He had been my doctor since I was born. He examined my ankle and shook his head.

"He's going to need surgery to remove these varicose veins."

"Varicose veins? He's only twelve."

"It's unusual, but not unheard of."

"I have football tryouts." Why couldn't he just let me finish? We only had one more day.

"I can't release you to play until this is fixed."

That's not fair. Now everyone will tease me about this.

Dr. Bailey made me an appointment for Wednesday with a surgeon in Fort Smith. When we got home, I called Coach.

"I have to have surgery."

"There's always next year," he said. "But I have an idea that you might like better. I need another team manager to help me. You would take care of equipment, clean the locker rooms, keep statistics. Stuff like that. I still have Roger—who's a ninth grader—but I need one more."

If I was manager, I wouldn't be on the football team, but I'd be a part of it. Maybe it would be enough to get the idiots off my back.

"Well, uh, I'm not sure." He didn't say anything back. "Coach, you still there?"

Did I mess up by not saying "yes" right away? Will he change his mind? I'm so stupid.

"Steve, you weren't makin' the team. You worked hard for three straight hours. No matter what I threw at you, you didn't quit. There are just too many good athletes for the few slots I have. This way, you can withdraw for health reasons, and the others won't see you bein' cut. The best part is you won't have to take PE."

Not having to take physical education sealed the deal. I wouldn't have to get undressed and shower in front of the others.

"I'm in. Thanks, Coach."

"Can you come tomorrow? Roger's on vacation this week."

"I'll be there."

The next morning, I got to the baseball field before any of the other kids. Coach gave me a clipboard with the names of everyone trying out.

"When I tell a person to have a seat, put a check mark next to their name."

Coach put them through many of the same drills as the day before. One by one, he told guys to sit. He called Jeffrey's name, and my stomach cramped. I'd have to see him every day at practice.

"Steve, how many is that?" Coach asked.

"Fourteen," I said.

"If I didn't call your name, better luck next year," Coach said. "For the names I called, make your way to the gym to get equipment and a locker."

A few of his cuts surprised me. In my opinion, some of the guys he kept were worse than the ones he cut. But what did I know?

"Sissy Simmons is now Coach's pet," one guy said loudly as he walked by. I looked down so I didn't have to watch others stare at me.

"Larry, what did you say?" Coach walked up to the guy.

"I was just having a little fun, Coach." He laughed and looked around at the guys stopped behind him.

"You all go on to the gym. I wanna have a discussion with the comedian here."

Larry squirmed as he stood there. "Coach, I was just teasin'."

"Oh, I *know* what you were doin'. I do *not* tolerate harassment of team managers. This isn't grade school. If you want to act like a child, then you're not ready for my team. If I hear you say anything like that again, you'll be sittin' in the stands watchin' football instead of playin' it. Now get out."

With his head hanging, Larry took off running toward the gym.

"Steve, if *anyone* on the team harasses you, you tell me."

"Coach, I don't wanna be a tattletale—"

"Steve, was I not clear?"

"Tellin' on them will make things worse."

I'd never heard Coach laugh before, so he surprised me. "You're part of my staff. If they don't like it, they can go join band."

Chapter 35

Moving On Up

November 1987
Detroit, Michigan
Age 27

GETTING BACK WITH **E**THAN **significantly** improved my work. I finally got Marcotte to trust my work again. He threw more projects at me week after week—press conferences, media interviews, campaign planning.

One of my clients was the SOUTHEAST MICHIGAN HOSPITAL COUNCIL (SEMHC). They paid a few hundred dollars a month as a retainer—a small amount compared to other clients, but still enough to complete small projects.

At the end of October, I got a call from Jane, the SEMHC public relations executive. I'd always liked her. She knew more about healthcare PR than anyone I ever ran across, including the MHA people I'd worked for.

She wanted to meet with me at their offices in Southfield. My calendar for the day had cleared, so I made the fifteen-minute drive from downtown. Her request intrigued me because she gave no hint as to the meeting's subject matter.

Maybe she's gonna fire FRANCO.

SEMHC had corner offices in a new one-story building. The trade association represented all but a few of the hospitals in southeastern

Michigan—including the Detroit metropolitan area. When I arrived there, Jane escorted me to her office and closed the door. After a few pleasantries, she got right to it.

"I'm leaving SEMHC, and I wondered if you'd be interested in the job."

"Excuse me?" Of all the reasons I imagined for her wanting to see me, that was the least anticipated.

"You have the education and experience. Mike Marcotte sings your praises."

Thank goodness I cleaned up my act after getting back together with Ethan. But that would be three jobs in a little over two years. What will people think?

"Tell me about the job."

For the next half hour, she explained what the position entailed and how she worked with the other staff. When we both ran out of things to say, Jane stood—and I expected her to show me out.

"It sounds like you would be a good fit. So, with that out of the way, Don would like to speak with you."

"*Now?*" Talk about being blindsided.

"Sure, why not?"

Jane led me to her boss's corner office where Don was sitting behind a five-foot-long mahogany desk. I'd met him when I worked at the MHA, where they always spoke highly of his abilities.

"Have a seat, Mr. Simmons."

Jane hightailed it out of there and shut the door.

Don pointed me toward two wood-framed chairs flanking a square table in the corner. I lowered myself into one and he took the other. His office didn't have a paper or file out of place. About ten or so years older than I was, Don had thick black hair and a wide, bushy mustache.

"Mr. Simmons, Jane says you're the person she'd like to replace her when she leaves next month."

"That's very nice of her."

"Tell me a little about yourself."

I gave him a mini biography, hitting all the high points I recalled from the résumé I used to get the Franco job. We discussed my background, and he tossed some hypothetical crisis PR questions at me.

"Don, why I would want to work here?"

The question surprised him, but it changed the narrative away from me. We spoke for almost an hour. The job would be different from my work at the PR agency. At SEMHC, I'd have nobody to delegate anything to. The association used an outside printer for their newsletters, annual meeting material, and annual reports, but I'd be responsible for all copy and design. I'd be the liaison with the PR departments at the member hospitals.

My title would be vice president of public relations, misleading because I'd be a department of one. The other two staff members held the titles of vice presidents in their respective areas of expertise—also departments of one. For support, the organization had an executive assistant and a receptionist.

As the meeting wound down, I lobbed a bomb into the middle of the room.

"I'm gay and live with my partner. Your conservative members might have a problem with it. I don't go around announcing it, but I won't lie about it either. Will that be a problem?"

"Of course not. The more relevant question, Mr. Simmons, is will you come work for me at an annual salary of $40,000."

Holy fuck. Almost twice my FRANCO salary. Breathe, Steve, breathe. Count to five. One. Two. Three. Four. Five.

"I would have to give FRANCO two-weeks' notice."

"Understandable. What do you say?"

"When do I start?"

I didn't finish meeting with Don until 4:30 p.m. It didn't make sense to drive back to the FRANCO offices in Detroit, so I left a message there for Marcotte. On the way home, I stopped at a Chinese restaurant to pick up a double helping of General Tso's Chicken.

Ethan and I had something to cele—.

Oh, shit. I accepted the job without discussing it with him. Why do I keep doing things like that?

Steve, it's too late now. Besides, he doesn't have to know you accepted. Lie to him.

I'll just add it to the long list of lies.

You can't keep doing this. You're going to drive him away.

I know.

Chapter 36

Poking the Bears

APRIL 1989
FARMINGTON HILLS, MICHIGAN
AGE 29

I N THE TWO YEARS Ethan and I had been back together, Mark and Wayne remained silent. Maybe they were content with my happiness because I'd had zero blackouts—not that I knew of. Surely Ethan would have noticed if I'd disappeared in the middle of the night or showed up wearing clothes reeking of cigarette smoke.

We recently moved into a new apartment in Farmington Hills, nearer to both of our jobs as well as his family. Ethan had come out to them more than a year earlier. Since then, we had a great relationship with his mom and two sisters. Unfortunately, his father had passed away before we met.

By 9 a.m. on a Monday in mid-April, I'd been at my desk for two hours when the phone rang. I picked it up after the first ring, a habit of mine.

"This is Steve."

"Hey, buddy. Sorry to interrupt your morning, but I have a huge favor to ask."

Oh, hell. Nick.

My former WAYNE STATE UNIVERSITY debate student had become my closest friend in the area other than Ethan. After the stunt Nick pulled when I first arrived at WAYNE STATE UNIVERSITY, I couldn't fathom as to why we became and remained friends.

Because you had a crush on him.

I just wanted to be his friend.

That's a lie. You wanted to be his lover.

We never spoke about why he claimed I made a pass at him when it had been the other way around. Since that day, the two of us pretended it never happened.

"What can I do for you?" I asked.

"The LSAT is coming up. I wondered if you'd help me study."

I'd helped two students study for the LSAT the summer before the rape behind TIFFANY'S, so I knew how to do it. I'd planned on taking the exam that fall, but everything fell apart for me. I didn't even start my master's thesis, although I finished the classwork.

"I'm swamped." Ethan would kill me if I put anything else on my plate. "I don't see how I could fit in the time."

"Once a week on Saturday afternoon. That's all I need."

Why do I always say yes when someone asks me to do something? I put their shit first and let my responsibilities suffer.

"Okay, but under one condition," I said. "You have to study the way I tell you to."

"Agreed."

"Let me do some research and I'll give you a call back this evening."

On my way home from work, I detoured up Orchard Lake Road to Barnes & Noble where I bought three LSAT workbooks containing practice tests. Thumbing through them made me wonder if I should take the exam. This could be my chance to attend law school—something I'd always wanted to do.

I rushed home from the bookstore to make dinner. Ethan walked in just as I put the chicken breasts in the oven. After a quick kiss, he passed through the dining room—a nook next to our galley kitchen.

"What are these?" He held up one of the LSAT books.

"Nick wants me to help him study for the LSAT. I picked those up on the way home."

"Ah. For a minute I thought they were yours."

Steve, are you sure you want to tell him?

"As a matter of fact, I was thinking about taking it myself."

Would that be a smart thing to do? Think of the stress. Why poke the sleeping bear?

Ethan appeared from around the corner with a blank stare, the kind you give a kid who's about to stick his finger in the frosting on a cake. I'd seen his what-the-hell-are-you-thinking look before.

"Law school?"

"If I get a good LSAT score, I might think about it."

"How would you pay for it? It's not like you've been saving money."

Ouch, that hurt—but he was right. Despite almost doubling my salary with the new job, I hadn't saved a cent. In fact, I splurged on a new Acura Legend and purchased expensive ski equipment without consulting him, but I couldn't explain the circumstances.

To be fair, you didn't lease the car or buy the ski gear. Wayne did.

Only I know that, though.

And that's your problem. All your fucking secrets.

With my lease payment, insurance, student loans, rent and utilities, and other expenses, I lived paycheck to paycheck.

"I'd get more student loans, I guess."

"Where would you go?"

"I'd love to go to Michigan, but it's not practical." It took at least an hour to get to Ann Arbor, and that was in very little traffic.

"WAYNE STATE UNIVERSITY, then?"

"That's my only realistic choice." We had two private law schools in the Detroit metropolitan area, but they cost too much. "Anyway, it's just a thought."

"You can't afford it."

He said it again. "You," not "we." I guess we're not in this together.

Steve, what do you expect? You spend every cent you make.

We couldn't pay our bills on his salary alone, thanks to my spendthrift ways. If I wanted something, I bought it, always keeping myself in debt.

"Again, it's just something I'm considering. I might not even get a good LSAT score."

He pulled me into a hug. "Look, we've got a good life together. If you start saving money, we can do anything and go anywhere. Law school would mean substantial changes. As hard as you work now, imagine how it would be if you're an attorney. I don't want to lose you to that." He swatted me on the butt and smiled. "I'm gonna shower. Dinner smells good."

I didn't deserve him—never did, and never would. Despite my mistakes and shortcomings, Ethan stood beside me. I loved him for that and hated myself at the same time. Keeping my mental disorder from him put an emotional distance between us. I feared he'd leave if I told him everything about me. How would I get past losing him?

The idea of law school excited me. My work as a public relations executive had become pedantic. Ethan was right, though. We simply couldn't afford it—I couldn't afford it. If I'd been reducing my expenses and saving, maybe I could have gone.

Why risk triggering my MPD? My job paid well, I had a wonderful man who loved me back, and I'd put the blackouts behind me.

But, if I ace the LSAT, Ethan will support my decision to go to law school, won't he?

In typical fashion, I registered for the next LSAT the same time Nick did—behind Ethan's back. It would be in two months at WAYNE STATE UNIVERSITY LAW SCHOOL.

For the next seven Saturdays, Nick and I snuck into the law school classroom where the test would be administered. I figured we'd do better on the exam if we completed the practice tests in the actual room where we'd take the LSAT. With each practice exam, we got better at the individual sections. We reviewed our wrong answers after each session.

The day of the exam, Nick was fidgety and kept averting his eyes around. I'd never seen him that nervous. We wished each other "good luck" and went into the classroom.

The exam lasted several hours with a short break in between each section. Nick avoided me during the breaks. I figured he needed space, so I gave it to him. Once we finished the final portion, I stumbled out of the lecture hall to find him leaning against the wall.

"It wasn't as bad as I expected it to be." The exam questions mirrored the ones we'd practiced answering repeatedly. Although I struggled with a few of the complex analytical ones, I found most to be easy. "I'm glad I took it with you."

"Speak for yourself."

"I'm sure you did fine, Nick. Nothing we can do about it now, anyway."

We went our separate ways in the parking garage, me back to Ethan and Nick to wherever. Could I quit my job and go back to school? It all depended on my test score.

Shouldn't it depend on whether you can afford it?

My phone at work rang a few weeks later. I grabbed it before the second ring—a quirk of mine.

"Have you checked your mail?"

"No, Nick, I have a job."

"Smartass. I got my exam score. Yours is probably in your mailbox."

I gave the office an excuse so I could leave work at four. The five-minute drive home gave me little time to consider what I would do if my scores were high.

When I got to the apartment, I jogged up the sidewalk to our mailboxes outside the building's entrance. Our box contained one piece of mail—a letter with a return address of "Law School Admission Council."

Shit, Steve, it's here.

My gut told me to rip it up and pretend it never existed. I could continue with my good, decent life instead of upending it for my own personal gain. If I didn't open the letter, Ethan would never know.

Tear it up. You know that's the right thing to do.

I tucked the envelope into the inside pocket of my suit jacket and went upstairs to our apartment. After a hot, relaxing shower, I tackled dinner. With no leftovers to heat, I could either fix something or order take-out. My stomach craved Chinese.

No wonder you're broke all the time. You have to stop eating at restaurants so much.

Sometimes, I hated listening to my conscience. I found some chicken in the freezer and put it in a bowl of water for it to thaw. When the door opened, I jumped. I didn't expect Ethan to be home for at least a half hour.

"You scared the shit out of me. What brings you home early, not that I'm complaining." He looked delicious as usual.

"I wish I were early. It's been a long day."

Ethan shuffled past me in the small galley kitchen and stopped at the table. I looked at my watch.

Fuck. He wasn't early at all. Maybe I just lost track of time.

The chicken breasts had thawed already. I patted the meat dry and put it in a glass baking dish. After seasoning the chicken, I slid the pan into the oven.

"You took the LSAT?" Ethan shouted.

I stiffened. How did he find out? Caught, I had to own up to what I did.

"Sorry. I thought I'd try it."

After washing my hands, I slipped around the corner. Ethan stood at the table with the opened LSAT envelope in one hand and its contents—an unfolded sheet of paper—in the other.

"Why didn't you tell me?" he asked.

"Uh, I—"

"Congratulations, I guess." He handed me the results, dropped the empty envelope on the table, and walked toward the bedroom. No kiss, no hug.

How did Ethan get the results? Did the envelope fall out of my pocket?

You know the answer to that. Plus, Ethan would never open your mail just as you wouldn't open his. Someone else got the envelope from your suit pocket, opened it, and placed it on the dining room table for Ethan to find.

The upper right-hand corner of the paper gave me the answer. Mark had drawn his signature smiley face with horns.

Mark, you son-of-a-bitch.

I had a blackout and didn't know it. No dizziness, no confusion. It was the McDONALD's burglary all over again. That was why the chicken had already thawed.

As for the LSAT, I'd received an almost perfect score, placing in the ninety-ninth percentile of everyone who had taken the exam. I found it impossible to celebrate, though.

I'd awakened my alters.

Chapter 37

Risking It All

O N A Saturday in early February, I accompanied Ethan to an audition for the male lead in a play being staged by the Novi Players theatre group. He had been in community theatre productions before we met.

We waited outside the room where the director was holding the try-outs for *See How They Run*, an English farce set in 1943. Ethan and I read lines together to prepare him for the audition. He wanted the lead, Lance-Corporal Clive Winton.

"You got this, babe," I said to encourage him.

"We'll see."

A young, slim woman with long hair opened the door. She reminded me of Catherine O'Hara, but with brunette hair flowing to her waist.

"Who's next?" she called out.

Ethan went in, and the woman motioned for me to follow.

"Oh, I'm not auditioning," I said.

"Are you with him?"

"Yes, but I–"

"Come watch, then." She had me sit at the back of the room near the door.

The director—with frazzled hair and a patchy beard—sat behind a desk at the front of the room. Ethan read two scenes with the Catherine O'Hara lookalike. She was exceptionally good, but so was Ethan. He read his lines with more confidence than in practice, but the woman performed Penelope Toop much better than I did.

"Excellent job, Mr. Feldman. We have your phone number. I'll be in touch by the end of the day."

If Ethan smiled any bigger, he'd pull a muscle. He practically skipped to the back of the room. I opened the door and held it for Ethan.

"*Wait*," the director shouted.

Good. He's gonna offer Ethan the part. We turned and walked toward the man's desk.

"Are you here to audition?" he asked.

"Who? Me?" His question took me by surprise. "No, I'm just with him."

"I have two parts to fill. Please come read for me."

"I only got a B in drama class." My senior play in high school didn't count because I didn't perform in it—one of my alters did.

"Amuse me and audition," the director said.

"I...I can't."

"Go read," Ethan said. "We can be in the play together."

He took a seat, and I approached the desk. The woman handed me a script opened to a page I knew well: another scene between Clive and Penelope. At least I was familiar with the lines. The reading went well, and the woman even performed better than she had with Ethan. Instead of two scenes, the director had us read four.

When we finished, I thanked the director and turned to leave. *I shouldn't have done this. It's not right.*

"Mr. Feldman, could you join us?"

He'd better be offering Ethan the part now.

"I'd like you both to be in the production. Mr. Feldman, you'll be The Intruder. Mr. Simmons, you'll be Clive Winton. Rehearsals begin tomorrow at one."

Oh, no. I can't take Ethan's part.

"Please give him the role of Clive," I said. "I can be the intruder."

"I offered the role to you, not him," the director said, polishing his glasses with a handkerchief. "If he wants to be The Intruder, the part is his. If you don't want to be Clive, I'll continue with the auditions. I'm sure there's someone in the hallway who'll be glad to take it."

"Take the part, and let's go home," Ethan said flatly. "I don't mind."

I didn't believe Ethan for a second. He had been thrilled after his audition. Now he looked defeated, the light in his eyes dimmed. *What have I done?* If someone else had gotten the lead, at least Ethan would be happy with a secondary part. For me to be the one who got it, though, seemed insulting.

The damage is done. You can either be in the play with him, or he can be in the play by himself as a supporting character. Either way, he knows the director preferred you for the lead. You should never have read for the part.

"It's the Kobayashi Maru," I said.

Ethan nodded in full understanding of my *Star Trek* reference. A no-win scenario.

"What?" the director asked.

"Okay, I'll do it."

"Great. Auditions are finally over. I'll see you tomorrow."

Although we'd parked in front of the theater, the walk seemed like a mile. We didn't speak until inside the car.

"Babe, I'm so sorry. I shouldn't have read for him."

"It's okay."

When I slid my hand over to touch his, he pulled it away and stared straight ahead. Nothing was okay—not in the least.

I got home from work one afternoon in March and opened our mailbox. In addition to our regular junk mail, I received a packet from WAYNE STATE UNIVERSITY LAW SCHOOL.

They said acceptances arrive in packets while rejections come in letters. I sat on the couch and waited for Ethan to get home. The unopened mail from WSU weighed heavily on my legs—and my conscience for going behind his back. When he walked in, I held the 10"x14" envelope in the air.

"What's that?"

"Guess."

"Law school? You got in?"

"I don't know. I was waiting for you."

When he settled beside me, I opened the end of the envelope and pulled out the contents—several pages and a brochure. The letter on top began with, *"Dear Mr. Simmons, We are happy to inform you...."*

"Yes." I turned to Ethan and kissed him. Even though I didn't expect him to be jubilant, the forced smile he gave me showed his true feelings. I'd seen it before—polite and expected, but not genuine. Although I didn't doubt he was happy for me, he obviously had reservations about me going to law school. It had to be the financial impact it would have on our lives.

That's just short-term, Steve. Keep your eye on the bigger picture. Ethan will come around eventually.

Mark hadn't made an appearance since he opened my LSAT scores. I pushed self-doubts into a deep hole. My MPD had been under control—somewhat. Gone were the nightly excursions to gay bars and morning surprises next to me in bed.

They're not the problem anymore. You are.

My sex life with Ethan had been nonexistent for two years. I always made excuses. "I'm tired" or "I'm not feeling well."

I don't know why I avoid sex. I love Ethan, but I can't fuse love with sex. The two concepts are mutually exclusive for me. But the love I have for him outweighs everything else—including sex.

You're lying to yourself. You don't love him more than your own self-interest. You're selfish to the core.

I don't mean to. It just happens, no matter how much I try to stop it.

Then why don't you make love to him more than you do? Why do you masturbate whenever you can to the stories in magazines hidden under the waterbed mattress? You'd rather get off fantasizing about having sex with strangers than with your own partner. If you love Ethan so much, why do you push him away?

Because I'm filthy, tainted. I allowed myself to be used and violated since I was four years old. He's the sweetest, loveliest man I've ever known. He deserves someone worthy of him—someone who hasn't been repeatedly raped, someone clean. When we have sex, I can't get those others out of my mind. I see myself through Ethan's eyes and want to vomit. I'm a whore and always will be. It's easy to have sex with strangers because they don't matter. They give me a little attention and an orgasm, which is all I need. Ethan deserves better.

Then why are you with him?

Because I don't want to be alone.

It's not fair to him.

"Yes, I know."

"Did you say something?" Ethan stepped back into the living room from the hallway.

"Sorry, I was just thinking out loud. Go shower and I'll work on dinner."

"Nope, we're celebrating. Come shower with me, then we'll go out to eat."

Even after everything I did to get into law school, he still treats me like I'm special.

"I'll be right there."

"At least you have sufficient time to secure and properly train a replacement," my boss, Don, said after I gave him my five-month notice. "You know what the position requires, so go forth and find me another Steve."

He took it much better than I expected. I went to my office and shut the door.

What have I done? I make a good living in my job. How can I throw it away for the unknown?

Steve, that's not what you're worried about. Mark and Wayne disappeared for two years. Everything in your life was perfect, but you weren't satisfied. You poked the sleeping sociopath and his doppelganger man-slut—and they're back. It's not too late to change your mind. Tell Don that you want to stay. Maybe they'll disappear again.

This job isn't intellectually challenging. I want more.

But at what expense? You might lose everything—including Ethan. Will it be worth it then?

He said we'll always be together—and he'll never break a promise to me.

Are you sure?

Chapter 38

More Cover-Ups

Thank God I found my replacement at work. Mary would start on Monday, April 30—less than two weeks away.

On Tuesday, April 17, I was writing our monthly newsletter when Viola, the receptionist, called to say I'd received a package up front. Ever since we announced to the member hospitals that I was leaving SEMHC, friends and colleagues had been sending cards, flowers, and the occasional small gift. I stepped into the lobby, and Viola pointed to a white box with the word "Dell" on the side.

"Holy shit. Did someone send me a computer?" I laughed at the ludicrousness of the suggestion.

"Maybe it's from Ethan," Viola said.

"In my dreams." I carried the box to my office and shut the door. When I pulled the paperwork from the plastic pocket on the side, my stomach tightened.

Oh, no.

My body tingled all over as goosebumps broke out. Payment for the computer had been charged to my American Express credit card two weeks earlier to the tune of $4,000. I didn't have the money to buy a computer.

None of this makes sense, unless...oh shit. It had to be one of them.

Once I found the number for DELL customer service, I picked up the receiver and started dialing. Then the old familiar dizziness overwhelmed me.

Motherfu—

———————————

My head throbbed as if being kicked over and over. It couldn't be a hangover because I'd put my drinking days behind me, unless...Mark or Wayne.

I opened my eyes. The red numbers on the clock said 6:55 a.m. *Damn, time to get up.* When I reached for the button to disable the alarm, I discovered it already had been turned off. *Good thing I woke up or I'd be late to work.* Ethan stirred next to me and mumbled something. I swung my legs off the waterbed and pulled myself to a sitting position.

"It's time to get up," I said. "Gonna jump in the shower." Maybe hot water would infuse life into me.

"It's Saturday. Do you have to work?"

Saturday? No. Please, God, not again.

My watch confirmed it was April 21. I'd lost almost four days. The significance of what it meant punched me in the stomach like a blow from Harry's steel-toed shoes. I took three long strides to the bathroom, pushed the door closed, and knelt barely in time for my stomach contents to hit the toilet water. After the heaving stopped, I cleaned up and brushed my teeth.

They're back, and it's my fault. Why did I do it? I didn't need law school. We were happy. I was happy. Ethan is everything I ever wanted.

Liar. If that is true, then why did you pursue law school?

The weight of it all smothered me. I crawled into bed and cuddled against him, the warmth of his body reminding me of everything I'd put at risk. Being with him stopped my alters, sending them away for whatever reason.

Why didn't I do as he asked? SEMHC is an excellent job.

Because you're selfish.

I wanted more for us—a home we could call our own. The kinds of things successful attorneys can buy.

You have him. What else did you need?

I'm in trouble and don't know what to do.

The smell of his hair calmed me. I overacted, as usual. Compared to other times I'd blacked out, four days were *nothing*. Besides, I never expected Mark and Wayne to disappear forever.

Steve, you're an idiot.

"Sorry I woke you, babe. I was a little disoriented."

"Are you okay? I heard you getting sick in there."

"Yeah, I'm fine. Just an upset stomach."

"We drank too much." He rolled over to face me, the waterbed tossing me like a boat adrift in a storm. "But it was worth it. We haven't had sex like that in a long time."

Thank you, Wayne. I'm worthless as a lover, so feel free to do it more often.

"You deserve better than me." Although the truth, the words revealed more than I should have. He could never know the real Steve. My transparency would end us for sure.

"Don't put yourself down." He stroked my hair and lightly kissed me. The gentleness of his touch reminded me of our first time together, when we lay against each other for hours.

"I love you," I whispered. *You need to say those words to him more often.*

"If you loved me, you'd let me get back to sleep."

He rolled onto his right side and scooted back against me. I put my left arm around him, not wanting to let go. If he felt tears falling onto his neck, he didn't say anything.

You didn't need law school.

I know, but it's too late. Wayne, you should take over for good. Give Ethan what I can't.

Give him what you can't or what you won't?

We woke up two hours later and went out to breakfast—to a little restaurant serving the best eggs, bacon, toast, and hash browns for under five dollars each. Ethan loved bacon, despite being a Conservative

Jew who grew up in a kosher home. Afterward, I asked him stop at SEMHC on the way home.

"I forgot to bring a file home. It'll just take a minute to find it. You can come in or wait in the car."

Fortunately, he chose the comfort of his Nissan. I looked around my office for hints as to what happened over the past four days. The first thing I noticed was the DELL computer had disappeared.

I hope to God that you sent it back.

I picked up the pile in my inbox and sorted through the papers. About halfway down, a colorful logo caught my attention.

Oh, fuck.

Don had approved two invoices for almost $4,000 from a company called PR For You. Those invoices represented three big problems. First, they were fake—and I should know. PR For You was my sole proprietorship—started last year so I could perform side work for extra money.

Second, someone had forged Don's name. I knew his signature as well as my own. He always made a little squiggly curl at the top of the D in his first name. The two signatures on the PR For You invoices had no such curl. They might be good enough to get by Debbie—who would have no reason to think them forged—but I knew better.

The final problem stared at me from the upper right-hand corner on each invoice—a smiley face with horns.

Mark, you embezzling, forging son-of-a-bitch.

What was I going to do? Mary started her job in one week. During her training, the vendors we used surely would come up. If she stumbled across PR For You, she'd ask questions I wouldn't be able to answer.

What am I gonna do?

Steve, you're gonna do what you always do—cover up the shit.

Paperwork left trails. As the only administrative assistant to four of us, Debbie kept meticulous records. She always made copies of my department's invoices for three files in the office: my department vendors, accounts payable, and company vendors. The original went to the MHA in Lansing, an affiliate organization we paid to manage our finances and cut the checks.

The copies here in the three company files had to disappear.

A quick check of my department vendors turned up nothing. I hurried to the lateral file cabinets lining the walls of the outer office. After finding the PR For You folder among the company vendors, I pulled the file and slipped inside it the two invoices from my inbox. I'd shred the folder and its contents at home.

Once I found the April accounts payable file, I started to pull it out when I noticed the March folder behind it had a rubber band around its contents. Curious, I removed it. Debbie had put a rubber band around the stack of invoices from March. On top was a list of numbers for checks sent to the vendors. Debbie—always efficient and thorough—had gone through the list and reconciled payments for the month.

Of course, she did. I am so screwed.

If I removed the April invoices, she'd notice them missing. The only way to conceal the embezzlement and fraud would be to wait until after Debbie reconciled the payments and hope she never had a reason to look through the file again.

If she ever noticed them missing, Debbie would investigate—and she would discover that the vendor files were missing. That would lead to her requesting the original documents from the MHA, and then Don might notice his forged signatures.

Dammit, there's no way to hide the fraudulent payments.

I returned the accounts payable files and closed the drawer. If Don never noticed his forged signatures and nobody ever investigated PR For You, I should be fine. I would get caught for sure if I destroyed the invoices in the accounts payable file. By taking the vendor files, I could keep Mary from discovering PR For You. Mary would never have a reason to look at old accounts payable paperwork.

You hope.

Ethan would be getting impatient outside, so I grabbed the company vendor file.

When we got home, I excused myself to the second bedroom we used as an office. Our cheap shredder would take, at most, two pages at a time. Once I destroyed the PR For You vendor file, I'd feel better.

I opened the folder and picked up the contents.

You've got to be kidding me.

The file contained falsified PR For You invoices dating back to February 1989—a month after I created the company. In the upper right corner of each, Mark had left his calling card.

Mark had submitted twelve fraudulent bills over the past year without me realizing it. I should have noticed it sooner, but monetary management had never been my strength. Ironic given I originally was an accounting major in college. I kept bank balances in my head and never reconciled checking accounts. Every month, I tossed unopened statements into a shoe box.

It took me a few minutes, but I finally found the box of PR For You statements. Opening them would have exposed Mark's embezzlement long ago. He deposited each check from SEMHC in the PR For You checking account and withdrew the cash a few days later. In total, he'd embezzled and laundered more than $9,000 through the account.

What did he do with the money?

You are so fucked, Steve. If SEMHC ever audits its vendors, they'll find the theft. This is too big for them to miss.

They won't if they believe the invoices were legitimate.

Why do you keep covering up his crimes?

If I don't, I'll go to prison.

Maybe you belong there. For your entire adult life, you've made one shitty decision after another.

Mark hadn't thought this through. PR For You could be traced directly to me. No product had been produced, no services rendered, and no itemized invoice submitted. If anyone at SEMHC asked me what the company did for us, I couldn't answer. All they had to do was check the Oakland County records to see who registered the DBA. Mark had done something I couldn't cover up no matter how much I wanted to.

Mark, you're an idiot.

I never expected my mental disorder to go this far. Mark's ability to switch without me noticing had evolved to a dangerous point. Other than losing the past four days, I didn't recall any missing time in the past year and a half. Yet, Mark had been switching all that time, creating the documents, forging signatures, depositing checks, and making withdrawals.

You can't trust yourself now.

Whether he realized it or not, Mark framed me. Everything related to PR For You could be traced back to documents with my name on it—bank account, debit card, mailbox, and the Oakland County DBA filing.

For the next five days, I couldn't keep food down. My head pounded like a bass drum, and no over-the-counter pain medicine helped. I tossed and turned each night. Somehow, I managed to hide my stress-induced illness from Ethan and my coworkers.

I stopped by MAIL BOXES ETC. every day to see if the SEMHC checks for the latest two invoices arrived. My American Express bill would be due soon, and I still didn't know where the damned computer disappeared to. On Thursday, the checks came in the mail.

Despite a little voice inside screaming "don't do it," I deposited the checks in the company bank account. I'd have access to the funds in three business days. As soon as I could access the money, I'd pay off the Amex bill. Then I'd close the business down, including the mailbox. Something had to be done to keep Mark from embezzling again.

You know that won't stop him. You need professional help.

They'll put me away.

Good.

As usual, I beat Ethan home. He worked too hard for the lousy pay they gave him. I retrieved the mail and climbed the two flights of stairs to the second floor. Going without food had zapped my energy. By the time I got to our door, I could barely move.

I dropped the mail on the bedroom floor and collapsed on the waterbed—in dire need of food and sleep in that order. Could I stand long enough to cook? After changing out of my suit, I stumbled to the kitchen and sorted the mail. Other than junk mail—which went in the recycling bin—we'd received two letters. One was from our renter's insurance company—and it appeared to be a check.

What the fuck is this?

I opened the insurance company envelope and pulled out a check for just under $4,000. The memo line said, "Insurance proceeds for DELL 316LT computer."

On the endorsement side, the check stated, "Must be signed by both insureds."

The hole keeps getting deeper and deeper. Now I have to forge Ethan's signature.

In the home office, I found copies of old paperwork with Ethan's signature. It took me a few minutes of practice, but the end result looked close to his. I didn't want it to be perfect. If it looked forged, he'd have plausible deniability.

What the hell did Mark do?

Don't be naive. Mark must have stashed the computer somewhere, reported it stolen, and filed a fraudulent claim.

You don't know that. Someone might have stolen the laptop.

Do you hear yourself? This is Mark we're talking about.

You're right. He has the computer hidden somewhere.

By forging Ethan's name, I kept from implicating him in the fraud. It was the least I could do—literally. Once I deposited the check, I could pay the Amex bill.

How am I going to stay out of jail?

You're not. They're eventually going to catch you.

Mark, how could you be so sloppy? It's as if you framed me on purpose. Don't you realize if I go to prison, so do you? We're the same damned body!

———————

By the end of July, I got Mary trained in the position. She had great skills and would make a fine replacement. Smart as a whip, too, but she never asked about PR For You. Maybe I dodged a bullet.

On my last day, Don took me to lunch. I prepared myself for him to bring up the checks with his forged signature, but he said nothing. Before I left the office for the final time, he gave me a going-away gift that made me cry: a black leather catalog case with my initials stamped in gold on the top.

What have I done?

Chapter 39

Proof Is in the Pictures

My left leg didn't bother me anymore. The surgeon removed the stitches yesterday and cleared me for athletics—not that I took part in any. Being manager for the junior high football team was as close to school sports as I got.

In three days, the team would play their season opener, so they practiced hard under the hot September sun. I had several responsibilities as team manager, including picking up dirty towels after the players showered.

Seeing Jeffrey every day at practice made me nervous. What if he said something to the other guys? After what I did with him—things I considered a price for our friendship—he never hung around me at school, never involved me with his other friends. He ignored me, except for the occasional stare.

Nobody on the team bothered me since Coach Stewart gave Larry a dressing down at tryouts. Too bad Coach didn't have sway over the rest of the student body. Didn't the other students get tired of calling me Sissy Simmons? It was only Tuesday, but I'd had enough of the week already.

While the players showered, I put away equipment and swept the floor. I hastily collected the damp towels, trying not to let my eyes wander as the guys dressed.

You're not gay, Steve, so stop looking or they'll think you are.

As I finished my chores, one locker stood open. The owner must have drowned in the shower. I went around the corner to check on him and caught Danny drying off. He looked up and smiled before I could scurry away.

Stupid, stupid, stupid. I should have known better than to go see who was still showering.

Danny came out of the shower room and dropped his towel. I walked by, snatched it, and ran to the laundry room. He'd finished dressing by the time I returned.

"Grab your stuff, Mr. Manager," Danny said. "I'll give you a ride home."

"You don't drive, Mr. Second String." My mouth had a mind of its own. It was going to get the crap beat out of me someday.

"My brother's pickin' me up."

"That's okay. I'll walk."

Even though Mom picked the three of us up from school every day, I told her not to wait for me. I'd walk the fifteen minutes it took me to get home.

"You're not afraid of me, are you?" Danny asked.

"Why would I be afraid?" Okay, he did scare me a little, but I also didn't know anything about his brother.

"Then grab your stuff and come with us."

Crap, I walked into that one. If I didn't let them take me home, Danny would have something else to tease me about.

"Okay. I'll be right back." I ran to the office and got my books. Out front, the back door of a big sedan stood open. Danny waved me over to sit in the back seat behind him.

"This is Billy, my brother."

The driver turned to look at me—and winked.

He made a U-turn. The tires squealed as the car lurched forward. Billy let out a howl and drove like a crazy person away from the school. At the intersection, he turned right instead of left.

"I live in the other direction."

"We're just gonna go for a little ride first," Danny said.

Oh, no, this is what I was afraid of. Where are they taking me?

"Just let me out. I'll walk."

"No can do," Billy said. "We're gonna have some fun and blow off some steam. You're one of us now, Mr. Manager."

I had too much drama in my life. Something always went wrong, catching me in the crossfire. If I got home late for dinner, Mom and Dad would be pissed.

The car turned down a road—if you could call it that. It was more of a field that had been worn down with two tracks for tires. We drove for two hundred yards before stopping next to an old barn behind trees blocking sight of the road.

"It's playtime," Danny said. "You gotta join us."

They jumped out of the car and slammed the doors shut. Billy opened the back door.

"Let's go."

"I'll just stay here."

"No need to be rude. We invited nicely."

Reminder to self—carry a switchblade from now on.

I set my books on the seat and got out. Danny and Billy led me into the barn. The building had bales of hay stacked eight high with several loose ones on the floor.

"It's party time," Billy called out.

He pulled a rolled-up cigarette out of his pocket and lit it. He took a long drag off it and held it out for me.

"Uh, no thanks. I don't smoke."

It smelled different than Mom and Dad's cigarettes. Still, I didn't want to try it. Inhaling smoke was gross.

The two of them kept puffing on the funny-smelling cigarette, passing it back and forth. I found a soft pile of hay and lay down. When the sound of metal clanging like belt buckles got my attention, I sat up and froze. Danny and Billy were naked. *Shit.*

"Y'all are crazy. I'll be in the car." Before I could get to the barn door, Billy had his arms around me from behind.

"You're gonna miss all the fun. Come join us."

I shook my head, but he dragged me to a blanket that one of them had put on the barn floor. *Why did I agree to go with them? I knew they'd hurt me in some way.*

"Why are you doing this? Please, let me go."

Danny held me down while Billy removed my shoes, pants, underwear, and shirt. He even took off my socks.

"We're here to party," Billy said. "I think you like what you're seeing."

Although I'd got excited, I tried to ignore it—but it wouldn't go down.

"Please, stop. I wanna go home."

"I'll take you home, but don't you wanna have fun with us first?" Billy asked. "Your dick sure wants to."

Steve, you're a coward. Fight back. Do something. They might stop calling you Sissy Simmons if you'd stand up for yourself.

I can't.

"We just wanna be your friends," Danny said.

"But you have a girlfriend," I said.

"That bitch doesn't put out," Danny said.

"I don't either."

"My good buddy Allen says you do," Billy said. "You remember him, don't you? He said you're the best piece of ass he's ever had."

First Mr. Jones, and now them? Allen, you were supposed to be my friend.

"If you take me home, I won't say anything. I'll just tell Mom that practice ran late."

"You ain't gonna snitch anyway." Danny lay on top of me, holding me down.

When he kissed me, I tried to pull my head away but couldn't. I closed my eyes and tried to ignore the stirring feelings in my crotch.

How can I like what he's doing? I'm so confused.

Danny got off me. For a minute, I expected them to let me go or take me home. Instead, they flipped me over and spread my legs. I first felt something wet before a sudden sharp pain in my ass made my body tense.

At least Allen had been gentle.

The pain subsided, and dizziness hit me. I floated away. *It's about damned time.*

Billy stopped the car at my house. Dad's truck wasn't parked in front, so I didn't miss dinner.

What did they do to me?

The taste in my mouth answered that question. Numbness and shame filled me. Should I tell Coach what they did?

If you tell him, he'll tell others—including Mom and Dad. You'll be teased and ridiculed. They probably won't believe you anyway.

I pulled the door handle to get out.

"Not so fast," Danny said. "Remember, we have these."

He held up Polaroid pictures of me in different positions having sex with them—on my knees, face down, on my back. You could clearly see my face but never theirs.

What am I gonna do?

"Don't snitch, or these show up at school," Danny said.

Billy laughed and grabbed the pictures from his brother. "You're our bitch now."

Oh, God. My life is over.

Chapter 40

Desperate Times

OCTOBER 1991
FARMINGTON HILLS, MICHIGAN
AGE 31

Our waterbed looked like a study table at the library with two treatises open and class notes—printed out and spiral bound—on my lap. My tax midterm the next day would be tough, but it was an open-notes test.

The DELL 316LT laptop computer had become my secret weapon to good grades. During class, I typed directly into a study outline. I was the first student at the law school to take notes that way. Other students complained at first—saying it made too much noise, that it gave me an unfair advantage—but the dean and professors sided with me.

As I suspected, Mark had hidden the computer and filed the fraudulent insurance claim. It reappeared before I started law school. I had a difficult time explaining where it came from.

"Where did you get that?" Ethan had asked when he saw it on the dining room table.

"I got it from the sales rep when SEMHC bought the new copier." It was the only cover story—flimsy as it was—I could devise. Even though the copier cost $20,000, no sales representative would give a gift worth $4,000. Ethan appeared skeptical—no big surprise since the lie was a whopper—but he dropped his inquiry.

With notes and books spread over the waterbed, I picked up a previous tax exam and reviewed the questions. Grades in law school meant everything, so I put every minute I could into studying. After two semesters, I ranked second in my class—deprived of the top spot thanks to an A- in legal writing.

My grades had already helped me secure a coveted summer associate position for next year at HONIGMAN MILLER SCHWARTZ & COHN, one of the top law firms in Detroit. That could be a steppingstone to permanent employment there.

Because I had to study for the tax midterm, Ethan had gone out for the evening to attend an art event with our friend Levi. School responsibilities made it difficult for me to socialize. When I did, one of my alters had a way of taking over, insulting our friends and causing strife among them. For the life of me, I didn't know why Mark and Wayne did it.

I apologized profusely for "my" behavior—blaming it on stress—but my standing with them had substantially diminished. I eventually encouraged Ethan to go have a good time with friends instead of staying at home while I buried my head in books. It seemed like a fair compromise.

As I thumbed through my taxation notes, the thump of the apartment door closing interrupted my concentration. Ethan came into the bedroom and sat next to me on the edge of the waterbed. I pushed my crap aside and moved over a little to give him some room.

"How was the exhibit?" I asked.

"I'm not happy."

"That bad, huh? What happened?" His eyes had a sadness to them, almost as if he'd been crying.

"With *us*." His voice cracked. "I'm not happy with us."

"I don't understand." *Yes, you do, but you don't want to face it.*

"Something has to change in our relationship, or I'm leaving."

Please be joking—or be a nightmare. That's it. I fell asleep while reading the boring tax laws.

Steve, you have only yourself to blame.

My erratic behavior hadn't been easy for him. How had I missed all the signs? I screwed up last June when I got arrested for driving under the influence—a DUI—while coming home from Nick's apartment. Ethan and I worked through that—at least I thought we had.

Mark and Wayne have fucked me over. Ethan thinks I'm the one responsible for it all.

Do you hear yourself? You are the one responsible. It is all your fault. Stop blaming your alters when you could have prevented this.

"Babe, you can't just walk in and do this to me the night before my biggest midterm. You've never said *anything* about being unhappy. Nothing."

Don't be so naive and stupid. He didn't have to shout it from a rooftop. You've seen it all along but chose to ignore it.

I reached out to hold his hand as he sat on the edge of the bed, but he pulled his back and stood.

"You have six weeks to fix it, or I'm moving out."

"What? Six weeks? I have midterms and finals. Law review. Moot court. The Jessup competition in Chicago." The tears ran down my face in waves. "What am I supposed to do? I went to law school for us. You can't just drop it on me like this."

You knew he'd do this when you got back together.

I didn't think it would happen.

You didn't follow your gut, and now everything is falling apart.

How can he do this to me the night before my midterm?

You did this to yourself.

I leaned back against the headboard as Ethan took a comforter and pillow from the closet.

"I'll be sleeping in the living room."

"No, please don't."

Wake up from this nightmare, Steve. Wake up.

I didn't make it to the bathroom in time. The vomit splattered over the closed toilet, hitting the wall, and running onto the floor. I lifted the white plastic lid as the rest of my dinner and Diet Coke landed in the toilet bowl. My knee slipped in the mess, and I fell sideways to the floor. Covered in bile and partially digested food, I curled up in a ball and shook.

Without Ethan, I have nothing. He's everything to me.

Then why did you go to law school? Why do you keep the truth from him?

I can't tell him. He'll know how disgusting I am.

Why aren't you being his lover? You haven't had sex with him in a year. You're no more than a roommate who has never put him first. He loved you, and you sabotaged it. You spent all your spare time in the past fourteen months studying. The person who's supposed to be everything to you has been nothing more than a footnote. You forgot about Ethan.

I didn't mean to—and now I have six weeks to fix it. How can I do that? I don't even know where to start.

The dizziness hugged me as an alter came to the front. I welcomed the break. Maybe I'd never come back.

That would be best.

The warm body next to me moved. How many times will this happen? Waking next to a stranger always gave me an uneasy feeling. When he got out of bed, the water in the mattress bounced me around. Either I was home, or Wayne found another person who owned a waterbed.

God, please let the guy be Ethan. If Wayne brought someone else to the apartment, that'll be the end for sure.

I opened my eyes.

My gorgeous love walked across the room to the closet. He didn't sleep in the living room after all.

How did I let it get this far?

You need to tell him the truth—all of it. It's the only way you're gonna keep him.

He will never understand. He will never forgive me for waiting five years to tell him something so important.

Steve, he's a psychologist. He'll understand. If you can't be straight with him, you're gonna lose him.

It will destroy any trust he ever had in me. Telling him about Wayne and Mark will look like I'm making excuses for everything. Keeping it secret is my only hope of keeping him.

And how is that going?

"Out of bed, sleepyhead. We should get on the road."

On the what?

A push of the button on my watch displayed the time and date. December 20, 1991.

Shit. It's been two months. I missed the tax midterm and all my law finals. Did I drop out? I obviously didn't go to the Jessup competition. On the bright side, Ethan is still here—and it's been more than six weeks.

"When do we need to be there?" It would help if I knew where we were going and for how long.

"We can't check in until two, but we might hit snow. If we're early, we can walk the dunes."

The dunes narrowed it down. We'd talked about going to Saugatuck someday, so that had to be it. When we left the apartment, I let Ethan walk ahead of me to see which car we'd take. He stood behind my Acura, so I opened the trunk for our bags. An unfolded map rested on the passenger seat.

"Why are you taking 94?" he asked.

Good question. Mark or Wayne had highlighted a route for us to take. I agreed with their choice.

"I'd rather stay on a southern route where it's a little warmer."

We played the radio all the way there. Our conversations covered nothing substantive. I wanted to ask about law school, the status of our relationship, how he felt about me. *Try asking him about what Mark and Wayne did for the past two months?*

A few minutes after noon, we found the bed-and-breakfast in Saugatuck. A sweet middle-aged woman greeted us. I stayed by the door with the luggage while Ethan paid for the room.

"Do you have a reservation?"

"It's under Feldman. Four nights."

"You're welcome to stay through Christmas if you'd like. It's off-season, so we have vacancies."

"We'll think about it."

Ethan got our key, and we carried our luggage upstairs. Our room surprised me: a four-poster bed, cream walls with stained trim, and dark hardwood floors. The Art Deco style *en suite* bathroom had a shower large enough for two people, claw-foot iron tub, and pedestal sink. Part of me desired to spend our entire time in bed having decadent sex, but another part wanted to do anything but that.

Over the next three days, Ethan and I walked the dunes along Lake Michigan, went to art galleries, and ate too much delicious food. He bought a framed pencil drawing—a sphere filled with detailed abstract figures. It cost a small fortune, but he loved it.

We talked a lot and cuddled on the bed even more. What we didn't do was make love. He wanted to, but I again made excuses—and hated myself for it. How could I care for someone so much yet not want to have sex with him?

You have to let him go. You don't deserve him. He should be with someone who isn't tainted by all the bullshit.

But he's all I have—all I've ever wanted.

If he's with you, he's the one who has nothing. Think about him for a change.

On Christmas Eve morning, I awoke next to the man who saved me, for whom I'd give my life if necessary.

You keep lying to yourself. You've always put yourself first.

I can't just let him go.

That's exactly what you must do. He saved you, now return the good deed by walking away.

Ethan had been the only stabilizing constant in my life—and I screwed it up. Going to law school had been poor judgment. Nick blew up my life by asking for help on the LSAT.

Stop blaming Nick and accept responsibility for once in your life. You're the one who took the test behind Ethan's back. You're the one who decided to quit a great job and go to law school.

I stroked his cheek with my left thumb as he lay facing me. His thick brown hair, high cheekbones, and stylish mustache gave him a beauty that far exceeded my own. Why had I subjected this wonderful man to my chaotic life without letting him make an informed decision?

Because he never would have wanted you.

We stared into each others' eyes for a brief eternity. The warmth of his gaze enveloped me, causing me to smile, which he returned.

"I'm sorry for everything," I whispered. "I love you and don't want to lose you."

He paused for no more than two seconds, but it was long enough to create an uncomfortable moment like a knife twisting in my gut.

"I love you, too," Ethan replied. "I don't want to lose us."

Does he mean it, or is he trying to convince himself?

What do you think? The relationship is a lie.

"We should get back." He slid out from under the warmth of the down comforter. A moment later, the sound of urine splashing the toilet water broke the silence. "Brrrrr. It's cold."

"Come back to bed, then. I'll keep you warm."

Instead of taking me up on the offer, he put on underwear and unrolled a pair of socks. Defeated, I followed suit.

We checked out and got on the road. The drive turned out to be a lot more pleasant than the one four days earlier. Although the music played like before, this time we talked. We also communicated nonverbally by holding hands. We'd turn and smile at each other, something I missed between us.

A few minutes before noon, we reached Allen Park on the outskirts of Detroit. The area had a winter storm while we were gone. The plows had pushed the snow to the side where piles stood a few feet high in places.

Whatever I'd sacrificed—to focus on us, to fix what I'd broken—had been worth it. We were going to be fine, even if it meant dropping out of law school.

We passed the eighty-feet-tall Uniroyal Giant Tire located next to the interstate. Ethan pulled his hand off mine.

"This isn't working."

"What?" He wasn't trying to adjust the radio or use the CD player, so I had no idea what he couldn't get to work.

"Us."

"*What?*" I swerved the car, almost hitting a snow pile on the off the road. "You said we were fine."

"But the closer we got to Detroit, the more my unhappiness returned. Nothing has changed."

As soon as we unloaded my car, Ethan got into his and drove away. He didn't say where he was going or when he would be back. I cried, screamed, and threw things.

If he leaves, what will I do? Where will I go? I can't do this alone.

Maybe he'll come back and be fine. Just give him space.

I sat in the living room, numb inside. When I looked at our little Christmas tree—which he put up for me—I got an idea. I found things throughout the apartment that represented something to both of us. Sentimental items such as small gifts we'd given each other over the years. He could open them as presents and be reminded of our love.

You seriously think manipulating him will work? It's a horrible plan.

For the next two hours, I wrapped "gifts" and added them to the real presents under the tree.

What did Mark and Wayne buy for Ethan during my time away? Did they try to fix the relationship? Maybe I did wrong things in Saugatuck.

You wouldn't have sex with him, that's what you did. You're damaged beyond repair. You're an emotional husk. You can't be intimate with someone you love. That part of you died when you let Tom make you believe it was normal for a four-year-old to suck his dick—or when Allen fucked you every night after the tornado—or when your cousin Lonnie forced you to give him a blowjob in Granny's house—or when Jeffrey coerced you into a sexual relationship—or when Danny and his brother raped you for two years—or when Gary knocked you out and tied you up before sodomizing you—or when the guy raped you behind Tiffany's and you—

"*Stop it.*" The wrapped re-gift hit the far wall and shattered. "*It's not fair.*"

Steve, you're only capable of having sex with someone you don't care about—and you know it. Strangers, one-night stands...rapists.

I lay awake on the waterbed until after midnight waiting for Ethan to come home. At some point I drifted to sleep. The burst of sunlight woke me a few hours later. Once I was dressed, I ventured to the living room where I found Ethan putting the sofa bed away.

"Good morning," I said. He nodded without smiling—not a good sign. "It's Christmas. Let's open the presents."

While he brewed himself a pot of coffee, I separated the gifts into the ones for him and the one for me. The one.

I guess it's better than getting none. We might have exchanged gifts during Chanukah.

Instead of getting on the floor beside me, he sat on the sofa. I first handed him the larger of the two unknown gifts, which he unwrapped. A book. Not a bad choice, either.

"Thank you. Your turn."

I ripped the paper. A beautiful pair of leather gloves with fur lining. "I love them. Thanks."

The second gift he opened was a pen and mechanical pencil set. *Wow, could that be more generic?*

"Now for some special gifts." I handed him one of the re-gifts. When he opened it, he looked quite confused.

"It's the key chain we bought at Six Flags Over Mid-America," I said. "We had so much fun there riding the Screamin' Eagle." Roller coasters got my adrenaline pumping.

I handed Ethan another re-gift—a little red heart charm. It meant a lot to me, so it should also mean something to him.

"You bought that for me in Trapper's Alley after one of our dinners in Greektown," I said. "I've had it on my key chain ever since."

He set the two items aside and leaned back. "What are you doing?"

"I'm just reminding you of what we mean to each to each other."

"*Meant.* That's in the past, just like those objects."

The words crushed everything inside me. They sounded so...final.

"Please, Ethan, don't."

"I'm moving to Rachel's. You and I will divide our things. I'll pay January rent, but then you're on your own."

My breathing froze. I couldn't inhale or exhale. This had to be a nightmare.

Wake up, Steve. Just wake up. And breathe.

"I know I've screwed up, but please don't leave. You're all I have."

"Not my problem."

Leaning back on the couch, he remained calm, seemingly undisturbed by his words. His cool demeanor cut me like a surgeon's scalpel aimed at my emotional center. Somehow, he pushed everything we had into a hole and buried it.

"You promised you would *always* be there for me."

He stood and brushed pieces of wrapping paper off his pants.

"Things change."

Things change? What the hell does that mean?

All the information in my head crashed around in a state of utter chaos. My beloved Ethan—the man who gave me purpose, who gave me the confidence to go to law school, who saved me from myself—was leaving me.

I grabbed my coat and ran from the apartment into the freezing weather. My feet—in tennis shoes instead of snow boots—pressed through the seven inches of snow as I crossed the lawn in the direction of Twelve Mile Road. With my mind focused on one goal, I paid no attention to the surroundings.

When I reached Twelve Mile Road, I headed east toward Orchard Lake Road. My hands, ears, and feet stung from the cold, but I brushed aside the pain and pushed forward. The sidewalk had been cleared, so I picked up pace. I reached the intersection in no time and turned right. Once I crossed the entrance to westbound I-696, I had clear sailing to the overpass.

The Michigan Department of Transportation had installed a fence on top of the low concrete barrier along the overpass. It was supposed to keep people from doing what I planned. A few cars flew along the interstate. I grabbed the fence and stepped onto the concrete barrier so I could pull myself over and into the traffic below. When I put my right arm over the fence, dizziness hit me. I lost my grip and fell backward toward the concrete.

Dammit, guys, let me do it. Please.

Chapter 41

Too Little, Too Late

December 1991
Farmington Hills, Michigan
Age 31

My body throbbed, reminding me of my encounter with Harry's steel-toed shoes. *Why am I sleeping on the floor? Not ideal, but I've woken up in worse places.* The glowing numbers on my trusted watch informed me it was December 26, so I lost less than a day. The sun wouldn't rise for another hour.

I should be on a cold metal tray in the morgue. Did I run off in the cold, snowy conditions to see if Ethan would come after me? Or did I really try to kill myself? Both statements had truth in them. I wanted to die, but I wanted Ethan to save me. Instead, my alters kept protecting me from myself.

My eyes adjusted to the dark enough to recognize my white computer and the glow from the surge protector. I doubted Ethan would have made me sleep in the office, so Mark or Wayne must have made the executive decision. *Idiots. You could have used the sofa bed.*

I turned on the light and found clean clothes folded neatly on a chair. After putting on shorts and a T-shirt, I stepped into the hallway. Our bedroom door was closed, so I opened it a crack. The sound of Ethan's light snoring made me want to crawl in bed with him.

That's never happening again. He's gone.

If God condemned me to relive the worse moments of my life in some sort of sadistic time loop, the past two days would top the list.

I sat on the couch and waited. An hour later, he walked into the living room, dressed for work and carrying his briefcase.

"I'll be out of here this weekend. Make a list of the things you want to keep, and I'll do the same."

"Babe, I beg of you, please don't do this."

"It's done."

"Tell me what to do, and I'll change. Please, I can't lose you."

"Steve, to be blunt, I'm not attracted to you anymore. You gained too much weight."

Ouch. I was thirty pounds heavier than when we met, but I was far from fat.

"Fine, I'll go on a diet."

"That's not enough."

What happened to the kind, considerate Ethan I fell in love with? The one who first had sex with me while Anita Baker sang "Sweet Love" on the stereo. The man who told me everything would be alright after I got the DUI. The man who left little notes for me to find on the days I had exams. Where did he go?

Steve, how can you be so naive? You, Mark, and Wayne beat him down. You destroyed the love he had for you. You just had to go to fucking law school, didn't you?

After he left for work, I stripped and crawled under the covers on Ethan's side of the bed. His scent on the pillow stimulated memories of us holding each other, our legs intertwined. I remembered how he'd roll on top of me while gently pressing his lips to mine. Soon I'd no longer be able to smell him, so I breathed deeply to cherish all he meant to me.

My tears soaked his pillow as I let out all my heartache. I drifted off to sleep, hoping I'd wake from this nightmare.

After lunch, I crawled out of bed and returned to the couch. Ethan wanted me to make a list of items I wanted to keep, but that signaled finality. Maybe if I told him about the abuse, he'd have a change of heart.

Steve, you're pathetic. You already tried to manipulate him. He's a psychologist, remember?

When he got home from work, I stood to face him. "Can we talk?"

"We have nothing to talk about."

He tried to get around me, but I sidestepped to block his way. "Please, just listen."

If you tell him now, he won't believe you. Even if he does, he'll think you're disgusting.

"I'm fucked up in the head. You think I don't know that? I was molested—*raped*—for *years* as a child." My mouth dried out, causing my lips to stick together. I sucked the inside of my mouth to generate saliva. "I was raped...twice...in college. Babe, I'm broken, and it's not my fault."

He raised an eyebrow and unclenched his jaw. "Why are you telling me this *now*?"

"I've kept too many secrets. I'll get help to fix me. I'll even convert to Judaism. You already know I met with the rabbi."

"It all sounds too convenient." Ethan shook his head. "It's over. Nothing you do or say can change that."

"But I'm telling you the truth." *Just not all of it.*

"Sure, you are. Now move."

"I need help."

"Then get it."

His eyes held no sparkle when he talked about me—about us.

It's over, Steve.

I stepped aside to let him through.

After Ethan showered, we made a list of how the property would be divided. I let him have whatever he wanted. Over the weekend, his friends—no longer *our* friends—helped him move to his sister's condo.

With all his things out of the apartment, he left his keys on the kitchen counter and walked out the door. No hug, no good-bye, no "see you later," no hope.

Ethan was gone.

January rolled around, and I barely noticed. I languished for days without realizing time had passed. I should speak to someone, anyone, who might understand.

When Ethan and I moved in together in 1987, I wrote a letter to Mom explaining how I'd met a wonderful man who loved me as I loved him.

"It won't last," she wrote back. "Men always leave."

Wallowing in self-pity, all alone in our apartment devoid of him and his property, I became little Stevie who needed his mama. I dialed the number from memory.

Why are you calling her?

I need...I want...to talk to her.

"Hello."

The sound of her voice made me angry, sad, and warm all at once. "Hey, Mom."

"Someone must have died if you're callin' me."

"Close. Ethan left me."

"Well, I told you it wouldn't last, but you never listen to."

Why couldn't she be a mother for once and console me? *What did you expect? She's not the one you shouldn't have called.* I hung up on Mom and dialed again.

"Hello?"

"Hi, Estelle. It's Steve."

"*Steven.*"

She smiled at me with her voice. It made me warm all over like a hug.

"*Cliff, it's Steven.*"

My uncle picked up the other line, and I spoke to two people who loved me more than my parents ever did—or would. How could I have missed so many opportunities to visit my aunt and uncle over the years? I had let fear or selfishness or both keep me away.

"Ethan left me."

I didn't have to tell them anything else. My aunt and uncle expressed what loving parents would say to a child who's hurting.

"I'm so sorry," Estelle said. "I really liked him."

"So did I," Cliff said. "Steven, I'm gonna go and let Estelle take over. It was good talkin' to you."

"Bye, Cliff."

I'd always been closer to my aunt, and he knew that. Besides, she and I could talk about mushy stuff better than he could with me.

They had met Ethan the summer before I started law school. He and I made the seventeen-hour drive to Arkansas, a trip I didn't think he'd ever want to take. The long ride gave us time to talk and enjoy ourselves. In Fort Smith, we got a room at MOTEL 6 and made plans to take Mom to lunch the next day.

When we went to pick her up at 11 a.m., she had alcohol on her breath and was smoking a cigarette. I opened the front passenger-side door for her because Ethan volunteered to sit in the back.

"Mom, there's no smoking in the car."

"Then I ain't goin'."

She slammed the door and went back inside her apartment, leaving me standing there dumbfounded, numb, and embarrassed. After a minute, Ethan wrapped his arms around me from behind.

"It's okay," he said as I failed to hold back tears.

We got in the car, and Ethan rubbed my back. After a few minutes, I called Estelle from the car phone.

"Come on over," she said without hesitation.

When we pulled up to their house, Estelle and Cliff welcomed Ethan with hugs. We spent a lot of time at their house over the next two days. One afternoon, they took us to lunch along with my brother and sister—but not Mom. I had no further contact with her until I called her that day after Ethan left.

Sitting on the floor in our empty apartment, I cried on the phone with Estelle. She gave me consolation and understanding in return—something Mom should have done.

"We could tell he loved you," Estelle said. "What happened?"

"It's complicated. I messed up. Didn't pay him enough attention. Gained too much weight. Didn't show him enough love." The list went on and on, but I could never tell her all of it. "It's killing me inside."

"Everything's goin' to be okay."

Even though I didn't believe her, the words made me feel better. Her soothing voice talked me down from the proverbial ledge. Eventually we moved on to another topic I didn't particularly want to cover.

"How's law school goin'?"

And, just like a parent, she went for the jugular without even realizing it. I didn't mind because it made me feel normal.

"I haven't seen last semester's results, so I don't know."

By the time we hung up, she convinced me to get dressed and go check my grades. Although I didn't take any of my finals last term, maybe one of my alters did. If not, then there wouldn't be another semester for me.

The professors posted grades in the basement beneath the library near the lockers and student lounge. My heart skipped a beat when I found my student number on the Constitutional Law grades. By some miracle, I scored the highest grade. The same with Criminal Procedure. Whoever sat for the exams did better than I would have.

I didn't hold out hope for Taxation. That, by far, had been my most difficult class, especially with a midterm and final. When I found the list of grades, I closed my eyes.

Please, God, give me a passing grade.

What a silly prayer. God wasn't a law professor. When I found my student number on the posted grades, I decided miracles did happen. I didn't get the best grade in the class, but I somehow earned an A.

How could Mark or Wayne get an A in every one of my courses? They somehow kept me in school and protected my class rank.

Law school is all I have now. Is it enough? I hate being alone and broken.

Would things be different if I'd told Ethan everything after we first met?

Steve, are you kidding? You would've scared him away.

That would have been a good thing. I wish I'd never met him or convinced him to come back. So many shitty decisions in my shitty excuse of a shitty life.

When I returned to the apartment, I sat on the floor where the couch used to be, with my back against the wall.

Why did I go to law school? We were happy.

No, you were happy. Nobody wants to be in a sex-free relationship with someone who never pays attention to them.

If Nick had never called me about the LSAT, none of this would ever have happened.

Stop blaming Nick! This was all your fault, no one else's. You would have lost Ethan no matter what because you're a disgusting piece of trash.

I know.

Chapter 42

Bittersweet Finish

JANUARY 1992
DETROIT, MICHIGAN
AGE 32

When classes resumed in January, I applied for a $5,000 private loan through the law school. I needed money to get an apartment and help pay bills until the summer position started at HONIGMAN MILLER. Because of my low credit rating, I had to have a co-signer on the loan application. I telephoned Ethan.

"I'm not co-signing for you."

"Ethan, please. It's only five grand. You won't get stuck with it." I didn't want to get argumentative with him.

"Do you promise to pay it back?"

"Of course. Once I graduate, I'll have plenty of money."

I took the application to him at his sister's house, where he completed the form. Once I submitted the loan application, I tried to focus on classes and regain my confidence.

In mid-January, I bought a Doberman puppy and named him Rufio after the doomed character in the movie *Hook*. He reminded me of Major. The Farmington Hills apartment manager found out and threatened to evict me. I was moving, so I didn't give a shit.

The loan came through, and I located a pet-friendly place in Clawson near where Ethan and I first lived. Loading the rented moving truck with my furniture on February 1 made the break-up real—permanent—destroying any hope of salvaging our relationship.

I hadn't been able to eat much since the day he moved out. My diet consisted of Diet Coke, milk, and orange juice. When I forced myself to eat solid food, it wouldn't stay down long.

In the first two months of the semester, my weight dropped from 190 pounds to 140. I nodded off in my classes, and the notes I typed didn't make much sense. One day, a classmate—Diane—approached me.

"Steve, you have *got* to eat a cheeseburger. Seriously."

"I'm not hungry."

"Did I ask if you were hungry?"

Diane didn't give up. She and I served on the WAYNE LAW REVIEW together, but we had never been close until after that day. Her guidance, advice, persistence, and stubbornness got me eating again. After a few meals, I stopped vomiting. She saved my life—but eating didn't solve the reason behind my subconscious hunger strike. Losing Ethan had taken away my will to keep going, and not even Rufio could get me past that.

Diane and I latched onto each other. She invited me into her home to meet her husband, Brad, and three children. After that, I had dinner with them once a week or so. We spent more time around each other at law school, too. Having her as a friend meant a lot to me in my time of need.

With her encouragement, I also sought professional help. I contacted the mental health department at HENRY FORD HEALTH SYSTEM in Detroit, which set me up with a psychiatrist for antidepressant medication. That doctor then referred me to Dr. Fields—a psychiatric resident—for therapy. I finally had someone I could tell about my blackouts, my alters, and everything that had happened to me since childhood.

Except I didn't. I couldn't.

My deception continued—this time to someone I should have told everything. She could have helped me. I spent week after week talking to Dr. Fields about Ethan, law school, and my mother, but I left out all the other shit I'd been going through since the blackouts started. Even though I told her what the babysitter did to me in Kentucky, I didn't mention any of the assaults that happened after that. Embarrassment and shame won out—but that wasn't all.

Telling Dr. Fields the truth about *everything* would create a paper trail for people to find later. Once I finished law school, I'd have to disclose my psychiatric history when I applied for admission to the bar. I couldn't risk anyone discovering what my alters did—and what I did to conceal their debauchery and crimes. Dr. Fields might throw me into the loony bin, even though that's where I belonged.

So, I talked about everything *except* what mattered most.

Are you saying Ethan didn't matter most?

My alters are the reason he's gone.

No, you *are the reason he's gone.*

I survived the semester but did get an A- in professional responsibility—ethics. The irony wasn't lost on me. With only two A-grades thus far, I moved up a spot to number one in my class.

A bittersweet victory, at best.

My summer internship at HONIGMAN MILLER went well. I continued to socialize with Diane and her family. Inclusion made me feel part of their happy home. She had gotten a summer position with another of Detroit's top law firms.

Mark and Wayne didn't behave themselves over the summer. Waking up with strange men and finding extra money on my dresser became a regular routine. I tried not to let it affect my work, and I seemed to have succeeded.

In August, HONIGMAN MILLER offered me a permanent job to commence after graduation—which I accepted with mixed emotions. Working at the firm had been a dream because of what it would do for me and Ethan. I still loved and missed him. If he called and asked me back, I'd run to him without any hesitation.

Because you're a pitiful loser.

Wrong. I still love him.

One morning, shortly after the fall semester of my final year began, a professor pulled me aside in the hallway.

"Did you get an offer this summer?" she asked.

I leaned against the wall and nodded. "HONIGMAN MILLER."

"Fabulous, but you might want to rethink that. There's a prestigious Chicago firm looking for top graduates."

Did I want to interview for another job? In another city? I'd look like a douchebag if I changed my mind. Plus, I liked the HONIGMAN MILLER attorneys. They had been so easy to work for.

"I don't know. I've already committed."

"Mr. Simmons, you shouldn't pass up this opportunity. HONIGMAN MILLER is an exceptional firm, but Jenner & Block is one of the top law firms in the country. At least look at their posting. I think HONIGMAN MILLER would understand. Besides, you've earned it."

You can get away from all the bad memories here. It won't hurt to check them out.

"Thanks, I'll look into it."

I went to the career development office and found the Jenner & Block posting. The firm specialized in litigation and had 300 attorneys in their Chicago office.

What the hell. I might as well try.

Before noon, I faxed a cover letter, transcript, and résumé to them. The Jenner & Block hiring partner called me that evening with an invitation to visit them that Friday. She said they'd have a plane ticket waiting for me at Detroit Metro Airport. I telephoned Diane.

"What are your going to do if they offer you a job?" she asked.

"I'd be crazy to turn them down, don't you think?" Their starting pay and bonus were almost $20,000 more than HONIGMAN MILLER's. It would be more expensive to live in Chicago, but I needed a change—a fresh start.

Mark and Wayne will sure love it.

Early the following Friday, I flew into Chicago's O'Hare International Airport. After getting a map of downtown Chicago, I took the Blue Line train into the city and found IBM Plaza. I waited in the reception area on the forty-second floor. A dark-haired woman—a few years older than me and almost as tall—escorted me to her office.

For the next hour, I answered questions and asked a few of my own. I met several more partners and a few associates. The experience turned out to be quite pleasant. By the time I got home late in the afternoon, the hiring partner had left a message on my answering machine.

"Please call me," the message said, offering no other information.

My fingers shook as I pushed the numbers on my phone. We quickly dispensed with pleasantries, and she got right to the point.

"Steve, Jenner & Block would like to extend an offer for you to join the firm upon graduation. We'll cover your bar review course and bar exam expenses. We'll also set you up with a job to do pro bono work in Chicago until you get your license."

Hmm, what should I do?

"I'm going to say yes, but first I have to withdraw my acceptance from HONIGMAN MILLER."

"That's fair."

Surprisingly, at 5 p.m., I got in touch with the HONIGMAN MILLER hiring partner before he went home for the weekend.

"I'm sorry, but I have to withdraw my acceptance." My stomach tightened as I second-guessed giving up the job I'd wanted since I started law school. *Ethan's gone. Your future with him is dead. It's time to move on.*

"What on Earth for?"

"It has nothing to do with you," I said. "I went through a messy breakup in my second year. It's screwing with my head, and I have to get away from Detroit for a while."

Just for a while? Stop hanging on, Steve. Let it go.

"Understandable, but we hate to lose you. If you return to the area someday, please look us up."

As soon as I got off the phone with him, I called Jenner & Block. It was just after four o'clock Chicago time. The hiring partner answered her direct line.

"I officially accept the offer," I told her.

"Wonderful. We'll be in touch."

Steve, are you sure? You'll be leaving your new friends and an area you love.

I have to get out of Detroit and away from Ethan. I can't live near him as long as I'm miserable without him.

The next week, I learned that I'd received the Richard B. Gushee Writing Award for the best student work to be published in the WAYNE LAW REVIEW. It shocked me. Although I wrote an excellent piece, I expected someone else's would be better.

How can you be so screwed up and still cruise through law school?

By December, my finances reached a critical point. My car payment and insurance costs—thanks to the DUI—became unsustainable. Because the dealership wouldn't take the car back without me paying the balance of the lease, I filed Chapter 7 bankruptcy.

The court served all my creditors with the filing—including the company where Ethan co-signed for my $5,000 loan. I braced for the fallout from that. After all, I still loved the guy and didn't want him to suffer because of my financial problems.

How can you still love him after what he did and said?

Because he was right.

At the apartment one evening in February, the phone rang. I figured it either was someone looking for Wayne or the phone call I'd been dreading.

"Hello?"

"Bankruptcy? Really?"

The yelling made my ear ring. I sat on the bed because I knew the call would get nasty. When I rested my head on the pillow, I closed my eyes and wished he was here.

"Ethan, I had no choice. It was the only way I could get rid of the car without them coming after me for the rest."

"Didn't you give any thought to the five-thousand-dollar loan? They want it *now.*"

"I'm sorry, I really am." The guilt nauseated me. No matter what had happened, he didn't deserve to get stuck with my debt.

"You *promised* you'd pay it off. *Promised.*"

"Are you listening to me? There was nothing I could do—unless you wanted me to be homeless."

Why do you feel so bad? Stick it to the asshole.

But I still love him.

You're not getting him back, so why do you care?

Because I don't want to hurt him.

"Your word's not worth anything, is it?" he asked. "You make promises and then do whatever you want. And you wonder why I left you."

He's right, you know. Everything is your fault.

Why is he being so cruel? It's not like I wanted to file bankruptcy.

Ethan's words came back to me—the cruel ones from last Christmas when I reminded him of his assurance that we'd always be together.

"Yes, I promised, just like you promised we'd always be together. Guess what, and this should sound familiar to you. *Things change.*"

When he hung up on me, I laughed for the first time in months before I realized how much I'd hurt and betrayed him.

The dean let me know in May before graduation that I would be finishing first in my class and that the faculty had voted me *summa cum laude.* Someone said the vote had been unanimous, but that was just a rumor.

All my life, I found it difficult to brag about anything or feel confident in what I did. Despite the blackouts and the breakup, I won the top moot court, law review, and academic awards—the first person ever to do so at the law school. I did the impossible under conditions that should have crushed me.

But all the accolades turned out to be hollow. With Ethan gone, the reason for going to law school vanished.

On May 5, 1993, at Masonic Temple in Detroit, I walked across the stage and proudly accepted my diploma as *summa cum laude* graduate of WAYNE STATE UNIVERSITY LAW SCHOOL. Before I left Detroit, I got a copy of my law school transcript and tracked down Mike Pfau's address. I put the transcript in the mail to him along with a note.

See, motherfucker, I don't have to cheat to make the top grades. I'm still smarter than you.

Steve Simmons

Chapter 43

Debauchery and Murder

July 31, 1993
Chicago, Illinois
Age 33

Rufio ran on and off the love seat, around the dining room table, over me as I sat at the end of the sleeper sofa, back to the floor, and then on the love seat again. I learned to let him release the energy however he could as long as he didn't break too many things.

I lucked out finding the 801 South Wells apartment building. The area just south of Chicago's Loop had everything I needed—including a small pet supplies store. Living with a Doberman on the fifth floor had its challenges, but it had worked out thus far.

The weekend was the first free one since taking the Illinois bar exam. I had no problem with any of the questions, but I wouldn't find out until October if I passed. My concern had to do with the Character and Fitness Committee. I had the DUI from 1991 and bankruptcy during my last semester of law school. Just so I wouldn't get caught lying, I also disclosed my minor-in-possession conviction from 1977 as well as the shoplifting convictions from 1979 and 1984. Even though I didn't want to tell them about getting caught for Mark's petty theft, I had to because lying to the Committee would be worse.

You're not telling them about your mental disorder and the McDonald's burglary, so you're still lying to them.

If I tell them the truth, they'll never let me practice law.

Rufio finally ended his sprints with a sloppy, noisy drink from his bowl. Then he jumped on the couch and rested his head on my lap.

I stroked his ears. Within a few minutes, his breathing deepened, and he fell asleep. Soon his eyes began to flutter, and his legs twitched. *What are you dreaming about? Hopefully, it's better than the ones I have.*

Nightmares haunted me. I wasn't sure which ones were worse: reliving Ethan leaving me, seeing the baseball bat shoved up Gary's ass, and having my face plastered against a concrete-block wall while getting brutally raped. In one dream, I kept squeezing Kevin's neck until the only sound he made was a death rattle.

I slipped out from under Rufio and wandered to the kitchen for my nightly ritual. Even though I'd tell myself, "Only one glass," I wouldn't stop until after three or four. Wine from the box's spigot filled my glass in no time.

There I was, home alone on a Saturday night, watching my LaserDisc version of *Terminator 2: Judgment Day*, and drinking wine while sitting on the couch with my dog. It could be worse, I guess.

I got up to get my second glass of wine when the familiar dizziness hit for the first time since I moved to the Windy City.

Oh, shit. Here we go.

The smell hit me first—a mixture of odors I knew all too well. Wayne had previously ventured into the world of group sex and BDSM in Detroit when I was in graduate school. That was BT—Before Tiffany's. My slutty alter had a knack for giving me the reins while being whipped, tortured, or tied-up in a sex sling.

This time, he deposited me on a stool inside a closet with gloryholes on three sides. Men on the other side of two holes had their junk planted in the grip of my hands. From the taste in my mouth, I concluded that Wayne had been busy. At least I had my clothes on—a T-shirt and pair of light gray tennis shorts.

I released the gentlemen and opened the door.

Holy shit, Wayne. You found the mother lode of debauchery.

My booth was merely one in an entire row of them. In front of me, a naked old man stood in a cage, a spiked black dog collar around his neck. A spiral staircase descended to a lower floor. Dozens of men filled the area around me.

Wayne, where the hell did you dump me?

Curious and stimulated at the same time, I ventured around to explore. Down a long hallway, I found a theatre room with hardcore gay porn playing on the screen. Men of various ages, sizes, races, ethnic backgrounds, and states of dress busied themselves in the seats and along the walls. Sodom and Gomorrah were amateur locations compared to this place.

A hand squeezed my ass, causing me to clench and turn. An attractive man smiled back at me—maybe an inch taller, near my age, slim, with his hair in braids hanging nearly to his shoulders.

"Hello, handsome," he said. "Haven't seen you here before."

"Oh, thank God."

For a second, I half expected him to call me "Wayne" and wonder where I'd been. I hadn't noticed any missing time in the nearly three months since moving to Chicago, but I didn't trust my alters. If they wanted to hide something from me, they usually found a way.

"An odd response," he said, one eyebrow raised. "You from out of town?"

"I just moved here. I'm not sure what to make of this place."

His eye contact made me feel both self-conscious and excited. We stood next to each other and watched the porn for a few minutes. Not knowing where this would go, I checked my pockets for condoms. Nothing. *Damn you, Wayne. What were you thinking?*

"Did you lose something?" the guy asked.

"Nah, was seeing if I brought something."

"Poppers?"

He held up a little brown bottle. Amyl nitrite. Based on my prior experience, sniffing it would override all my inhibitions and judgment—something I desperately needed while also wanting to avoid.

Giving in to temptation, I removed the lid and inhaled deeply with each nostril.

The effects hit me at once.

Steve, what are you doing? Go home. Nothing good can come of this, and you don't have any protection.

I handed the bottle to the guy, and he took a couple of whiffs. When he nodded toward an open door to a private booth, I followed. *One only lives once, right? When in Rome....*

We had fun, and I needed it. When we finished, I descended the stairs to the bottom floor. The exit took me through a theatre where a nude man masturbated on stage while men sat in the audience.

I have to leave. This is wrong.

When I got outside, I found a cab across the street and gave the driver my address. As we pulled away, I looked back at the sign of the establishment where I just had unprotected sex with someone who never told me his name.

BIJOU.

I never heard of it.

At my apartment, Rufio greeted me silently at the door. I threw my clothes in the hamper, douched a few times, took a quick shower, and brushed my teeth—twice. When I crawled into bed, I glanced at the clock. The sun would be up in three hours. I set the alarm for 7 a.m. and drifted off to sleep.

Dumping me in the Bijou became a regular thing for Wayne to do. He also had a penchant for area bookstores. My fear of getting sick weighed heavily on me.

Why doesn't he understand the need to use condoms? We're gonna get HIV if he keeps this up.

Steve, you're just as guilty.

I know, but what does it matter? I'll always be a worthless whore.

Then why worry about getting sick? Just enjoy yourself.

Ironically, during the summer, I worked at AIDS LEGAL COUNCIL OF CHICAGO to provide *pro bono* legal services to people with AIDS or HIV.

My job at the Jenner & Block offices began in September. The Illinois Bar Association granted my law license on November 4. My first assignment was "document review"—going through a client's files to find documents for a lawsuit—which comprised almost all my billable hours. At night, Mark or Wayne took over and did whatever they wanted. Most nights I got no more than a couple hours of sleep.

On February 4, 1994, I awoke before sunrise. While my bagel toasted, I jumped in the shower for a quick rinse to wake me up. I didn't know what time Wayne or Mark got us home, but I needed more shuteye.

How much longer can I keep this up? Every night. Every damned night. Between the two of them, I never get enough sleep. I'll run out of luck eventually. Either Wayne will get us infected with HIV or Mark will get us killed while trying to steal something.

After walking Rufio in the freezing cold, I caught the River City shuttle, which dropped me on East Wacker across the Chicago River from IBM Plaza. I walked into my office at 7:30 a.m. to find on my chair an assignment due by the end of the day. No document review for me—although I'd rather be looking through documents than updating citations for a five-year-old brief.

By noon, I'd finished the brief, so I sat at my desk to eat a tuna sandwich I bought off the lunch cart. I almost dropped my Diet Pepsi when the phone rang.

"Hey, Steve. It's Sarah. You'd better sit down."

I hadn't heard from my law school classmate since graduation. She and I survived law review, HONIGMAN MILLER, and the Cedar Point roller coasters together. Her voice sounded flat, strained.

"What's wrong?"

"It's Diane Arnold's husband, Brad. He's been murdered."

"What?"

"It happened in Mexico. They found his body yesterday. That's all I know."

How could he be murdered? Although I managed to hang up the receiver, it happened in slow motion.

"Nooooooo."

I shoved everything off my desk and threw random things against the wall. With papers flying everywhere, I kicked client files that were stacked on the floor next to my desk. My office chair fell over, and I pushed it into the door with my foot. As I tried to do the same thing to a box of documents, I slipped and fell onto the mess, my arms and legs flailing and kicking. Then I curled in a fetal position and couldn't stop crying.

The familiar dizziness hit me, and I welcomed it like a large glass of wine. *Thank you.*

———————

I "awoke" in a hotel room two miles south of Diane's West Bloomfield home. At least Wayne left me a detailed note explaining what he did.

When I had my breakdown after learning about Brad, Wayne took over. He straightened up my office and told the firm I'd need at least a week off. After boarding Rufio, my virile doppelganger drove us to Farmington Hills, Michigan, where he switched back to me.

Diane had so much to deal with that I stayed out of her way. I did what I could to distract her kids and make sure everyone ate. The day after Brad's funeral, I bid Diane farewell and returned to Chicago. The Arnolds had always been kind to me and served as an adopted family.

Yet, you lie to them and keep secrets.

They'll cut me loose as a friend if they know the things I've done—and continue to do.

Steve, when it all comes tumbling down—and it will—they're going to find out anyway. Then it'll be too late for you.

Going back to work after more than a week in Michigan seemed senseless. My job had no point. All I did was help corporations to get more money or keep their coffers full. When I decided to become a lawyer, I never realized the career would be so tedious and unfulfilling. I had done nothing worthwhile since joining the firm.

You had everything and gave it up. You traded Ethan for a life you hate.

I know, and I'll never forgive myself for it.

Chapter 44

No Way Out

Mom and Dad surprised us last week with a brand-new tri-hull boat and a camping trailer that would sleep all five of us. They said we would no longer have to take the big tent and cots camping, but I'd have to share a bed in the camper with Mike.

"Can we take the smaller tent for me and Major?"

"Don't you want to sleep in the camper?" Mom asked. "We can tie him up outside to watch the campground."

"That's mean. I'd rather sleep in the tent so he can stay with me." *Will she really tie him up outside where he's all alone? That's not very nice.*

Dad backed the boat onto the carport and the trailer on our front lawn. It gave me an idea. "Mom, can I move into the camping trailer?" *Steve, you're crazy. She'll never go for it.*

When she tilted her head and scrunched her forehead, I thought she was gonna yell at me. "Move into the camper? Why?"

"I just thought it would be nice to have my own room. Major can sleep with me."

"Okay, but put your plastic sheet on the bed."

I spent Saturday cleaning the inside, running an extension cord to an outlet, on the carport, and adding a small space heater. I happily let my brother have our bedroom all to himself.

The first night in my new room, Major conked out right away. He kept me warm enough that I didn't have to turn on the heater. I slept better than I had in a long time—and I didn't pee the bed.

I still ate, watched TV, and showered in the house, but I slept and did my homework in the camper. The 14'x8' living space made me feel safer and at ease than I ever had—other than when I stayed with Aunt Estelle and Uncle Cliff.

A few days later, I overheard Mom and Dad talking about going to Blue Mountain with the Winslows again this year. Jeffrey continued to be a problem, expecting to do sex things when he came around the house or when we camped together. He always found ways to get us alone—and I couldn't resist his requests. I didn't look forward to another summer of that.

One Monday before school let out for the semester, a note fell from my locker when I opened it. I grabbed the piece of paper off the floor before anyone else could. Once I got settled in class, I read the message.

> *Billy will pick you up in front of the gym after the buses*
> *leave. Don't be late.*

My stomach tightened. *Please, God, not again. What am I going to do?* I ripped the paper into tiny pieces and stuck the remnants into my science book.

Damn. Will it ever end?

Steve, you have to tell someone.

Who? If this gets out, I'll be humiliated. They'll call me all sorts of names.

They call you names now! Tell Coach. He'll know what to do.

He'll see the pictures and think I'm a homo.

Had you rather be raped?

No, but what choice do I have?

Chapter 45

Three Dogs

R ufio and Dallas chased each other through the knee-high grasses in the field next to River City. After we braved the sub-freezing temperatures at the end of November, the 50° Fahrenheit weather seemed like a heatwave.

I rescued Dallas—another Doberman—in August. His growth had been stunted as a puppy because the breeders abused and neglected him. The authorities shut down the breeder, and I got a playmate for Rufio.

The dogs finally got their exercise, so we headed back to the apartment. As we crossed the street, a barking sound caught my attention. A homeless guy was beating his yellow Labrador retriever with his cane. I'd seen him with the dog several times before and had even given him a small bag of food.

"*Hey, stop.*" Even if the dog *was* his, I couldn't stand idly by and let him abuse it.

My two Dobermans took off toward him, dragging me along as they strained the leashes. The homeless man took off, leaving the injured dog tied to a pole. Michelle—a woman in my apartment building—arrived and checked the dog while I held onto mine. She owned two Rhodesian Ridgebacks who were dog show champions.

"He's cut on his back in a few places," she said. "And there's some blood on his head. I think he needs stitches."

"Can you watch him for a couple of minutes?" I said. "My vet closes in an hour. I'll take these two to the apartment and come back for him."

She nodded, so I took Rufio and Dallas to the apartment. I grabbed an old collar and leash for the injured dog. Fortunately, the vet worked until 1 p.m. on Saturday, and we could walk there in a few minutes. The Lab let me put the collar on him and remove the rope. He walked the three blocks with me, staying by my side the entire time.

The veterinarian took us back right away. He stitched up three cuts and gave the dog two shots—antibiotics and the rabies vaccine.

"He's malnourished, but in good shape," the vet said.

"How old do you think he is?"

"No more than two. He's intact, too, so you should think about neutering him."

We scheduled surgery for Monday morning. I couldn't return him to the homeless guy, and I refused to take him to a shelter. If I could integrate him with Rufio and Dallas, I'd keep him. I never wanted three dogs, but the universe had other plans.

The vet put a plastic cone around the Lab's head, and I walked him back to my building. I couldn't bring him to the apartment without all three dogs first meeting and interacting in a neutral place. I stopped by Michelle's place on the fourth floor.

"I'll keep him, if possible," I said, "but I have to see if he and my two get along. Can you help me introduce them?"

"Of course."

She took the Lab outside to the field, and I met her there with mine. They did the expected sniffing and rubbing—but, surprisingly, still no growling. His being intact concerned me. If it made him aggressive even after the neutering, I wouldn't be able to keep him. Fortunately, the three got along quite well. But how would they react in the apartment?

After letting them play together in the field for a half hour, Michelle and I took them to my place. All three walked in, and my two didn't show any territorial aggressiveness whatsoever.

We let them off the leash, and I held my breath. The Lab sniffed around the apartment while mine watched.

God, please don't let him pee to mark his territory.

About fifteen seconds later, Dallas took off and the other two went in pursuit—over the living room furniture and around tables. Cushions went flying. Michelle patted me on the back and laughed.

"You'll never be able to own anything nice," she said.

"Shit. I guess I have another dog."

You keep saving others, Steve. When are you going to save yourself?

Chapter 46

Paranoia

T he nurse took my blood pressure while the doctor shined a light in my eyes. They told me the name of the hospital, but I forgot it already. When the medical personnel stepped out, a uniformed police officer appeared. He looked to be in his thirties, maybe younger.

"Mr. Simmons, can you tell me what happened tonight?"

"Officer, I was gonna ask you the same thing." Each word caused a sharp stab in my head.

"So, you don't remember?"

"If I could remember, I wouldn't be asking you."

"Mr. Simmons, I'm just trying to help. What's the last thing you remember?"

"Leaving work on Friday. I'm an attorney at Jenner & Block."

The officer laughed. I didn't think it was particularly funny, but maybe he didn't like attorneys.

"Are you sure it was Friday?"

Uh, oh. I should have first asked what today is.

The nurse returned to take my blood pressure. Only then did I notice the IV in my right arm, the bag hanging next to the bed.

"Officer, could you cut to the chase? What happened to me?"

"You were found unconscious on a sidewalk across the street from Ann Sather Restaurant on West Belmont around 2 a.m. Do you remember being there?"

"I'm in that area often."

"But you have no memory of being there tonight?"

"I already told you that. I can't remember shit."

A cute doctor walked up and shined a flashlight in my eyes. "You suffered a concussion. I'm not surprised you have memory loss."

If he only knew the extent of things I didn't remember, then we'd be having a different conversation. The concussion gave me a great excuse, which I found to be quite ironic.

"A witness said a man stepped out of an alcove and punched you," the officer said. "He then proceeded to kick you until someone intervened. You're a very lucky man."

Lucky? I'm lying in a hospital emergency room after being assaulted. I'm not sure what's so lucky about any of it.

"What day is this?" I asked.

"It's four-thirty on Sunday morning," the officer said.

Holy crap. I hope it's the Sunday after I left work. If I asked for the date, it might look weird. It could be the Arkansas foreign language competition all over again.

Then I remembered my watch. I would look silly checking the date, so I decided to wait until nobody could see me.

"The guy must have hit me real hard."

The officer laughed and gave me a business card. He'd written something on the back.

"Leave a message if you think of anything. The number on the back is for the police report. Have a good day."

I closed my eyes and tried to recall something—anything—that would explain what happened. Nothing came to mind.

The hospital released me back into the wild at sunrise. I found a cab near the ER and went home. According to my watch.

Damn, I hope the dogs went out Saturday. Surely Mark or Wayne would at least do that.

Rufio, Dallas, and Armand nearly knocked me down when I opened the door. I didn't smell any messes, so they had to have gone out the day before. I put on their leashes and took them to the field across the street. In seven months, Armand had become a well-loved member of the family. The homeless guy who beat him hadn't been around since the rescue.

The weather was so nice, they didn't want to come in. One mention of food, though, and they nearly dragged me back to the apartment.

My head throbbed, and the pain medication was wearing off, but at least I could lie in my own bed. After showering, I took some Tylenol and crawled under the covers. As the bed sloshed around, I couldn't get my mind off the assault.

Was it a random incident, or did someone target me? If they assaulted me specifically, then why?

You know the answer to that. It has to be because of Mark or Wayne.

I hope it was random. If it wasn't, they'll come after me again.

Chapter 47

Targeted

T he switching got worse after my ER visit in June. From the time I got home from work each day until the moment my alarm went off in the morning, Wayne or Mark usually had control. Many times, I didn't even make it home before one of them took over.

On Saturday, July 22, I decided to socialize with the firm's summer associates—law students between their second and third years. I'd become friends with a few of them, including Dani, a woman from the Chicago area. She and four others came over to my apartment for drinks and to watch *Star Trek: Generations* on LaserDisc. We had a great evening gossiping, drinking wine, and talking about their future. Dani invited everyone to her nearby apartment for the following Saturday.

Almost immediately after the summer associates left at 11 p.m., I blacked out and didn't "wake up" until 2:30 a.m.—in the hallway outside my apartment. Either Wayne went gloryhole trolling at the Bijou or Mark had been up to no good. I wanted to take a shower and hit the sheets. When I pushed the door open, I detected something very wrong: my dogs didn't greet me.

"Rufio? Dallas? Armand?"

They still didn't run to me, but I heard whimpering and scratching behind my closed bedroom door. How could they have gotten in there? I never let them in there because their sharp nails could pierce the waterbed. Did Mark or Wayne put the dogs in there before they left? If so, why?

Cautious, I stepped farther into the apartment and stopped when I got past the bathroom. The beveled-glass top to my dining room table had shattered. Thousands of glass pieces covered the carpet. I checked the bedroom to make sure my three "kids" were okay. Until I cleared the glass fragments, I couldn't let them out. I canvassed the apartment to make sure the person who broke my table had gone. Convinced the vandal had left, I picked up the phone and dialed 9-1-1.

Two uniformed officers—a man and woman—arrived twenty minutes later. They inspected the door and looked around the apartment. Then one watched me while the other asked questions.

"Were you home when this occurred?"

"No. I was out and got home about two-thirty."

"Did you leave your door unlocked when you left?"

"It locks automatically when it closes."

"Does anyone else have a key?"

"Only the building manager." I didn't like where the questions were headed.

"The door and lock haven't been tampered with. How did someone get in?"

Good question, and one I couldn't answer, unless—

Did Mark or Wayne destroy the table? To what end? Is it possible one of them lost their temper?

All I could do was shrug. The officers looked at each other.

"You said someone put your dogs in the bedroom. What kind of dogs do you have?

Oh, great. This is the question that will bring their investigation to a close. It's also a question that points in a direction I have to consider.

"Two Doberman Pinschers and a Labrador retriever."

The moment of silence that followed made me want to hide.

"Mr. Simmons, have you been drinking tonight?"

"It's Saturday night. What do you think?"

"How much?"

"Two glasses of wine." I had no idea how many drinks Mark or Wayne had wherever they went.

The officers gave me a card with a number to call for a copy of the police report. Once they left, I got the broom and three trash bags that I put inside each other. Maybe the glass wouldn't puncture them. As soon as I began sweeping up the mess, I jumped back.

No, it can't be.

The pile of glass had concealed a hammer that looked just like the one I kept in the bedroom closet. How did it get there?

Steve, to be so intelligent, you're actually quite stupid. How the fuck do you think it got there?

It took me more than an hour to clear the floor of glass. The vacuum cleaner removed the smaller shards. Convinced I had gotten it all, I let the dogs out and checked my toolbox in the bedroom closet. As suspected, my hammer was gone.

There's only one thing that makes sense. Whoever destroyed my table has a key to the apartment—and my dogs know them.

Just stop, Steve. If it walks like an alter and talks like an alter, it's your fucking alter.

Fine. Mark or Wayne did it. But why?

If one of them did do it, they had to have a reason. I also had to consider that someone had it out for me. My dogs might let someone come in if they'd once been here with any of us three.

Okay, Wayne and Mark, did one of you do it? If not, did one of you give a key to someone?

On Monday, I paid the apartment management to change the lock on my door. If someone did have a key, it would be worthless now.

Steve, they can still get into the building with the old key.

That evening, I had the three dogs on leashes as I walked around the building. Michelle headed toward us on the same sidewalk with her older dog. Our dogs had played in the field together and never showed aggressiveness toward each other. As we passed her, Armand jumped Michelle's dog unprovoked. Then he lunged at her as I tried to pull him back.

"*Armand, stop.*" I dragged my three away from Michelle and her dog. In the kerfuffle, Armand bit Michelle's dog several times. Armand then aimed his growling and snapping toward Rufio. Dallas hid behind me.

"*Armand, no.*" He sat and whimpered. I turned to Michelle. "Take your dog to the vet now. Of course, I'll pay for everything."

I pulled out my wallet and gave her my Visa card. *Please let him be okay.*

She took off with her bleeding dog while I took my three upstairs. Rufio had one superficial cut I treated with a triple antibiotic. Dallas suffered no injuries. Once in the apartment, Armand ran to the couch.

The vet had told me to watch Armand for possible outbursts because he was abused, I never expected it to happen—especially after all these months. I loved my dogs so much that I'd never harm them, but Armand's sudden change worried me.

You know what you have to do.

I can't do that. I just can't.

You have to.

The next morning, I called my administrative assistant to say I'd be late to the office. Then I gave Armand a big hug and attached the leash. As I walked him through the Printer's Row area, he was rambunctious and happy. I couldn't stop crying.

How could I keep an unpredictable dog around Rufio, Dallas, and others in the building? Armand wagged his tail and seemed so content now, but he could turn into a killer for whatever reason.

When I got to the veterinarian's lobby, the doctor came out.

"Steve, you're doing the right thing. He could hurt or kill another dog or, worse, a person. Do you want to come back to be with him while I do it?"

"I'm sorry, but I can't."

Because you're a fucking coward.

I am.

The lovely dog had become part of my family. Somehow, I failed him. As I walked home alone—bawling like a newborn—I kept telling myself that Armand might not attack again, that I didn't have to put him down.

But what if you're wrong?

The next day, Dani went with me to the animal shelter where I adopted a Doberman/Rottweiler mix I named Gabrielle—Gabby for short. Impulsive, yes, but I told myself, "Take a life, save a life."

Unmotivated to do any work, I went through the motions the rest of the week. One of the junior partners—Thomas—had given me an assignment on Wednesday to write a legal brief by Friday. I made little headway on it. Having Armand killed ate away at me.

You failed him. He loved you, and you let him down.

I know, and I didn't even go back to say good-bye.

I concluded by Friday I'd overreacted in putting down Armand but would have to live with the decision. At 5 p.m., I went down a floor to the conference room where the firm had "happy hour" each week. I needed a glass of wine and snack before heading home. Just my luck, I ran into Thomas at the bottom of the stairs.

"Where's my brief?" he asked.

"Sorry. It'll be on your desk first thing Monday."

He shook his head and walked away. My constant fuck-ups at work would be my undoing. I grabbed a plastic cup and filled it two-thirds full of Cabernet. Dani caught me as I headed to the sandwich table.

"Don't forget about the party tomorrow."

Dammit, I almost did. "I'll be there. Do I need to bring anything?"

"Nope. Just you."

Even though I liked the summer associates—especially Dani—I didn't want to go. But she had accompanied me to the animal shelter on Tuesday, so I could at least attend her get-together. I filled a plate with snacks and returned to my office.

After working at the firm all day Saturday, I went home and showered before Dani's party. At least she lived only five minutes away by cab. I got to her Presidential Towers apartment at 8 p.m. With the 90° Fahrenheit temperature outside, the cab's air conditioning didn't keep me very cool. I welcomed the frigid air when I stepped into the high rise's lobby.

The evening passed quickly, and I had a blast. We played spades, drank wine, and gossiped even more than before. Just before midnight, I bid them adieu and left. I stood on the street looking for a cab.

"Hey. I wanna talk to you."

A man yelled from about fifty yards away. He headed in my direction on the sidewalk. Instead of escaping to the Presidential Towers, I crossed the street to flag an approaching cab. It drove past me, leaving me vulnerable. The man stepped into the street and blocked my route back to the apartment complex. I froze as he drew nearer, my feet unwilling to run in any direction.

Oh, no. Is he gonna drag me behind a building and rape me? Will he stab me as soon as he reaches me? Maybe he has a gun. Why can't I move?

"Why are you bothering me? I don't even know you."

"You don't *know* me? That's a joke. We got some things to settle."

"Tell me what you want?" It had to be because of something Mark or Wayne did.

The man approached me, crossing the lanes and getting closer.

Chapter 48

Damaged

July 1995
Chicago, Illinois
Age 35

Every slight movement of my head caused an explosion from the neck up. I opened my eyes to the sight of a white ceiling. I turned my head a little sideways and regretted it at once.

"Hel—"

Damn. I can't even speak without my head exploding. What the fuck happened?

My right hand held something, maybe a remote control. I found a button and pushed it. With luck, it would notify a nurse. I waited for eternity—at least it seemed that way.

"You're awake. Good."

A woman I couldn't see very well stood next to my bed. She had dark hair, but that's about all I could discern. Without my glasses, I was practically blind.

"Mr. Simmons, I'm Nurse Owens. Do you know where you are?"

"Hospital." When I whispered it, my head didn't hurt as badly.

"Are you in pain?" the nurse said, checking my vitals.

Talk about an understatement. It hurt worse than the tonsillectomy I had a year earlier.

"Hell yes. Head."

"I'll be right back."

Millennia later, she returned—at least I believe it was the same one. She had dark hair like the other nurse.

"I'm adding Toradol through your IV. You should be feeling the effects almost immediately."

My body buzzed all over and had a sense of floating. It didn't stop all the pain in my head, but it helped.

"How do you feel now?"

"Better." I tried to focus. "Where am I?"

"You're in the ICU of Northwestern Memorial Hospital. I'll be right back with the doctor."

Sure, you will. Several days later—okay, it seemed that long—a young doctor with black bushy hair appeared next to the bed.

"Glad to see you're awake. I'm Doctor Singh. Mr. Simmons, an ambulance brought you in early Sunday morning."

"What is today?"

"It's Monday. You were unconscious and unresponsive when you arrived here. An MRI found a subdural hematoma in the left frontal lobe. You're currently in the ICU. We're taking you for another MRI in a few minutes to see if the hematoma is expanding."

True to his word, two orderlies showed up and wheeled me away—and out of the hospital, pushing me across the street to another building. When we got to a room with the MRI, a man injected me with a sedative. I must have fallen asleep after that because I awoke back in the hospital. Then again, maybe I switched and didn't notice.

I again pushed the call button in my right hand. *Oh, God, the dogs. Don't forget about the dogs.*

"Did you need something, Mr. Simmons?" a nurse said.

"Dogs. I have dogs. And I have to call work."

"You're not doing anything. Tell me who to call and what to say."

The nurse brought a phone in and called my apartment building. With Michelle's help, the manager arranged to have my dogs boarded at Burnham Park Animal Hospital. Then the nurse called my administrative assistant at Jenner & Block to let her know I was in intensive care.

With that taken care of, I drifted off to sleep.

The next morning, Dani paid me a surprise visit. My memory still had holes, but I remembered more than I did the day before. About the incident, though, all I recalled was the guy yelling at me and crossing the street. After that, nothing.

"I feel horrible you had just left my place," Dani said.

"Nonsense. It could have happened anywhere."

Yeah, especially if someone is out to get you. Since the police didn't catch the guy, I will still be in danger once I get out of the hospital.

"I still feel bad. Why would someone do this?"

"No idea."

Liar. It's likely the same person who vandalized your apartment and beat you up on Belmont. You might not know why, but you know it's because of your doppelgangers.

Dani stayed for a while, but I couldn't say how long. As soon as she left, I pushed the nurse call button and waited.

God, please let it be Toradol time.

The doctor stopped by my room on the morning of August 7—day sixteen in the hospital. I'd been transferred to a regular room a few days earlier.

"Mr. Simmons, it all looks good. The subdural hematoma stabilized without the need for subdural evacuation."

"What's that?"

"Surgery. You were truly fortunate."

"Tell my head that." I had the nurse keep the curtains closed because bright light pierced my eyes like a lightsaber to the head.

"I'm sending you home today with three prescriptions—a two-week supply of corticosteroids to control brain swelling, a month supply of Toradol for pain, and a prescription of Tegretol to control seizures. I made an appointment for you—"

"Seizures? I haven't been having seizures."

"You had generalized tonic–clonic seizures—"

"Four *what?*"

"Grand mal seizures. You had four in the first twenty-four hours after admission. You've also been having absence seizures—petit mal seizures—since then."

Damn. What's gonna happen to me?

Face it, Steve. Part of your brain died because of the injury. Maybe it's the part with Mark and Wayne. If anything positive comes from this, that will be it.

The injury left me with persistent vertigo, so I had to use a cane. So many thoughts swirled around in my mangled mind. *Will I be able to play tennis or softball again? Can I walk the dogs?* When it came down to it, those two things were more important than returning to work. That told me a lot about the career I'd pursued at the cost of my relationship with Ethan.

Why do you keep thinking that? Your lies and deception about your mental disorder destroyed your relationship.

The discharge nurse showed up to my room at 10:15 a.m. with a bunch of papers to sign, some pills to take home, and prescriptions for my pharmacy.

"Someone will have to pick you up."

I laughed, which I regretted at once when my head began throbbing.

"Nurse, there isn't anyone who can pick me up," I said. "Either send me home in a taxi, or one of you can drive me there."

Since I hadn't been mugged, I still had money in my wallet—at least enough for a cab.

"Who'll be staying with you at home?"

"Rufio, Dallas, and Armand. Uh, I mean Gabby. Armand is no longer with us."

"That's good. Roommates?"

"Yes, the four-legged kind. Two Dobermans and a mutt."

The nurse told me I couldn't be alone for a few days. I laughed again at the expense of my head.

"That's not happening."

They put me in a cab, which let me off in front of my apartment building just before noon. With Michelle's help, I went to get Rufio, Dallas, and Gabby after lunch. They almost knocked me down when the veterinary tech brought them to the lobby. I got on my knees so the three of us could have a hug. They soaked me in licks, and I loved it.

I maxed out my credit cards paying for the boarding. Thankfully, my excellent health insurance covered my entire hospital stay—including the ambulance. If Mark and Wayne would stop draining my bank account, I could afford to pay everything off in a month or so.

As requested by the hospital, I followed up with my primary care physician a few days later. She referred me to a neurologist who would test my cognitive abilities. After two weeks, he cleared me for work.

A week after returning to the firm, my right wrist hurt so bad I couldn't turn a doorknob. I thought using the cane caused the pain. My doctor had an X-ray taken.

"It's a broken scaphoid in your right wrist," she said.

"How's that possible?"

"It's a common injury when someone falls. They instinctively put out their arms to catch themselves. It must have happened in the assault, and the steroids masked the injury until you stopped taking them."

Of course. The assault was the gift that keeps on giving.

She referred me to a specialist at Northwestern Memorial Hospital. I couldn't seem to stay away from that place. In late September, I had wrist surgery and returned to work a few days later—with a cast from my bicep to my knuckles. I'd ordered a signature stamp before surgery because I wouldn't be able to sign documents with my right hand for several weeks.

On the positive side, I expected the cast to keep Mark and Wayne at bay for a while.

You hope it does.

Chapter 49

Challenges

Mom and I finished cleaning the lunch dishes when Dad walked in. He wore a nice pair of jeans—meaning no holes or grease—and a short-sleeved dress shirt I had never seen before. He never wore clothes like that on a Saturday.

"I'm going to Bud's for a couple of hours. He's working on his car and needs help."

That couldn't be right, but I kept my mouth shut. Dad had been acting weird for weeks. He worked late almost every day, rushed to answer the phone when it rang, stopped smoking, and started wearing cologne. But he would never, *ever* wear good clothes to help someone work on their car.

In the past few weeks, Mom and Dad argued about everything—and I expected one to start in the kitchen with me trapped between them. Mom remained surprisingly quiet. Dad glanced toward her when he opened the door to the carport. It slammed behind him. I put down the dish towel and turned to leave the kitchen.

"Steven, follow him and see if he goes to Bud's."

What the hell? "How? On my bike?"

"Yes."

I nodded, raced out the door, and jumped on my ten-speed. If I ever had to choose sides between my parents, I'd pick Mom's every time. Dad and I never talked or did anything together. Why would I want to live with someone who treated me like furniture?

Peddling as fast as possible, I followed at a distance. He turned left, left, and right, which was exactly how you'd get to Bud's house from ours. Instead of pulling into his friend's driveway, though, Dad drove past it and turned right a block later. At first, I thought he would double back, but he didn't. I waited another ten minutes before heading home.

I found Mom sitting at the table with a cigarette dangling from her lips. In front of her, another cancer stick burned in an ashtray next to her purse.

"He drove past Bud's and turned right two blocks later. I don't know where he went after that."

"That's okay. I know where the son-of-a-bitch is."

She snuffed out the extra cigarette, grabbed her purse, and left, slamming the carport door behind her.

Mom and Dad returned a half hour later screaming at each other. I hightailed out the back door where Major got excited to see me. Hunched below the kitchen window, I listened. It seemed Mom found Dad at her beautician's house—in bed together.

Their argument scared me because I thought they would start hitting each other. I took Major around to the front of the house and into the camper. With the door locked, I cracked one of the windows to see if I could still hear them. Two years old now, Major had a lot of energy and wanted to play all the time. He jumped on and off the bed in a frenzied manner as I held my ear to the screen while trying to hear Mom and Dad argue.

Fifteen minutes later, I heard the distinctive rattling sound of carport storm door slam shut. Dad stomped out of the carport and down the driveway with Mom a few steps behind.

"Don't you fuckin' come back, you son-of-a-bitch," she screamed.

"You wanna live here, good luck payin' the goddamned bills," he said.

Anytime Mom used the F word, it was best to stay out of her way. They've had arguments before where Mom took off walking—and I usually chased her down—but nobody had ever been kicked out of the house.

When she picked us up from school on Wednesday, I had to move a large brown envelope when I climbed in the front. She had on a nice pair of slacks and a flowered blouse. Instead of tennis shoes, she wore a pair of black pumps.

Mom hadn't dressed up since she went to a funeral a few years before. As soon as we got home, I turned on the TV to watch *Dark Shadows*. She went to her bedroom—probably to change clothes—so I sneaked into the kitchen and found the envelope on the counter. The return address said, "attorney-at-law." A quick peek inside confirmed my suspicions. Divorce papers.

Although Mom never said we had money problems after she filed for divorce, everything pointed to it. We had to sign up for the free lunch program at school. One night, she called one of her sisters, Aunt Geneva.

"Bobby ain't givin' us a dime until a judge makes him...Uh-huh...I sent my résumé out, but I haven't had a job in ten years...Welfare? Absolutely not...I just need a hundred dollars to get us through the month...Why not? ...Go to hell."

Mom slammed the receiver down so hard I thought she broke it. She came into the living room carrying a drink that probably had booze in it. I let Major out to do his business and said good night to her before we went to the trailer.

"Wanna go to Fort Smith with me tomorrow?" she asked.

"I have school."

"You can miss one day."

That obviously wasn't her first drink. Whenever she had too much alcohol, Mom slurred her words a little.

"Why can't you take Mike or Sharon?

"You can afford to miss it. They can't."

She had never asked me to miss school before. Even though I wanted to get another perfect attendance certificate, I agreed to go.

I slept in the house that night because we had to leave early. It was warm for the last day of February, so we didn't need our heavy coats. We got to a small white building in Fort Smith at 6:30 a.m. and sat on the steps. The sign on the door said ARKANSAS DEPARTMENT OF SOCIAL SERVICES.

The office didn't open until 8 a.m., so we had time to kill. It didn't bother me getting there early. I had brought a book along—*Dragonquest* by Anne McCaffrey. Although it was still fairly dark, the building had lights on outside bright enough for me to read.

I got lost in the book about dragon riders. When Mom blew her nose loudly, I jumped and dropped the paperback. That was when I noticed her crying, so I put my arm around her.

"It'll be okay, Mom."

She bawled for a few more minutes until others started showing up to stand in line. By the time someone unlocked the door, at least a dozen others had joined us.

"Stay out here. I shouldn't be long."

"Okay. I'll be in the car."

Almost an hour passed before she finally came out. She stopped to light a cigarette before heading to the car. Her eyes were bloodshot red. Once she got in, Mom passed an envelope to me.

"They approved food stamps, but nothin' else."

We went straight to WINTON'S IGA where she filled a grocery basket. When she removed a booklet from the envelope and handed it to the cashier, the woman rolled her eyes. She tore out some of the stamps and handed the booklet back to Mom.

"I need a carton of Winston Menthol Lights," Mom said.

The cashier left the register for a moment and returned with the carton of cigarettes. Mom gave her a ten-dollar bill and got change back. Once the sacker put our groceries in the basket, he walked away. Other sackers pushed the groceries they bagged outside to the shopper's car, but we had to do our own.

"Mom, why isn't he takin' our groceries out?"

"He must be lookin' for a tip."

As I pushed the basket away from the checkout counter, I heard a man behind us say something about welfare cheats. I'd never hated my dad as much as I did at that moment.

Does he love us?

Chapter 50

Consequences

After the head injury and wrist surgery, I worked every hour I could manage. The cast kept Wayne and Mark out of action for a few weeks, but it came off in November. Free once again, Wayne resumed his nocturnal debauchery. I believe he got off on shocking me by switching back in the middle of his escapades.

One night in December, I awoke in a sex sling surrounded by eight men wearing leather. I appeared to be in the home of someone who had a BDSM room. Three sex slings hung from the ceiling. Whips, paddles, and other torture devices hung on one wall. Although Wayne might have agreed to the gang bang, I did not. Cuffs held me in a four-point restraint and a ball gag muffled my screams.

Please let me go. Don't do this. Doesn't Wayne know this—for me—is rape?

The more I squirmed to resist, the more the men smiled and rough-handled me. They raped me repeatedly. When they finished and released the restraints, I found my clothes and got the hell out of there.

At home, I cleaned myself out with saline water several times and hoped for the best. I'd lost dozens of acquaintances to AIDS in the previous ten years. The disease terrified me.

Why does Wayne put me in those situations? Doesn't he understand that—from my perspective—those men repeatedly raped me? How can I not have HIV after that? Wayne's playing with a loaded gun pointed at our collective heads.

The next day, the health department tested me for HIV. The nurse said it took weeks for the infection to be detected, so I'd have to repeat the test. Thanks to Wayne, I'd have to get tested monthly and wait up to two weeks for the results.

Why can't my alter change his risky behavior.

Stop pointing at Wayne. How many times have you knowingly had bareback sex? You're a hypocrite.

My drinking increased after that night, but it didn't stop Wayne from doing what he wanted, the effects be damned.

A week later on Tuesday evening, Wayne switched back to me—naked, in tennis shoes—while sitting on a stool at the counter of a nonfunctional bar with empty shelves. I appeared to be in a banquet room the size of a basketball court. Instead of being filled with tables and chairs, however, the room contained two dozen men—also very naked and also wearing tennis shoes. Old, young, middle aged, fat, skinny, buffed, flabby.

A few leaned against one of the six mirror-covered pillars while others wandered around. Each of the men held a white cup in one hand, and many pleasured themselves with the other. I held an identical cup. It had no odor, but touching it cleared up the mystery: a water-based lubricant. A plastic display case next to me on the countertop held business cards with black and red printing on them. "Chicago Jacks," they said. I'd found one of those cards in my jeans a week earlier. At that time, I didn't give a shit about what it was. It didn't take a college degree to figure out the theme of the party.

Where was I and how did I get there? More important, where the fuck were my clothes? I prayed the locker key attached to my left wrist with a rubber band could answer that question.

As I got my bearings, I noticed guys using a door to my left. It had to be the exit or a bathroom. I ditched the cup and made a beeline for it. The door led me to a room with lockers. I breathed a sigh of relief when the key opened one that contained familiar clothing.

"Wayne, are you leaving so soon?"

I turned to see a portly man several years older than I was.

"I have to work early." My watch said it was still Tuesday evening, so I hadn't missed any days at work. After dressing and bundling up, I walked up the stairs to the building's exit. Chicago had several inches of snow on the ground, and the temperatures were supposed to drop into the single digits. Luckily, I found an L station across the street and took the train home.

No wonder I can't be intimate with men I like—at least not for long. I feel dirty, disgusting. Why would anyone want to be with me?

If Mark resumed his crime spree, he kept it hidden. Besides, with Wayne's nightly debauchery, Mark didn't have time to do what he wanted.

My work suffered horribly in the weeks that followed. The Tegretol made my brain foggy, and the lack of sleep magnified it. By early afternoon, I couldn't string two sentences together that made any sense. I made basic mistakes that took extra time to correct. My 1995 billables had come in well below the requirements. The head injury and wrist surgery set me back two months. My mental disorder—now called dissociative identity disorder (DID)—sabotaged the rest of the year.

In January, I got a bad feeling about work. Partners stopped giving me assignments, and most brushed me off when I asked for work. Given my inconsistent performance, I didn't blame them. I finally went into my supervisor's office in February to see what was happening.

"I know this past year was terrible, but am I okay at the firm?" I asked.

"You're just fine," he said. "Everyone understands."

"Are you sure?"

"Yes, Steve, your position at the firm is fine."

Although I wanted to believe him, part of me didn't. I continued to perform my work the best I could. The quality and quantity didn't meet Jenner & Block standards—or even mine—but I didn't know what to do.

You know what needs to be done. Tell Dr. Perry everything.

I'd been seeing a psychiatrist since I moved to Chicago in order to keep taking the antidepressants Dr. Fields had prescribed for me during law school. My appointments with Dr. Perry became a chore. He treated my depression with medication, but—just as with Dr. Fields—I kept from him the reason why I was depressed to begin with. My alcohol consumption at home also increased as I tried to numb myself.

In the second week of March, a senior partner called me into his office. I hadn't done any work for him, so I thought he was giving me an assignment.

"Sit down, Steve," he said. "We need to talk."

Here it comes. No good conversation ever started with those words.

"What's up?"

An inch-thick file on his desk had my name in big letters on the tab. He opened it and turned through a few pages.

"Your performance here at Jenner & Block has been sporadic."

"I know. A lot of shit has happened to me over the past year."

He took a deep breath and exhaled. "I'm not just talking about 1995. Before that as well."

"I was sick in 1994 for a few months and had the tonsillectomy. At the beginning of the year, my friend Brad was murdered."

"You missed a lot of work, and your billable hours have been low since you joined the firm. We can't see you advancing to make junior partner in the time frame we expect."

"You're firing me?" Law firms usually let associates go if they weren't going to make junior partner. I never expected it to happen to me, not after everything I gave up getting this far.

"We'll keep you on for a year to give you ample time to seek a position elsewhere. That way the other firms won't see it as a termination."

What did you expect? Your work has sucked.

"We know you've been battling cancer in recent months."

"Cancer?"

"That's what you wrote."

The partner passed me a printout of an email sent in my name. It went into great detail about health issues I'd had, including the latest diagnosis of lymphoma.

Where the fuck did they get the idea that I had cancer?

Where do you think?

"Sorry, my brain wasn't working there for a second." I handed the printout back to him. The sudden dizziness signaled an impending switch to Mark or Wayne.

Oh, no. Please don't fuck up everything.

I came out of the blackout sitting at my desk in the apartment. A box on the floor held the personal property from my office at the firm. My personal computer and monitor had been stacked next to it. A white envelope lay next to my computer keyboard.

It contained a check from the firm in the amount equal to four months' salary.

What the hell happened? What did you two do? And what am I gonna do now? The firm was giving me a year to find a job. A year! Now I have no job and no prospects. What good is this money when other firms will know I was fired?

I'm so screwed.

Chapter 51

Downward Spiral

With the implosion of my career at Jenner & Block, I fled from Chicago back to Detroit in May 1996. My DID had become so disabling that I needed familiarity and comfort. I sure as hell wasn't moving back to Arkansas or South Dakota. In the Detroit area, I had the Arnolds, Nick, and a handful of friends from my PR and law school days.

HONIGMAN MILLER made me an offer to work in their bankruptcy department, but I turned them down—and second guessed myself at once. Then I landed a job in the litigation department at MIRO WEINER & KRAMER—a small boutique law firm in Bloomfield Hills. The bulk of their work revolved around TAUBMAN CENTERS, the shopping mall giant based locally.

As soon as I returned to the area, I also began seeing Dr. Fields again. She now operated had a private practice out of a home office, which I sometimes found strange, especially hearing young children playing in the hallway on the other side of the door.

By January 1997, I hated my job and where I lived. The lease work I had to do for mall tenants proved tedious and simple. Even my worst performance at Jenner & Block exceeded the necessary capabilities for the job. For being a litigation department, we rarely did any actual litigation.

The dogs and I lived in a dump of a house in Farmington Hills. The fenced-in area covered about the same space as a bedroom in a single-wide mobile home—the perfect size for a human, but not so for two Dobermans and a mix-breed. The place was so bad even Wayne wouldn't bring a trick there, but I continued to wake in various beds throughout the Metro Detroit area.

On Saturday, January 11, the arctic blast that had plagued us all week continued to keep temps below 20° Fahrenheit. The dogs stayed outdoors just enough to do their business and not a second more. The five inches of snow we got mid-week covered the ground and many roads.

If I'd still been at Jenner & Block, I would have been in the office at least part of the day, usually working on projects due on someone's desk by Monday. Miro Weiner & Kramer didn't expect us to work weekends. That left me with few things to do when I had time alone.

In my previous session with Dr. Fields, I finally told her about Mark and Wayne. She responded by skirting around the issue and deflecting it to another topic. I still didn't divulge everything about them, but I opened the door.

The warm house kept me inside all day. I played with the dogs and watched TV. About 8 p.m., I got a little dizzy and my head began buzzing—signs of an alter's imminent arrival. Over the years, I'd become more adept at detecting the signs further in advance. It didn't help with asymptomatic switches, unfortunately, which Mark had perfected.

I'd put Dr. Fields's phone on speed dial for that reason. By pushing one button, I reached her machine.

"Dr. Fields, it's happening again. I can't stop it. I'm switching, and I don't know what to do. *Please help me.*"

I crawled out of bed and picked up the dirty clothes on the floor. They didn't have a smoky smell to them, a good sign.

After getting dressed, I fed the dogs and put on my winter outerwear so I could go outside with them. Strangely enough, I couldn't find my good winter hat. I'd worn it on Saturday when I went in the back yard with them. I had to make do with an older one not nearly as warm.

Once the dogs finished doing their business, I grabbed my keys and wallet. My stomach craved waffles, even if I had to brave the cold to get them. I stepped out the front door and stopped.

Where's my car?

Someone had to have hot-wired it—unless Mark or Wayne did something with it. I took off on foot to the police station, located about a quarter mile away. The frozen snow crunched under my feet.

By the time I got there, I couldn't feel my face. The freezing air had numbed the exposed areas. When I strolled in, a police officer behind the counter greeted me. I got straight to the point.

"My Chevy Blazer has been stolen."

I gave him my driver's license. He slid a form across the counter to me, and I began filling in the information.

"When was it stolen?"

"Sometime between 6 p.m. Friday and twenty minutes ago. I didn't go out the front of the house at all yesterday."

The officer took the completed form and began typing in the computer. A minute later, he wrote something on the back of a card and handed it to me.

"This has the police report number on it. Below is the phone number for the impound lot. Someone wrecked your Blazer in a hit-and-run last night."

"Oh, no, I hope nobody was hurt—except the asshole who stole it."

"They slid on ice and hit a pole. The driver fled the scene. Do you still have the key?"

"Yes." I held it up.

"Does anyone else have a key?"

"This is the only one."

"Interesting. The steering column hadn't been tampered with."

The officer stared at me for a few seconds. He didn't believe me, but he had no proof.

I phoned the number from my house and arranged for a tow to Knudsen Brothers Collision in Westland. Although my insurance paid for a rental car, the company I had to use wasn't open on Sundays.

On Monday, I got the car and drove to the collision shop in Westland. Whoever wrecked my car did a bang-up job—pun intended. The passenger-side headlight and fender had been smashed. It would take the shop at least a week to fix it. I opened the car to see if I left anything important in it.

Son-of-a-bitch.

That was why I couldn't find my good winter hat. One of my alters left it on the seat of the car.

Damn you, Mark or Wayne. Now I just filed a false police report.

At least they didn't switch back to you as soon as they had the wreck.

I still filed a false police report.

After all you've done, that's the crime that bothers you?

The lease on my Farmington Hills house would end at the end of May. I didn't want to rent it for another year, but I had procrastinated finding another place.

One night in April, I went to bed early because my alters' nightly activities had me dragging during the day. I prayed they'd let me get a full night of sleep for a change.

A piercing sound woke me from a deep sleep. I sat up in bed and tried to figure out what it was.

Oh, shit. The smoke alarm! I have to save the dogs.

After dressing in record time, I grabbed my wallet and keys off the dresser. My cell phone wasn't on the nightstand where it should be—and it wasn't on the floor. Before I opened the bedroom door, I put my hand against it. Warm, but not hot. Standing to the side, I gently pulled it open. No flames rolled into the room like in the movie Backdraft, but smoke poured in causing me to cough. Flames burned bright in the office across the hall. What the hell happened?

I found the dogs cowering under the kitchen table. After putting leashes on them, I took them out the front door. It took me a minute to get the car doors unlocked and open so they could jump into the back.

The Gateway tower computer I bought before leaving Chicago sat in the back of my car.

Motherfucker. This night keeps getting better. What the fuck is going on? Mark and Wayne, what the hell did you do?

I ran back into the house to dial 9-1-1. The line was dead. Before the smoke got too thick and the fire spread, I managed to get some belongings out of the house: suits, shoes, and a few other items of clothing.

The fire truck pulled onto my lawn and began dousing the flames. A fire inspector on the scene asked me a bunch of questions. Even though I answered them as best I could, my "best" included a book of lies.

"I got the dogs out and then went back in for my computer and some clothes. The phone was dead, so I couldn't call 9-1-1."

"A passing motorist called it in."

The dogs and I stayed until the fire department contained the blaze. I lost everything remaining in the house—thousands of dollars in property. If I would have had renter's insurance, the authorities would have investigated more thoroughly and might have concluded an arsonist started the blaze. I had no motive without insurance. As for the cause, I didn't have a clue.

I found my Motorola flip phone in the front seat under my day planner. Why did my alter take it from the bedroom? I might have needed it to call for help.

After letting the office know I'd be off work for the day and why, I found a place to board Rufio, Dallas, and Gabby. Then I called Diane.

"I'll be staying in a motel until I can find a place."

"Nonsense. You can stay in our extra room."

I didn't have the guts to tell her it would take a few paychecks before I could afford first and last month's rent plus a security deposit. Between Wayne's nightly trips to bars and my own overspending, I'd blown through the Jenner & Block money.

I moved my suits and a few other clothes into Diane's spare bedroom. An examination of my finances confirmed that it would take three paychecks—six weeks—before I could save enough to rent a new place.

Steve, you're a financial mess.

A week later, while I sat on a couch in Diane's den, she walked up and stood over me.

"I need you to leave."

We always joked around with each other, so I thought she was kidding, but she handed me a $3,000 check that proved otherwise.

"I can't take your money. I'll have enough saved soon."

Steve, you're lying to her. Can't you tell her the truth about anything?

"You can stay 'til tomorrow."

Shit. She wants me to leave right away. Mark and Wayne, what did one of you do?

I considered these people to be family. Somehow, I'd damaged the relationship—maybe irreparably. Unwilling to stay there until the next day, I packed my shit and checked into a motel an hour later.

The following day, I took off work again, cashed Diane's check, and went hunting for a place that would rent to someone with three dogs. Luckily, I found a house in Royal Oak.

Not knowing what happened with Diane worried me tremendously.

Maybe you overstayed your welcome, like a dead fish after three days.

I don't think so. She changed too abruptly. If my alters did something, I don't even have enough information to apologize for it.

It doesn't matter. When she finds out you've been lying to her all this time, your friendship won't survive.

Chapter 52

Sabotaged

My job had become a nightmare, thanks to my alters. For weeks, I'd been switching several times a day at work. It started out with a few minutes here and there, but then I began losing hours at a time. Neither alter left me any notes, so I had no idea what they were doing or why.

A few months previously, one of my supervisors assigned me the case of a professional athlete who had invested in the wrong company. It proved to be a pleasant change from reviewing leases for mall tenants. But my presence at work came in small bits as Mark and/or Wayne decided to practice law in my stead. I'd discover completed motions and briefs that I'd never worked on and court appearances I had no memory of attending. I was sifting through the mess one day when another litigation associate poked his head in my office.

"The word is you've been showing a handgun around the office today. You shouldn't do that. It's spooking people."

"A handgun? I don't even own one."

I used to have a SIG Sauer P239, but I sold that last year after it scared me having it around.

What if they bought another one?

"I'm just passing on the information," the associate said. "Be careful."

Once he left, I shut the door and began looking through my office. The credenza behind me contained nothing but files. I'd been in my desk all day, so I doubted it could be there. When I opened the bottom drawer, I gasped.

On top of my files, someone had placed a SIG Sauer P239—identical to the one I sold the previous fall, still in its original box.

How could they buy a gun without me knowing? They must not have had to take the safety course over again.

Don't be ridiculous. You've been missing so much time that they could have gotten a PhD, and you wouldn't have noticed.

After putting the gun in my briefcase, I sat and considered my options. The gun stunt had ended my chances at the firm. They would never trust me or feel safe with me around.

It will be the third job in sixteen months. Huge red flags.

A job hunter had reached out to me a week earlier to see if I would be interested in moving jobs. I called her, and she connected me to the hiring partner at the firm HILL & HILL, a medium-sized firm about a mile away. They were looking for a new associate with my experience.

I dropped off my résumé at lunch, and they interviewed me the following Monday. They had new offices, an energetic staff, and a large law library. At the conclusion of the interview, the partner gave me the "don't call us, we'll call you" speech, so I went back to work and waited.

Two days later, on August 20, I took my softball equipment to work for the firm's annual game against the TAUBMAN CENTERS employees. They played it the previous year while I was in Lansing taking the Michigan bar examination.

At 1:30 p.m., the phone rang.

"It's Stan from HILL & HILL."

Hearing the hiring partner's name gave me a sense of relief. *Please offer me a job. I have to leave this place before I have no career whatsoever.*

"We are extending an offer for you to join our firm," Stan said.

I did a little happy dance inside, although I seemed to be working my way down the career ladder.

"That's great news. What's the salary?"

When he said the number, I thought I heard it wrong.

"Could you repeat that?"

When Stan gave the number again, I realized my hearing was fine.

"What about bonuses?"

"Bonuses aren't guaranteed."

The job hunter had misrepresented the firm's salary structure. She said they paid the same level as the top Detroit firms and gave generous bonuses.

Why did I go through all that and get my hopes up?

"Is the salary negotiable?" I asked. "That's thirty percent less than I make here. I'm bringing experience from Jenner & Block in Chicago, plus I graduated at the top of my class. Can you at least match my current salary?"

How could I take *another* thirty percent cut with no bonus prospects? Their pay was half of what I would have made my first year at HONIGMAN MILLER.

"Consider the offer withdrawn."

The line clicked when he hung up, the sound of a proverbial guillotine executing my career.

What the hell just happened? How could they low-ball me like that? What do I do now? I'm so fucked.

The rest of the day dragged on. I couldn't go crawling back to HONIGMAN MILLER after having turned them down twice. At 5 p.m., I changed clothes for the slow-pitch softball game and drove to the park. A good competition would help me get rid of tension.

We played for a while, and I had a wonderful time. Then the "coach"—one of my supervisors—told me to pitch. That had been my position on the McDONALD's softball team. After three innings, a female player came up to bat. I threw a pitch, and she swung at it.

"Let her hit it," someone from the TAUBMAN dugout yelled.

I threw another pitch, and she swung again. Two strikes.

"Pitch it so she can hit it," the guy again yelled from the TAUBMAN dugout.

My anger started rising, but I breathed deeply and threw another pitch. The ump called a ball.

"Stop throwing the ball so high," my supervisor—the coach—yelled. "Let her hit it."

My competitiveness took over. I started to throw another pitch when the familiar wooziness hit me.

No, don't switch now. Please.

Whichever alter took over didn't release me until 9:30 a.m. the next day—sitting in my chair at work. I had no idea what happened at the softball game or thereafter, but I had a bad feeling.

At 10 a.m., my gut told me to call Stan at HILL & HILL, so I did.

"I apologize for the way I reacted yesterday. I'd like to accept your offer."

"There is no offer. We withdrew it, remember? Don't call me again."

That's that, I guess. I'll just have to hang on here.

A few minutes later, my supervisor showed up. If ever there was an "oh shit" moment, this was it because he never stopped by my office.

"You acted way out of line at the softball game yesterday. You can't tell our biggest client to 'kiss my ass.'"

Ugh, it's much worse than I thought. There's no way out of this that doesn't end with me being unemployed.

"Look, I'm sorry. I had an awful day, but that's no excuse for my behavior."

"No, it's not. The client said you called this morning and apologized."

Thank you, whichever of you did it.

"They accept your apology—"

"Thank God."

"—but you're fired. Please pack and leave the building immediately."

Fuck you, Mark or Wayne, whichever of you did this. What the fuck am I supposed to do now? You've sabotaged my career. Are you happy?

The security guy stepped inside carrying two empty boxes. He stood over me as I filled them with my personal belongings. It took all my might to keep from bursting into tears. When I had almost finished packing, he stepped away. I took the opportunity to phone the professional athlete client. His wife answered.

"I wanted to let you know that the firm just fired me, so you'll have a new attorney here. I'm sorry."

"We don't want a new attorney," she said. "Where are you going?"

"I don't know yet."

"Wherever it is, we'll stay with you. My husband will be back this evening. Please give him a call then."

Hanging my own shingle is the only option, and I have my first client.

Are you nuts? The stress will be your undoing.

I'll be representing a former professional athlete in a case that will bring in $2,000 a month. With a couple more clients, I'll be fine.

You're not anywhere close to "fine." You need help—and I don't mean secretarial.

I've tried talking to Dr. Fields. We're getting nowhere.

Try telling her everything for a change.

I can't do that. I just can't.

Chapter 53

Hitting Bottom

July 11, 1998
Royal Oak, Michigan
Age 38

It had been more than a year since Miro Weiner & Kramer kicked my sorry ass to the curb. They did the right thing just as Jenner & Block had done the previous year. Even if another firm would hire me, my mental disorder made it impossible to work at one.

What made me think I could practice law on my own?

I didn't have the knowledge, skills, or money to start my own one-person firm. The past year had been extremely difficult. My work for the athlete client barely kept me afloat. I took on cases I shouldn't have—such as medical malpractice, products liability, and racial discrimination. They required extensive discovery that I had neither the time nor money to handle properly. I had become a walking example of legal malpractice.

As for my mental health, I continued to rely on Dr. Fields. She either didn't believe I had MPD—now called dissociative identity disorder (DID)—or she had no idea how to treat it. I'd been seeing her two or three times a week for months without any improvement.

I had no business practicing law at all, but I had no option.

Yes, you do, but you won't consider it.

I cannot and will not commit myself to a mental institution. It's not happening.

If not for Diane and her kids, I would feel detached from everything. After I found another place to live, we resumed our social interactions—albeit strained ones. I still didn't know what caused the distance between us. My instinct told me Mark or Wayne did something, but neither they nor Diane gave any hint as to what happened.

On Saturday, July 11, I tried to sleep late, but the dogs had other ideas. Their barking finally won out. I crawled out of bed and got dressed. As with most Saturdays, I planned to grab breakfast at McDonald's, play with the dogs, and work the bulk of the day.

At the bottom of the stairs, Rufio, Dallas, and Gabrielle—two Dobermans and a Rottweiler mix—greeted me by rubbing against my legs and licking my hands. They bounced around like kids on caffeine while I poured food into their bowls. When I stood upright, bundles of money stacked on the dining room table grabbed my attention. My stomach churned and feet froze to the floor.

Mark, what the hell did you do?

It had to be him unless Wayne prostituted himself to some high rollers. A yellow Post-It Note on top contained writing in familiar penmanship.

I made a withdrawal from your bank branch yesterday.
This should help.
Mark

He added a smiley face with horns next to his name.

This had to be a joke. Maybe Mark made it look like a lot of money by putting singles in bundles with larger bills on top for me to see.

When have you known Mark to play practical jokes?

I picked up a bundle with a money strap around it and a hundred-dollar bill on top. It contained nothing but hundreds. The bills didn't have sequential serial numbers, so I doubted they could be traced.

What the hell was I going to do? Banks had cameras, and he robbed my branch of Standard Federal Bank. I spoke with tellers there every week. If I went back, surely they would recognize me.

You can mail the money back to them.

What a stupid idea. The shit probably has my fingerprints all over it, not to mention my DNA. I should shred or burn it all to get rid of the evidence.

Steve, you need the money for your cases. If you destroy it, Mark will just rob another bank.

I can't. Spending the money will make me no better than Mark. I can turn myself in, give back the money, and tell them I have DID. Then I'll get help.

You idiot. It will never work. You'll be imprisoned, or institutionalized, for sure.

When I counted the money, I couldn't believe it. $48,000.

It's a lot of dough. Okay, I might as well use it. Now I need a plan to launder the money.

Here's how you do it. Pay cash for everything when possible. Make small deposits at different Standard Federal Bank branches around the area. Never return to your branch for anything.

That might work.

I'd gone from law school valedictorian to bank robber in five-and-a-half years—not exactly the career path I'd hoped for.

You're a disgrace.

Chapter 54

Turning the Tables

The boat and trailer disappeared in September while I was at school. I didn't have to ask what happened to them. Once Mom filed for divorce, I knew they wouldn't be around much longer. Whoever took the trailer left my things in a box on the carport.

I had to move back into the bedroom with Mike. Poor Major had gotten used to sleeping with me, so it took him a few nights to adjust.

In the last week of school, I stood at my locker between periods when someone slipped something in my back pocket. I pulled the note out and unfolded it.

In front of the gym after school.

Dammit. I can't deal with Danny and Billy right now.

The rest of the day, I tried to come up with a way out. Were they bluffing? Would they really show the pictures to people? They could destroy me.

When the final bell rang, I meandered around other students as they got onto buses parked on the road. I sat in front of the old gym waiting for Danny. A few minutes after the buses left to pick up the high school students down the road, Billy pulled up in the Buick. Danny appeared from around the gym and got in the passenger seat. He whistled and motioned for me to come.

You don't have a plan, so what are you gonna do?

I'm gonna do what they say. I don't have much of a choice.

Their parents worked, which left Billy and Danny alone at the house for two more hours. Billy pulled the car around back—presumably so nobody would see me get out. I followed Danny up the back porch. They had a nice place. It had to be twice the size of ours, with fancy furniture and nothing out of place. *Do their parents know their two sons are blackmailers and rapists?*

"This way," Danny said.

He led me to a bedroom with posters on the wall. The Rolling Stones, Led Zeppelin, Pink Floyd. It surprised me when he closed the door, leaving just us two together.

"I thought you'd be more of a Tony Orlando and Dawn fan," I said.

"Fuck you."

The Rolling Stones poster hung above his desk, which looked about six feet long. An IBM Selectric typewriter sat at one end. A stereo system occupied the other. On an entire wall of his room, shelving held hundreds of albums. I lifted the turntable lid.

"The *Dark Side of the Moon*. Not my cup of tea. I'm more of an Elton John and Jackson 5 fan."

"I have theirs too." He thumbed through some of the albums and pulled one out. A few seconds later, the music from the *Goodbye Yellow Brick Road* album filled the room.

There have been times when something caught me off guard, but nothing more than when Danny moved forward and planted a kiss on my lips. A long, sensual kiss, much different from the times he kissed me before. I broke it off and stepped back.

"What are you doin'?" I asked.

I loved the way his lips touched mine, but why did it have to be him?

"Isn't it obvious? I like you."

"You *like* me? I'm not a homo." I kept telling myself that like it would negate the feelings I had for men.

"I ain't either." Danny smiled and put his hand on my shoulder. "I just like fuckin' and kissin' you."

When he pulled me close, I fought the urge to push him away and run. This monster—who had blackmailed and raped me for almost two years—suddenly decided he *liked* me? Maybe I could use that to my advantage.

We removed each other's clothing and got on his bed. With every move he made, every touch I felt, I kept reliving the times he and his brother raped me—at least those parts I remembered. I hated the way he stimulated my body and so easily warmed me all over. When we finished, he lay next to me with his head on my chest.

"I loved that." It nauseated me saying that.

No, it didn't. You enjoyed every minute of having sex with your rapist.

"Me too."

Would my plan work? I had to give it a try. "Could you do me a favor?"

"It depends."

"Give me the pictures you and your brother took." It wouldn't hurt to ask, right? "You don't have to blackmail me anymore. I'll do this whenever you want."

"Billy ain't gonna like that."

I pressed my lips against his, moving my mouth around in an open mouth kiss. Our tongues danced with each other as I fought back the urge to vomit. When I pulled him on top of me and wrapped my legs around him, his body responded. Round two was slower, more sensual, intimate—and I despised every minute of it.

Liar. You wanted to do it—just like you want to do it again now.

The feelings confused and angered me. Did I enjoy it? Yes, and I hated it at the same time. Sweat covered both of us by the time we finished.

As I lay back, all five foot eight of him jumped out of bed and removed one of the albums from the rack. He brought it back to the bed and pulled out the contents. Six Polaroid pictures fell on the sheet. I picked up the blackmail material.

"Did you jack off to these a lot?" I asked.

"You bet."

I went to his desk and used a pair of scissors to cut up the Polaroids—especially anything identifying me. Once I brushed the tiny pieces into the trashcan, I was free. The bastards had nothing on me now. While Danny watched from the bed, I got dressed.

"Come on," he said. "We have time to go again before my parents get home."

"No, I don't think so." I slipped my feet into the tennis shoes and pulled the shirt over my head.

"Why not?"

"Because you're a fuckin' sicko. You raped me how many times? And now you expect me to be your boyfriend or some shit like that?" *You wouldn't really mind, would you?* "Never."

My mouth always ran faster than my brain. Before I could open the bedroom door, he slammed into my back, shoving me against the wall. I tried to face him, but he began punching me in the side and back.

Dizziness swept over me, and I blacked out.

Every part of me hurt, especially my sides and stomach. Danny must have beaten me good. How the hell did I get home? It didn't matter as long as I never had to kowtow to that asshole and his brother again.

I got dressed for school and went to check myself in the bathroom mirror. I had bruises on my left jaw and around my torso.

Damn, he got you good.

Nobody said anything when I groaned as I sat at the table. Maybe they didn't notice. Hell, it even hurt to swallow my cereal.

"I've never seen a dodge ball make that kind of bruise," Mom said.

"The ball didn't do it. It hit me and slammed my face against the wall." I must have blamed it on the cruel sport we play in PE. Hell, I didn't even take PE.

Will she buy it?

Does it matter if she doesn't?

We got to school a little earlier than usual because Mom had an appointment with her attorney before she went to work. I'd be glad when they finished the divorce. It stressed me out, especially not knowing what they were doing.

Danny and I had the same first period class. I got to the room and skimmed the day's assignment. As I read, others whistled and laughed at something, causing me to turn. A few students surrounded Danny, who had a black eye, busted lip, and stitches above his left eyebrow and on his chin.

Damn, I wonder what happened to him.

We made eye contact, but he quickly looked away. Did his brother beat him up because I destroyed the pictures? Had he been in a car wreck? Part of me sympathized for him. He liked me, and I threw it in his face.

He raped you. Raped.

Maybe we can be secret boyfriends after all.

He took his assigned seat which just happened to be next to mine. Now I knew why he picked it the first day of class. Surely, he could have found a better way than rape to show he liked me.

"What happened?" He might not answer me after I rejected him. But he turned sideways and leaned in my direction.

"Ain't you hilarious," he whispered. "I shoulda called the cops."

"That's a funny one." I kept my voice low, hoping nobody would hear us.

"Man, you're nuts."

The others getting in their seats didn't seem to be paying any attention to us. If they associated me and Danny as friends, they might ask questions.

"I don't understand. *You* attacked *me.*"

"You owe me a new typewriter and stereo, you fuckin' psycho. Stay away from me."

Fuck me. I beat the shit out of him and don't remember any of it.

That takes all the fun out of it.

Chapter 55

Broken

By the end of July, I'd blown through almost all of the bank robbery proceeds by paying personal and business expenses. I also purchased a new high-end laptop for Diane as repayment for the money she gave me. Although I should have given her the $3,000 in cash, I rationalized that buying the computer kept her somewhat insulated from the bank robbery.

She still benefited from the proceeds.

I didn't say it was a perfect plan.

As for Ethan, I could have repaid the $5,000 student loan my bankruptcy forced him to pay. I decided not to because of what he put me through.

You were worse.

"I can't function anymore," I admitted to Dr. Fields during a session a week after the bank robbery.

"You should take a mental health month," she told me. "How about August?"

"That's doable."

How the hell is that doable? You can't just tell judges and clients that you're stressed and need to postpone everything.

It turned out I didn't have to—one of my alters did. He told judges and clerks that I had lymphoma and needed to take four weeks off for treatment. The lie got court appearances rescheduled and filing deadlines extended. Something like that never stayed a secret because court clerks talked to attorneys, especially opposing counsel. I discovered the subterfuge when one of my former law professors called to see how I was doing.

Given my notoriety at WAYNE STATE UNIVERSITY LAW SCHOOL—at least among class members—I knew people would gossip. As a result, Diane found out through the grapevine—so I had to extend the lie to her as well. My alters backed me into a corner, and I did nothing to correct the falsehood. I had to act sick, appear sick, and always remember I was sick.

How long can you keep this house of cards standing? It's all gonna come crashing down, Steve. Prepare yourself.

In mid-August, Diane invited "sickly" me to an outing on the lake. I couldn't say no, so I went. Watching her and the two kids enjoying themselves waterskiing made me smile.

"Your turn," Diane said.

Apparently, I didn't appear at death's door to her.

"I don't think I can." It had been twenty-five years since I last waterskied.

"Steven Simmons," she yelled, "get in the water now before I collectively throw you in."

It would be futile to argue with her, so I put on a vest and jumped in. The warm water soothed me. Not too hot, not too cold.

"Slalom or two skis?"

"Slalom." Why not be a glutton for punishment, right?

It took a while to get the ski on and maneuver it inside the V of the rope handle. *This might be a bad idea.*

The driver, a friend of Diane's, took the slack out of the rope. The boat dragged me for a few feet before I yelled "hit it." Just as I broke the surface, I lost control and fell. Did I expect to get up on the first try? Maybe, but it didn't happen. The boat circled me, bringing the rope around so I could grab it. Once again, I put the single ski in the V of the rope.

"Hit it."

When the boat took off, I made sure to keep my legs tensed. I wobbled a bit as the boat pulled me out of the water. Skiing around the lake brought back some of the only good memories from childhood. Camping at Blue Mountain Lake, swimming, and roasting marshmallows over the fire. Of course, there was also my parents' drinking and arguing, and I could never forget Jeffrey's sexual encounters. I couldn't reconcile all the mixed feelings.

The boat pulled me around the lake. My balance held, and I crossed the wake several times. Still, I didn't dare try any tricks.

After the ski day, my shame became unbearable. The Arnolds made me feel like part of the family, and I lied to them.

In therapy, I told Dr. Fields about my switching, but she continued to sidestep it.

She thinks you're making it up. Tell her everything.

I can't do that. If she finds out how I went along with all the lies, she'd see how untrustworthy I've become.

She's your psychiatrist, and you won't even tell her the things she needs to know. What are you afraid of?

I'm afraid of letting everyone down.

Bullshit. You're terrified of people discovering everything that you and your alters did over the years. Then they won't like you. You'll have no friends, no therapist, nothing.

I just want to be normal.

Normal? That ship sank.

As failures went, I had no peers.

When September approached, I realized the month off work had done nothing to help me relax. Mark and Wayne didn't let me sleep. Bills I couldn't pay kept rolling in. Every day I got further behind on my cases. The things I'd done over the years began suffocating me. I couldn't look at myself in the mirror anymore without getting nauseated.

My dogs gave me joy, but that couldn't sustain me.

One Tuesday after therapy, I went home and played with Rufio, Dallas, and Gabby. Rolling around on the floor with them made me laugh and feel great. I needed that.

After I wore them out, I propped the side door open so they could get in and out of the house. I put up a gate to keep them in the kitchen. Following a long, hot shower, I walked up the stairs to my bedroom/office. I owed Diane an explanation, so I typed a five-page letter begging for her forgiveness. In it, I detailed everything as best I could. The abuse, the alters, the lies—I left out some details because there were too many to cover.

So that someone would find it easily, I put the letter in an envelope and on the computer keyboard.

Over the previous two years, I saved several bottles of prescription pills. Flexeril and Dolobid for the bulging disk in my lower back. Tegretol for my petit mal seizures. I had amassed more than 200 pills. No doubt the combination of these three medications would do the job.

I washed the pills down with Pepto Bismol—hoping it would keep me from puking. It took several minutes to take all the medications.

With everything down, I took a roll of duct tape and wrapped it around my head. I made sure the tape covered my mouth. If I did vomit, maybe I'd drown in it like so many dead rock stars have.

The dizziness hit as sleepiness gripped me.

You waited too late, guys. I finally beat you.

I opened my eyes to the sight of Rufio, Gabby, and Dallas licking and eating vomit off the floor. My head hung off the side of the bed. The duct tape had been removed from around my mouth. A perfect plan spoiled.

What happened? How could I not be dead? How did the dogs get up here?

My head hurt too much to answer my hypothetical questions. Rufio licked me in the face. Just my luck to live through a suicide attempt only to be licked by a dog that ate my vomit.

Oh, no. The vomit. It might kill them.

I swung a pillow at the dogs. "Get out. Downstairs."

They ran down the stairs, and I rolled over on my back. According to my watch, I'd been knocked out for two days. This had been the closest I'd come to succeeding, but it wasn't enough.

I can't even kill myself properly.

Chapter 56

Humpty Dumpty

OCTOBER 9, 1998
ROYAL OAK, MICHIGAN
AGE 38

Why did I keep wasting my time going to therapy? I wanted Dr. Fields to fix me with her $100-an-hour intellect, but she either couldn't do it—or wouldn't try. She threw bottle after bottle of antidepressants at me. All I had to show for it were receipts for tax deductions and a cabinet full of pills. Why didn't she try something else?

Because you lied to her for years, Steve.

When I began psychotherapy with her six years earlier, she must have thought I was just another person who had a shitty childhood that caused them to be sad all the time. I told her about my bad mother, worse father, bullies at school...oh, and about some of the sexual abuse.

But you left out the most important part, didn't you?

Two parts, actually. I neglected to tell her about my other two personalities—Mark and Wayne—until two years ago.

You still didn't tell her everything.

I told her enough.

Unfortunately, she didn't believe me.

Why should she? You're still lying to her.

Since my disclosure, I tried everything Dr. Fields threw at me: various antidepressants, more sleep, multiple sessions a week, less work. Hell, I even meditated. For someone who hated the quiet, that took discipline.

When I drove to her office for yet another session, I didn't want to go in. In fact, as I sat across the street in my car, I kept the engine running, ready to put it in drive and leave. But I rang her doorbell at exactly 9 a.m. We jibber-jabbered about nothing important for the first half hour before I broached the main issue again.

"I'm still having blackouts," I said, bracing for her to downplay them or blame them on something else.

"How often are you missing time?" She leaned back in her chair and stared in my direction, her blank expression divulging nothing. Her round, black glass frames were in stark contrast to her blond hair and pale complexion.

"I have to check my watch constantly to see what day and time it is."

"Drinking can cause blackouts," she said.

And there it is, right on time.

"Causality is the other way around. I drink *because* of the blackouts." I never should have told her how much wine I consumed.

Dr. Fields retrieved a legal pad from her desk and thumbed through it. Her shoulder-length hair fell forward as she turned the pages.

"Two weeks ago, you said, 'I drink at least three large glasses of wine every night.'"

"You're not listening. I drink to pass out so they *don't* take over. It's the only way I—"

Ding.

I wanted to smash her fucking timer.

"That's it for today, Steve." Dr. Fields opened her calendar. "Same time next Tuesday?"

Across the street from her office, I sat in my car for a few minutes trying to absorb the session. She always gets me worked up and sends me away before we finish our conversation.

Paying her two or three times week continued to kill me financially, but I kept hoping something magical would make my tormentors disappear.

As I prepared to drive away, the all-too-familiar dizziness sucker punched me in the brain.

Oh, no. Not now. My stomach lurched. I closed my eyes and leaned back. *Here we go again.*

The grim-faced cops pointed their guns at me from behind the barricade of police cars across the asphalted parking lot. Lots of guns.

Holy shit. Where am I?

Coming out of a blackout always left me disoriented, but this was a doozy. I glanced behind me, hoping the real target stood there. Nothing but a building with glass doors containing the words "Standard Federal Bank."

Are you kidding me? Another bank robbery?

The gloves I wore now made sense, as did the catalog case in my right hand. *Is it full of money? Think fast, Steve. Think.*

Half expecting bullets to pierce my back, I turned and ran toward the entrance. *Please don't be locked. Please don't be locked.* The doors opened and closed without any bloodshed—for now. In the bank lobby, I stopped at the blue-roped waiting line leading to the teller windows.

Where is everyone?

I ran down a hallway to the right and found an office with the door open. Once inside, I dropped the catalog case and pulled off the gloves. I noticed my initials on top of the case, a gift from Don when I left SEMHC. My body trembled.

Mark, how could you do this again? Like always, you switched back when things got tough, leaving me to clean up your bullshit. What am I gonna do? How am I gonna get out of this?

Who the fuck am I kidding? The only way I'm leaving here is in handcuffs or a body bag.

Gaps in the closed vertical blinds gave me a view of the police officers. Four of them milled around, while others kept their firearms pointed at the front door.

Why aren't they storming in? Maybe others are hiding, and the cops don't want to hurt anyone.

I sank to the carpet with my back to the desk. My watch said it was still Friday, October 9. I'd lost several hours after leaving Dr. Field's office that morning.

What's gonna happen to my dogs? They'll need food and water. They'll have to go outside. Will the police shoot them because they're Dobermans?

With both arms wrapped around my knees, I cried. Tears soaked the pin-striped, gray fabric of my best court suit. I guess Mark wanted to go out in style.

Something heavy in my left jacket pocket pressed against my leg. When I reached inside, a chill ran down my spine. A SIG Sauer P239 semiautomatic pistol. I ejected the magazine and counted the rounds. Eight plus one in the chamber made nine.

Dammit, Mark. You're obsessed with this handgun. How did you get another one? If the police know I'm armed, it explains why they haven't rushed in.

How did I let it get this far? Why didn't Dr. Fields help me? Why didn't she believe I had multiple personalities? She's a fucking psychiatrist, for Christ's sake!

After releasing the safety, I pressed the gun muzzle against my right temple.

My right temple chilled from the coolness of the P239's muzzle. Would my alters let me do it this time? One firm tug on the trigger, and my miserable life would finally be over.

Ethan, the last seven years have been so empty without you. Since the day you left, it's been difficult to stay alive. None of this is your fault, though. Some people broke me a long time ago. If anything, the five years you gave me kept me alive. I'm sorry for dragging you into my messed-up life—for hurting you.

That seemed to be my superpower—hurting people. All the stupid things I'd said and done over the years alienated everyone I considered to be friends. If I'd told someone about my blackouts when I was sixteen, none of this would have happened.

Bullshit, Steve. You could have stopped this at any point, but you chose not to.

If I'd told Dr. Fields about the first bank robbery and showed her the money, she would have had to believe me. How did it come to this?

You know how.

My life had been over for a long time. Once I made it official, everyone would be better off.

Mom, all I ever wanted was for you to love me as much as you loved Mike and Sharon. Estelle and Cliff, I let you down, and I'm sorry for that. Sean, Nick, and Diane, thanks for the friendship you gave me. I always wanted to give more back, but I was afraid.

Steve, stop wallowing and get it over with. On the count of three.

One. Two. Three.

Nothing happened.

Because you're a fucking coward. Neither Mark nor Wayne tried to stop you this time, and you still couldn't go through with it.

I can do this. One. Two. Three.

Unable to pull the trigger, I set the gun on the carpet.

What next?

Maybe I should tell my clients before someone else does.

I got my phone and began calling them.

"I can't represent you anymore. I've just robbed a bank, and I'm going to prison."

When I said that to two clients who answered, they thought I was joking. Three didn't answer, so I left messages.

Neither of the clients I spoke with expressed any concern for me, but I didn't blame them. I was a nut job who took their money and left them with nothing but a file in my office. If I could phone Rufio, Gabby, and Dallas, I would. Just as with Major, I'd never get to say good-bye to them.

You don't know that. You're crazy, after all.

Of course I'm insane. But nobody will believe me.

The telephone in the office rang, the high-pitched trill interrupting my thoughts.

"The bank's closed," I screamed.

"Please pick up the phone," someone said on a bullhorn outside.

"*Go to hell.*" I doubted they could hear me through the walls. "Mark, where are you now? Did it get too intense for you in here? *You goddamned coward. You robbed a bank and literally left me holding the fucking bag.*"

I stood and paced back and forth in the small office. There were two ways out of this. One involved handcuffs, and the other a body bag. I needed to speak with a good criminal lawyer, and I knew only one—Jordan, a former colleague and someone I considered to be the best criminal attorney I'd ever met. His executive assistant answered on the second ring.

"Hey, Marla, it's Steve Simmons. Is Jordan in?"

"I'm sorry, but he's on the phone."

"Please interrupt him, I need to talk to him now," I said. "It's an emergency."

"There's nothing I can do. He's talking to a client."

"Marla, I'm in a bank surrounded by police with their guns drawn. *Please put him on the phone.*"

She didn't say anything, so I must have gotten her attention. The more I paced, the more agitated I became. I'd normally be switching about now, but both my alters decided to hide. They tended to drop me in a shit storm and leave me there.

"Steve, it's Jordan. What's going on?"

"I just robbed a bank. Well, it wasn't *really* me, but that doesn't matter right now. The police have the building surrounded. I don't know what to do."

"Where are you?"

"I'm at Standard Federal Bank in Brighton."

"Hold on for a minute, Steve. I'll be right back."

I stood there, holding my phone, numb and on fire at the same time. Mark had blown up my life—our lives.

"Steve, are you still there?"

"I'm going to kill myself. That's the only thing I can do."

"Steve, listen. The phone is going to ring in the office. Pick it up. A police officer named T wants to talk to you."

"I don't know what to do. This is all screwed up. I should never have let it get this far."

"Pick up the phone and give yourself up. That's the best advice I can give."

The office phone rang again.

"Okay. Thanks, Jordan." I disconnected the call. The incessant ringing formed a melody in my head. Only one thing would stop it.

"Hello."

"Mr. Simmons. This is T with the Brighton Police Department. Are you okay?"

"I've been better."

"Please put down your weapon and come outside with your hands in the air."

"You'll shoot me."

"No, we won't, I promise. Not if you do as we say."

"I never wanted this to happen," I said. "Maybe I should just end it all."

"Please don't do that, Mr. Simmons. No matter how bad it looks, you haven't hurt anyone. If you surrender now, things will get better."

How does he know things will get better? Things won't get better.

This can end in one of three ways. I can go out with my gun pointed at the police and let them kill me.

That wouldn't be right, would it? How can I put that onus on innocent cops?

The second way out will be to eat a bullet. I already tried that and couldn't do it.

The third option seems the most reasonable. Surrender.

"Okay, T, I'm coming out. I'm leaving my gun in here."

Your life is over.

Once I placed my gun on the desk, I walked out the front door with my hands above my head. The police swarmed me. They handcuffed me and led me to a police car. As they put me in the back, my head slammed against the door frame, and I fell.

A fitting end to a lousy day.

After being booked at Livingston County Jail, I changed into an orange jumpsuit. An officer on the jail staff escorted me to a small, dark cell on the second level. Once inside, I sat against the wall and cried. I had no right to be indignant or upset with the cops or jail staff. I sealed my own fate by being complicit with every illegal thing Mark did.

My poor dogs. I hope the police don't shoot them when they search my house. Will I ever see them again? I have to. Once the prosecutors find out about my mental disorder, they won't press charges, will they?

Are you serious? You robbed a bank. The police aren't gonna let you out just so you can see a therapist.

I should have walked out of the bank with my gun pointed at the police to give them target practice.

This is all your fault. You could have stopped this years ago. Suck it up, Buttercup.

The cell had a sheet and blanket. I tied the sheet into a slip knot and secured the other end to the door. The makeshift noose fit over my head.

Here goes.

I sat down hard. The sheet tightened and held my torso off the floor. With my throat constricted, I gurgled and gasped for air. Then the dizziness hit me.

Assholes. You never let me finish.

———————————

The cold concrete floor of the holding cell made sleep impossible, as did the blaring intercom that never stopped. With no blanket, pillow, or clothes, I served as a naked freak show for anyone who bothered to look. Suicide observation, they called it.

How could I possibly hurt myself here? The eight-foot-square cage contained no hooks, doorknobs, handles, or bars to tie something onto—something I didn't even have. Besides, I was literally fewer than ten feet from the intake desk, the busiest place in the jail. The cell's clear wall and sliding door gave everyone who walked by a full view of my nude body.

They probably put my nakedness on display to humiliate me more than protect me from myself. The constant parade of people past my cell ensured I got plenty of attention. People laughed and commented as if I were one of P.T. Barnum's central attractions.

My silence and disinterest didn't dissuade them. Would they be disappointed to know their harassment neither demeaned nor embarrassed me? I survived "Sissy Simmons," multiple rapes, my mother, my stepfather, and many more indignities. Personal demons destroyed all my modesty, pride, and self-worth over the decades.

Bring it on.

Chapter 57

Stopping the Monster

NOVEMBER 1999
HOWELL, MICHIGAN
AGE 39

I WAS THE LAW SCHOOL VALEDICTORIAN who became a serial bank robber. The Detroit area media had a fun time with my case. After my arrest, people I considered to be friends—whom I'd never wronged other than lying to hide my mental disorder—distanced themselves from me like a cat covering their shit with litter. Former law school classmates told the media I was "strange," "odd," and "a loner" with no friends. They ran over me with a bus, backed up, and did it again.

Without a doubt, legally speaking, I was in a pickle. Days after my October arrest for the Brighton bank robbery, I became a suspect in the Beverly Hills, Michigan, robbery in July. Mark stupidly used the same *modus operandi*—disguise, fake bomb, fake accent—at both banks.

Most people didn't know that state governments stood at the front of the line to prosecute bank robberies. The federal government stepped in *only if* the state ceded jurisdiction to them.

The State of Michigan chose to prosecute me in Livingston County for the October 9 robbery of Standard Federal Bank in Brighton. They would have my trial first. Oakland County ceded jurisdiction to the US Department of Justice (DOJ), who would prosecute me for the July 10 robbery of Standard Federal Bank in Beverly Hills after my first trial.

After thirteen months in the Livingston County Jail, I finally got my day in court. Thanks to medication, junk food, and lack of exercise, my weight ballooned from a fit 180 pounds to 230. Friends had to buy me a suit with a forty-six-inch waist. My weight embarrassed me more than the fact I was on trial.

I fired my first attorney—a classmate who agreed to represent me *pro bono*—after it became apparent he was in over his head. After I threatened to represent myself, Judge Daniel Burress appointed a superb criminal attorney out of Ann Arbor, Don Ferris, to represent me. I pleaded not guilty, and Ferris gave notice of my intent to claim the insanity defense based on my multiple personalities.

We had an excellent expert witness, Cathy Frank, MD, the director of forensic psychiatry and psychiatric education at HENRY FORD HEALTH SYSTEM.

My trial began on November 1, 1999. I didn't switch to Wayne or Mark during jury selection, but it happened repeatedly as the trial progressed. Friends and clients testified for the prosecution. Some said I had mentioned robbing banks as a "joke," but I had no memory of ever saying such a thing. Did it happen? Probably. I switched so much in the last two years that most days seemed to last mere minutes.

The prosecutor argued I'd been planning for years to use dissociative identity disorder as a defense to the bank robberies. That would have taken a lot of foresight. They even introduced a manuscript I'd written in 1995—*The Murder Club*—as evidence, although that had no bank robberies in it.

As I listened to the witnesses describe what Mark did, the guilt buried me. I'd been quite naive—and delusional—after the police arrested me. Not only did I expect to be released soon, but I also believed the prosecutor wouldn't charge me with anything when they learned of my mental disorder.

"Board Rufio, Dallas, and Gabby," I had told Linda, my good friend whom I worked with at FRANCO. She stepped in to take care of my property after my arrest.

"You don't have the money to do that," she said, explaining that my bank accounts had been seized.

"I won't be in here long. Sell my car if you have to."

"We already sold it for money to hire the expert witness," she said. "Steve, you're going to be in here for a while."

How could I have been so stupid? I failed Rufio, Dallas, and Gabby. Major had been taken away from me through no fault of my own, but I had to bear all responsibility for losing my loved ones this time. Linda assured me they had been adopted into a good home, but it stung nonetheless.

I can still see them running through the house, jumping on me, making me laugh. They always looked at me with love. They depended on me, needed me, and I let them down.

The prosecution took a day to present the state's case against me. After they rested, Judge Burress called a recess. A guard escorted me into one of the rooms for attorneys and clients to meet.

A minute later, Dr. Frank walked in and sat across from me. A petite woman with short hair, Dr. Frank had a disarming smile that immediately made me like her. She not only believed in me, but she also treated me with respect. I tried to return the favor the best I could under the circumstances.

"Steve, how are you holding up?"

"I'm switching a lot, especially during testimony."

"Stress will do that. I wanted to speak with you because I'm not sure the jury is buying your defense."

"We haven't even put it on yet."

"No, but the prosecution preempted it. The jury's reaction tells me they are skeptical."

My own expert witness has no confidence in my defense. That doesn't bode well for me.

She's just being honest.

"I'm telling the truth," I said. "I can't control what Mark and Wayne do."

"I believe that, but you need to look at the bigger picture. You've spent all these years protecting them, especially Mark. For the most part, you kept him—and yourself—out of trouble along the way. Look where it got you. What do you think he'll do if you're absolved of this crime?"

Holy shit, I never thought of that.

For more than twenty years, Mark never had to suffer the consequences except for a few nights in jail. Every one of my bad decisions empowered him. The same with Wayne.

"I made sure they got away with everything."

"Yes. They knew you would keep them out of trouble."

"Shit. If I'm found not guilty by reason of insanity, they'll think they can get away with anything. Mark will be...more dangerous than ever."

"That's my concern."

You have to stop them here and now, Steve. You wasted so much time and energy to keep them—and yourself—out of trouble, and it did no good. By hiding your mental disorder and covering for them, you created monsters.

"Doctor, would you send Don in? I have to change my plea."

Dr. Frank nodded and gave me a knowing smile. "You're doing the right thing. Good luck, Steve."

Am I doing the right thing? God, I hope so. I'm so tired of fighting them, of trying to exist.

"Thank you for everything—for believing me," I told Dr. Frank. "I wish I'd met someone like you twenty years ago."

I wish I'd done lots of things twenty years ago.

The door opened at the far end of the room. Don joined me at the table. "So, Steve, what's next?"

"Let's get this over with. Change my plea."

"Just like that?"

"Just like that."

"I'll see if the prosecutor and I can come to a plea agreement."

"No *quid pro quo*, no deal. Just tell them I'll plead guilty."

"Let me do my job, Steve."

"Fine, but I'll take whatever sentence Judge Burress gives me. It's time I stopped helping my alters. After all the things they got away with, I deserve a long sentence."

The guard came to get me ten minutes later and escorted me into the courtroom. Once the judge came in, we all sat.

"I understand the defendant wishes to change his plea."

My attorney and I stood.

"Yes, your honor. My client wishes to change his plea to nolo contendere on Count I, Bank Robbery, and Count II, Felony Firearm."

"Mr. Simmons, are you entering this plea of your own volition?"

"Yes, your honor." Pleading "no contest," with no deal on the table, relieved and pleased me.

"On Count I, Bank Robbery, how do you plead?"

"*Nolo contendere.*"

"On Count II, Felony Firearm, how do you plead?"

"*Nolo contendere.*"

"Is the prosecution satisfied with the defendant's plea?"

"Yes, your honor."

"Then it is entered. Bailiff, please bring the jury in."

Judge Burress thanked the jury for their service and released them. I smiled, certain I'd made the correct decision.

Weeks later, the day had finally come for my sentence. It didn't matter to me anymore. Because of me, I no longer had a career. I lost Rufio, Dallas, and Gabby. Most of my friends, including Diane, pretended they never knew me.

We all stood when Judge Burress entered the courtroom. Over the next hour, the judge and attorneys went through the pre-sentence investigation report and other issues. Finally, the time came for the sentence.

"Will the defendant please rise."

If I refuse to stand, what would they do? Arrest me? I guess it wouldn't be prudent to test the judge's patience.

"On Count I, Bank Robbery, the court hereby sentences the defendant to a term of eight to twenty-five years. On Count II, Felony Firearm, the court hereby sentences the defendant to a term of two years to be served consecutively with the sentence imposed on Count I."

So, there it was. Ten-to-twenty-seven years.

Fuck you, Mark.

JANUARY 21, 2000
DETROIT, MICHIGAN
AGE 40

One more plea. I kept telling myself that. The two jurisdictions—state and federal—had been bouncing me around for fifteen months.

When the time finally came to go to federal court, they hauled me before a magistrate judge in the morning for arraignment. Then I appeared before Judge Patrick Duggan after lunch. I doubted he remembered judging me in the moot court finals at WAYNE STATE UNIVERSITY LAW SCHOOL. At that time, he praised my performance, calling me "very talented."

I probably shouldn't mention it to him.

"How does the defendant plead on the sole count of bank robbery?" Judge Duggan asked.

"Guilty, your honor."

Because of the agreement with the U.S. Department of Justice, I couldn't plead "no contest" as I did in state court. The U.S. Attorney insisted I plead guilty, which would limit my options for appeal—not that I would. I spent the next five months at the Milan Detention Center, a federal facility in Milan, Michigan. They returned me to Detroit in June for my sentencing. I appeared before Judge Duggan for the final time.

"On the sole count of bank robbery, the court sentences the defendant to seventy-one months to be run concurrently with the state sentence."

The federal sentence was a wash. It would run at the same time as my state time, thus ending before the State of Michigan paroled me. The DOJ transported me back to the Livingston County Jail to await transfer to the Michigan Department of Corrections.

Many in my position would be angry, bitter. I didn't ask to be molested and raped, nor did I choose to have multiple personalities. But having a mental disorder didn't put me in prison; how I mishandled it did. Sure, Dr. Fields could have done more to help me. In the end, her inaction didn't put me behind bars—mine did.

I made excuses, hid evidence, moved from state to state, changed jobs, perpetrated fraud, laundered money—all to keep my reputation and freedom. My own cowardice and foolishness did me in, not a psychiatrist's unwillingness or inability to treat me.

At many points along the way, I could have put a stop to everything my alters did. Instead, I let fear control me. That might have been a good excuse when I was a child, but it held no credibility when I reached adulthood. Going to a psychiatric facility—had it come to that—would have been more preferable than allowing my alters to hurt people.

Prison might be a good thing. Maybe I could come out on the other side as a person making better choices and more responsible decisions.

Only time would tell.

Epilogue

Becoming Me

PRESENT DAY
PALM BAY, FLORIDA
AGE 64

The State of Michigan paroled me on September 11, 2007. From the time of my arrest until my parole, I spent 3,260 days behind bars. In those eight years, eleven months, and two days, I never complained about my sentence—nor have I done so since. The three of us—me, Mark, and Wayne—got exactly what we deserved. In fact, I believed we should have spent more time in prison.

"Do you think we should let you out?" a parole board member asked at my hearing.

"No, I don't. My actions hurt a lot of people." And I wasn't talking only about the bank robberies.

While in prison, I completed all the necessary mental health and anger management programs, including a year in cognitive behavior therapy (CBT). In CBT, I divulged most of what Mark and Wayne did while also admitting my complicity. Even then I wasn't ready to divulge details about Allen, Danny, Billy, and the two adult rapes—more out of shame and embarrassment than anything else. I worked hard to put that pre-prison version of myself behind me so I could one day look in the mirror without becoming nauseated.

Upon release, the DOJ paid for me to see Charles Stern, PhD, a wonderful psychologist in a Detroit suburb with experience treating DID. His guidance—even though it lasted less than two years—helped set me on a path to controlling my disorder.

To date, Mark and Wayne haven't dropped the amnesia barrier. I have no memory of anything that ever happened while they were in charge. Mark said to my therapist, and in a note to me, that he and Wayne would never drop the barrier because I wouldn't want to know the full extent of their activities.

My parole for the State of Michigan lasted two years, which overlapped the DOJ's three-year supervision. I left Michigan in October 2009 and spent my last year of federal supervision in Arkansas. Since that time, I've not had a single blackout—that I know of. But Mark and Wayne are tricky.

In 2012, I met Grant, a wonderful man and U.S. Navy veteran twenty-three years younger than me. I guess that would make me a gay cougar. He accepted me with my flaws and shortcomings. I told him about my prison, mental health issues, my alters, and the things we did.

After eight years together, we married and moved to Florida. I'm happier than I ever thought possible. Dr. Frank and prison saved my life. I didn't like losing almost nine years of my freedom, but the alternative would have been worse.

Hiding my mental disorder from those around me turned out to be the biggest mistake I made—as a child, a teenager, and an adult. Fear dictated my actions from the first moment it happened: afraid of being institutionalized, afraid nobody would believe me, afraid of being teased.

If I'd told someone about losing time, the molestations, and the rapes, I might have saved myself years of heartache—and prison. Even after Mark's first felonies, I could have stopped further damage and destruction by my psychopathic and sociopathic alter. Concealing a mental disorder never ends well. I'm lucky we didn't kill anyone—or get killed.

As soon as I realized something was wrong with me, I should have gotten help from a qualified mental health professional. In not confiding in someone, I pissed away a large chunk of my life. My incarceration actually started when I was a child and ended when I went to prison. Only then did I free myself from the torment that controlled me for so many years.

In March 2011, Cliff passed away. On his deathbed, he asked me to take care of Estelle. I quit my job and moved in with her three days after the funeral. A few months later, a neurologist diagnosed her with Alzheimer's—but I never told her, thus honoring her request that she never know about it if it happened.

For more than six years, I served as Estelle's caregiver, friend, and son. She also fully accepted Grant into her life. When broken hips at ages ninety-five and ninety-eight kept her housebound, she fell in love with *Judge Judy*, *The Big Bang Theory*, and *Two and a Half Men*.

Estelle Dobson suffered a massive stroke on November 17, 2017, a month after her third hip-replacement surgery in two-and-a-half years. When she granted me health care power of attorney after I moved in, she had made me promise never to leave her in a vegetative or severely debilitated state. I sat by her bed in hospice for four days until she passed.

When Estelle died, I lost the one person in my family who had always been there for me. She told me a few months before the stroke that she and Cliff had one regret—not trying to adopt me as a child.

A day doesn't go by when I don't think of them.

My mother, Shirley Simmons, passed away in 2018. We hadn't spoken to each other since early 2011. The man I believed to be my father—Bobby Simmons—died two years later. As it turned out, he wasn't my biological father, a tidbit of information I discovered after submitting my DNA to Ancestry.com. That distinction went to Ernest "Pete" Holloway, a 62-year-old man my mother worked for. I asked "Dad" about it, but the information shocked him. My mother took the secret of my conception to her grave.

Michael and Sharon—my biological half-siblings—continue to live in the Fort Smith area.

Although my alters are dormant, they're still lurking. I have no doubt they'll return if I ever need them. As of now, I'm doing everything I can to keep my life the way it is—honest and happy. My alters also know that I'm willing to go to prison to set things right.

It took a long time, but I'm finally becoming the person I always wanted to be.

MEMOIR OF A MANGLED MIND

Acknowledgments

This book wouldn't have been possible without the help of so many people in my life, both during and after the events of this memoir.

Numerous beta readers, proofreaders, and memoir group members gave me valuable suggestions, advice, and mental health therapy throughout this writing journey: Sylvia Clare, Tim Depp, Jim Foohey, Annette Frazier, Mica Garrett, Lisa Grace, Elizabeth Gwathney, Jane Penland Hoover, Carolee Huffman, Ellen Kelsch, Kathleen Kline, Michael Tittle Marinelli, Sara Merchant, Julie Pompa, Linda Rathburn, Becky Rozman, Riet Scott, Michele Reichold Summers, Carol Wakeling, Kathy Woodward, and Terrie Mayka. I'm sure someone has been left out because many stepped forward to help.

Many thanks to Patrick Price, my developmental editor who insisted I self-publish this memoir should the traditional route not work. His editorial work provided me with the tools to polish the project. I also found his book proposal course invaluable when I began querying this project.

I would have been lost had it not been for Marion Roach Smith, whose webinars and online interviews taught me how to write and structure the book. Her personal words of encouragement after reading my manuscript helped quell my impostor syndrome—at least for a bit.

When I languished in finishing the project, Carolyn Hamilton—memoirist and book coach—gave me a much-needed kick in the ass, especially in writing the most difficult sections.

Literary agents Ann Rose, Jacqui Lipton, Lane Heymont, and Stefanie Rossitto at The Tobias Agency provided wonderful advice as I sought representation. Although my search proved unsuccessful, I found their insights to be invaluable.

I received unexpected help from my friend Joyce "Fenderella" Irby, one of the most talented musicians I've ever known—and who has the voice of an angel. Reading her memoir, *I'd Still Say Yes*, gave me the courage to include all the dirty secrets I'd so carefully protected over the years.

Three dear friends—the aforementioned Michael Tittle Marinelli along with Lisa and Jim Gunn—gave me mounds of moral support as I wrote this memoir, even if they didn't realize it at the time. Likewise to Lynn and Selina Rosen—who's an excellent author in her own right. They encouraged me to keep writing, a push that helped me pivot from fiction projects to this one.

A special thanks to Rabbi Craig Mayers of Temple Beth Sholom in Melbourne, Florida. He guided me as I completed an almost forty-year quest to Conservative Judaism. Rabbi Craig and the others at Temple Beth Sholom welcomed me with open arms, and their support gave me the spiritual strength to complete this book.

Dear friends Linda Rathburn and Julie Pompa—former colleagues at ANTHONY M. FRANCO PUBLIC RELATIONS all those years ago—never knew the critical role they played in my survival. They always looked out for me when I lost a little too much weight or acted somewhat irrational—which happened a lot.

Likewise, Don Potter and Jane Eckels—whom I worked with at the SOUTHEAST MICHIGAN HOSPITAL COUNCIL (SEMHC)—have been supportive friends for almost forty years. When my life fell apart, and I desperately needed help, Don stepped up, which makes me even more ashamed for what I did to conceal my alter's activities at SEMHC.

Thanks so much to Joshua Dressler, one of my former law school professors, who became a close friend afterward. He not only taught me about criminal law and procedure, but he also showed me what it's like to have a friend in the worst of times. His friendship never wavered.

Three law school classmates and former friends—Pam Jesue, Tiki McCarthy, and Lisa Waits—propped me up when my personal life imploded. I ultimately violated their trust in me, something I'll never forgive myself for. Tiki gave me family when I had none. The destruction of our friendship is one of my biggest regrets, but I have only myself to blame.

Several people at Jenner & Block pulled me through difficult times. I must give kudos to Dottie Zydek, my administrative assistant who surely thought I was batshit crazy—and she would've been correct. Howard Suskin gave me much-needed guidance and support as I struggled at the firm. Many thanks to J. Cunyon Gordon, a brilliant attorney and dear friend who mentored me on the ins and outs of being a gay attorney at the firm. She also got me hooked on sushi. The brief friendships I had with summer associates Steven Siros, Debi Neal, and Ellen Cox Call lifted me out of the dark void.

My former colleague Thomas Cranmer convinced me to do the right thing when I got backed into a corner. For that I'm forever thankful.

If not for the advice of Cathy Frank, MD, I might never have made the correct decision when it mattered most. Her advice saved my life—and stopped me and my alters from hurting others.

My attorney, Don Ferris, did for me more than I deserved, and he did so with utmost professionalism and tenacity.

Charles Stern, PhD, set me on the road to recovery. Without him, I don't know where I would be today. He gave me key coping skills to help keep my alters at bay. Everyone with dissociative identity disorder would be lucky to have him on their side.

Then there's Ethan. I couldn't appreciate the love and affection he gave me during my troubled years. Despite all my mishegoss, he opened his heart in ways I was incapable of providing. I'm sorry for all the pain I caused him and his family, especially Rachel and Hannah, who had been like sisters to me. Fortunately, Ethan found in Levi everything I wasn't and could never be.

My cousin—Linda Smith Parmer—has been a strong force in my life, especially in recent years. We lost so many years, but we reconnected at the right time.

Finally, last but not least, there's my husband, Grant. We met in 2012 when I was fifty-two years old, an age where I'd given up on love and companionship. He took a chance on me despite the baggage I carried. As I struggled emotionally while writing this memoir, Grant held me, loved me, and never let me fall. He's the light that shines on me every single day.

If I forgot to thank someone, I apologize. There are just so many who deserve recognition.

Made in the USA
Columbia, SC
25 January 2025

8885753b-1864-4e22-884f-fbe22b118a8bR01